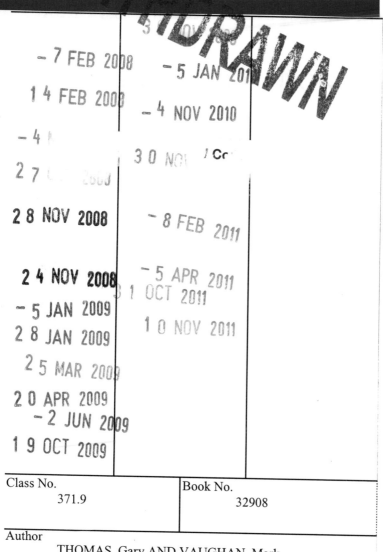

INCLUSIVE EDUCATION

Series Editors:

Gary Thomas, Chair in Education, University of Leeds, and
Christine O'Hanlon, School of Education, University of East Anglia.

The movement towards inclusive education is gathering momentum throughout the world. But how is it realized in practice? The volumes within this series will examine the arguments for inclusive schools and the evidence for the success of inclusion. The intention behind the series is to fuse a discussion about the ideals behind inclusion with pictures of inclusion in practice. The aim is to straddle the theory/practice divide, keeping in mind the strong social and political principles behind the move to inclusion while observing and noting the practical challenges to be met.

Current and forthcoming titles:

Shereen Benjamin: *The Micropolitics of Inclusive Education*
Ann Lewis and Brahm Norwich: *Special Teaching for Special Children – A
    Pedagogy for Inclusion?*
Christine O'Hanlon: *Educational Inclusion as Action Research*
Caroline Roaf: *Co-ordinating Services for Included Children*
David Skidmore: *Inclusion: The Dynamic of School Development*
Gary Thomas and Andrew Loxley: *Deconstructing Special Education and
    Constructing Inclusion*
Gary Thomas and Mark Vaughan: *Inclusive Education: Readings and Reflections*
Carol Vincent: *Including Parents?*

INCLUSIVE EDUCATION

Readings and reflections

**Gary Thomas and
Mark Vaughan**

Open University Press

Open University Press
McGraw-Hill Education
McGraw-Hill House
Shoppenhangers Road
Maidenhead
Berkshire
England
SL6 2QL

email: enquiries@openup.co.uk
world wide web: www.openup.co.uk

and Two Penn Plaza, New York, NY 10121-2289, USA

First published 2004
Reprinted 2005, 2007

Copyright © Gary Thomas and Mark Vaughan, 2004

A catalogue record of this book is available from the British Library

ISBN 10: 0 355 20724 3 (pb)   0 335 20725 1 (hb)
ISBN 13: 978 0 355 20724 4 (pb)   978 0 20725 1 (hb)

Library of Congress Cataloging-in-Publication Data
CIP data applied for

Typeset by RefineCatch Limited, Bungay, Suffolk
Printed in the UK by Bell & Bain Ltd, Glasgow

Dedicated to the memory of Marsha Forest

Contents

Series editors' preface

'Inclusion' has become something of an international buzzword. It is difficult to trace its provenance or the growth in its use over the last two decades, but what is certain is that it is now *de rigeur* for policy documents, mission statements and political speeches. It has become a slogan – almost obligatory in the discourse of all right-thinking people.

The problem about the sloganizing of 'inclusion' is that the word has become often merely a filler in the conversation. People can talk about 'inclusion' without really thinking about what they mean, merely to add a progressive gloss to what they are saying. Politicians who talk casually about the need for a more inclusive society know that they will be seen as open-minded and enlightened, and will be confident in the knowledge that all sorts of difficult practical questions can be circumvented. And if this happens, if there is insufficient thought about the nitty gritty mechanics, those who do work hard for inclusion can easily be dismissed as peddling empty promises.

This series is dedicated to examining in detail some of the ideas lying behind inclusive education. Inclusion, much more than 'integration' or 'mainstreaming', is embedded in a range of contexts – political and social, as well as psychological and educational – and our aim in this series is to make some examination of these contexts. In providing a forum for discussion and critique we hope to help provide the basis for a wider intellectual and practical foundation for more inclusive practice in schools and elsewhere.

In noting that inclusive education is about more than simply 'integration', it is important to stress that inclusive education is really about extending the comprehensive ideal in education. Those who talk about it are therefore less concerned with children's supposed 'special educational needs' (and it is becoming increasingly difficult to meaningfully define what such needs are) and more concerned with developing an education system in which equity is striven for and diversity is welcomed. To aim for such developments is surely uncontentious; what is more controversial is the means by which this is done. There are many and varied ways of helping to develop more inclusive schools and the authors of this series look at some of these. While one focus in this has to be on the place and role of the special school, it is by no means the only focus: the thinking and practice which go on inside and outside schools may do much to exclude or marginalize children. The authors of this series try to give serious attention to such thinking and practice.

The books in this series therefore examine a range of matters: the knowledge of special education; the frames of analysis which have given legitimacy to such knowledge; and the changing political mood which inspires a move to inclusion. In the context of all this, they also examine some new developments in inclusive thinking and practice inside and outside schools.

It is often said that the move to inclusive education is a continuing journey. This book of readings and reflections, edited by Gary Thomas and Mark Vaughan, chronicles that journey by mapping the diverse and shifting currents of thought that have led toward greater inclusion. The editors begin by placing those currents of thought in the context of discussions of rights, equity and justice. They then collect together articles and papers – some of them seminal, some of them illustrative of a theme – that represent significant shifts in academic and professional thought, before moving on to describe changes in legislation and innovations in inclusive practice.

Throughout, the benefits of progress to inclusive education are set in the context of the benefits to society of inclusion. As one of the texts in the book – a position paper from the British Psychological Society – puts it: 'a society which can nurture, develop and use the skills, talents and strengths of all its members will enlarge its collective resources and ultimately is likely to be more at ease with itself'.

The book will provide an important reference point for professionals and students in education, charting a history of accelerating progress toward inclusion and documenting major developments in the continuing journey.

Gary Thomas
Christine O'Hanlon

Preface

Recently, a certain indignation has been expressed by some education academics and teacher unions about the progress toward inclusion in contemporary education. That indignation seems to find its source in a concern that the move to inclusion is driven by principles and politics – or what has sometimes been called 'ideology' – rather than evidence that inclusive education works.

We hope that this book helps to attenuate that concern not just by giving examples of evidence demonstrating that inclusive education is indeed successful but, more importantly, by indicating that principles are – and should be – a central part of the argument in the move to inclusion. Arguments for inclusive education have valid political, practical and empirical contexts and we thought it important to provide for all students of education and for professionals in education some indication of the history and contexts of the changes that are currently happening in schools and colleges. We are telling a story of changing ideas and we hope that this story will be of interest not just to students but also to the general public and, in particular, to parents of disabled and non-disabled children.

The need for the book was first discussed in the offices of the Centre for Studies on Inclusive Education (CSIE). Around us was collected CSIE's library of books and resources about inclusion and its own extensive list of publications, a database and an archive that is probably unrivalled in its detailed chronicling of the journey to inclusion not just in the UK but internationally. These resources are in regular demand from students, academics, education administrators and parents for information about inclusive education in general or about specific projects that have provided a lead for others. This book draws on that rich collection as well as a wider academic literature.

This book is not intended in any way to present a comprehensive or definitive selection. Rather, it gives a taster of important sources on the move to inclusion, our selection being personal and idiosyncratic, dependent on our own knowledge of the literature and our own predilections. Lack of space has precluded the possibility of including every piece we would like to have included (several volumes would have been necessary), and almost all of the material chosen for incorporation in fact represents only an edited selection from the original. Given these limitations, we hope that the book will be used in two ways: first, as a charting of the progress of inclusion, giving a flavour of the changes that have been taking place and the general context of their occurrence and, second, as a guide to the kind of significant material that underpins progress with inclusion so far. Particularly where extracts have been used, we would encourage readers to go back to the original sources for a fuller understanding of the points that the authors have been making.

Collecting and collating material from some time ago, there is a problem that has confronted us and that is the changed use of language over the years. Only ten years ago, for example, there was common usage of the word 'handicapped' and the phrase 'the disabled', which are now avoided, and sexist language (always assuming 'he', when 'he or she' was meant) was the norm. Clearly, we have not been in a position to correct such usage where we have been quoting directly from the writings of others and ask that our readers bear with us in taking these writings as being of their time – times when the implications of using particular vocabularies had not been thought through and different conventions obtained.

More than most books, this one has depended on the goodwill of others in granting permissions. Formal permissions have been sought and are given below as well as in the main body of the text. It is worth noting that of the many permissions we have sought there has not been a single refusal, a fact that demonstrates the spirit in which those who work, write and publish in education operate.

The work of seeking permissions has required excellent administrative support and we are indebted to Gaye Denley for her assiduity in chasing them – particularly those from disappeared publishers. We are also grateful to colleagues at CSIE and Oxford Brookes University for their support, help and ideas. The trustees of CSIE have been especially helpful in providing encouragement to the project and in giving it sustenance.

Acknowledgements

The authors and Open University Press would like to thank the following for permission to reproduce extracts of copyright material. While every effort has been made to trace and acknowledge all copyright holders, we would like to apologize should there be any errors or omissions. These will be corrected in any reprint if the authors are informed of changes and so on. Permissions have been received for the following:

Part One

Equality by R.H. Tawney, published by George Allen & Unwin; *Theory of Justice* by John Rawls, published by Oxford University Press; 'I have a dream' speech by Martin Luther King Jr, reprinted by arrangement with the estate of Martin Luther King Jr, c/o Writers House as agent for the proprietor, New York, NY, copyright 1963 Martin Luther King Jr, copyright renewed 1991 Coretta Scott King; Needs, rights and opportunities in special education in *Needs, Rights and Opportunities*, edited by C. Roaf and H. Bines, published by Falmer Press; *Social and Educational Justice: The Human Rights Framework for Inclusion* by S. Rustemier, published by Centre for Studies on Inclusive Education (CSIE); *The Creatures Time Forgot: Photography and Disability Imagery*, by D. Hevey, published by Routledge.

Part Two

Asylums, by E. Goffman, published by Pelican; Special education for the mildly retarded – is much of it justifiable? by L.M. Dunn, in *Exceptional Children*; A critical examination of special education programs, by F. Christoplos and P. Renz (1969), in *Journal of Special Education*, 3(4): 371–9. Copyright (1969) by PRO-ED, inc. Reprinted with permission; Street level bureaucrats by Weatherley and Lipsky, published by Harvard Educational Review; *Reconstructing Educational Psychology* by G. Leyden, reprinted with permission; *Psychology and Special Education* by W. Swann, published by Open University Press; Integration and participation in comprehensive schools by T. Booth, published by *Forum*, Triangle Journals; *A Sociology of Special Education* by Sally Tomlinson, published by Routledge & Kegan Paul; *Educating Pupils with Special Needs in the Ordinary School* by S. Hegarty, K. Pocklington and D. Lucas, published by NFER-Nelson; *Educational Opportunities for All?* published by the Inner London Education Authority; *Achieving the Complete School* by D. Biklen, New York: Teachers College Press, copyright 1985 by Teachers College, Columbia University. All rights reserved, pp. 1–6, reprinted by permission of the publisher; Making the ordinary school special by T. Dessent, published by *Children and Society*; *Action for Inclusion* by J. O'Brien and M. Forest, published by Inclusion Press; Normalisation, needs and schools by S. Carson, in *Education Psychology in Practice*; Reviewing the literature on integration by S. Hegarty, in *European Journal of Special Needs Education*, 8(3), see website http://www.tandf.co.uk/journals/routledge/08856257.html; Changing the way we think about kids with disabilities: a conversation with Tom Hehir, in *Inclusion and Special Education* by E. Miller and R. Tovey, pp. 14–17 (Cambridge, MA: Harvard Educational Publishing, 1996). Copyright © 1996 by the President and Fellows of Harvard College. All rights reserved; *Deconstructing Special Education and Constructing Inclusion* by G. Thomas and A. Loxley, published by Open University Press; *Reasons Against Segregated Schooling*, published by CSIE; Does special education have a role to play in the 21st century? by M. Oliver, published by *REACH, Journal of Special Needs Education in Ireland*.

Part Three

Education: A Different Vision: An Alternative White Paper, published by Institute for Public Policy Research; *Inclusive Education: A Position Paper*, published by the British Psychological Society; *The Inclusion Charter* published by CSIE; *Inclusive Education – A Framework for Change* by A. Wertheimer, published by CSIE.

Part Four

Each Belongs: Integrated Education in Canada by L. Shaw, published by CSIE; *Mainstreaming in Massachusetts* by M. Vaughan and A. Shearer, published by CSIE; *Disability Equality in the Classroom: A Human Rights Issue* by R. Rieser and M. Mason, published by Disability Equality in Education; *Kirsty: The Struggle for a Place in an Ordinary School* by M. Vaughan, published by CSIE; *Everyone Belongs* by K. Jupp, published by Souvenir Press; *Bishopswood: Good Practice Transferred*, published by CSIE; *Developing an Inclusive Policy for Your School* by R. Rogers, published by CSIE; *Human Rights and School Change: The Newham Story* by L. Jordan and C. Goodey, published by CSIE; *National Study on Inclusion in America: Overview and Summary Report* by National Center on

Educational Restructuring and Inclusion (NCERI), published by CSIE; Interview with the headteacher, *The Making of the Inclusive School* by G. Thomas, D. Walker and J. Webb, published by Routledge; A seven year sentence by S. Harris in *National Integration Week Magazine*, published by CSIE; *Index for Inclusion: Developing Learning and Participation in Schools* by T. Booth and M. Ainscow, published by CSIE.

Introduction

This book has gone through several lives. Our intention at the outset was to produce a book that recorded significant international markers in the move to inclusion – the most important writings that had taken educational thinking in an inclusive direction. The first title mooted was thus *Moves to Inclusion: Turning Points on the Journey to Inclusive Schools*.

It then became clear, as we began to examine in more detail the project that we had so rashly proposed, that there weren't in fact any 'turning points' (although the moment when the word 'inclusion' was first used in educational contexts – in Canada in 1988 – is described here, see O'Brien and Forest, piece 21). Inclusion, it transpires, represents the confluence of several streams of thought, social and political as well as educational. Those moves to inclusion in fact come not from one direction – not, for example, solely from research about the effectiveness of special education and special pedagogy – but from several directions: from research, certainly, but more importantly from the imperative to greater social justice; from calls for civil rights; from legislation that prohibits discrimination; from the stimulus provided by original, distinctive projects started by imaginative educators; from the voices of people who have been through special education. All of these in their own ways have played their part in the changes that have occurred in the last quarter of the twentieth century and the first part of the twenty-first.

And if one is taking an international view, it is important to note that those varying ideas, while united in direction and general sentiment, germinated differently in different parts of the world. A social democratic political climate, for example, was a force behind the beginnings of mainstreaming in Scandinavia; communist local government played its part in Italy; the civil rights agenda was important in North America; and, more recently, an anti-discriminatory theme has figured largely in legislatures across the world.

So, with these varied starting points, key documents or mileposts were rare. There have been no major turns at the root of an international sea-change. Indeed, the currents that have shaped practice have converged, un-coordinated, from many directions. No one, in the early days of de-segregation, stated that their ultimate aim was *inclusion*. The move to inclusion has been slow, and often with a whimper from the educational establishment rather than a bang: no definitive event, no revelatory research finding has brought us to where we are now.

This mêlée of ideas and patchwork of progress presented a certain difficulty at first in the compilation of this book, for the varying themes and evolving practices have employed vocabularies in flux. As we noted in the preface, gendered language was once the norm; no longer. There used to be frequent use of the word 'handicapped', which is now replaced with 'disabled'. Often, there was discussion of 'the retarded'. And there is the change of ideas encapsulated by the move from the words 'mainstreaming' and 'integration' to 'inclusion'.

There are significant differences between inclusion and the ideas that have preceded it: mainstreaming and integration. It is clear to us that inclusion means more – much more – than these earlier ideas, to the extent that a book about inclusion is not a book about mainstreaming. (One should note here that 'mainstreaming' was the term used in the US for what tended to be called 'integration' in Europe and Australasia.) However, in tracing the origins of the ideas behind the current move to inclusion, it is equally clear that inclusion has its roots deep in the integration/mainstreaming movement. We have tried to show in this book that there has been a union of ideas culminating in inclusive thought and that the ideas that brought people to the wisdom of mainstreaming are but one strand in a much broader bundle of ideas having its lineage in notions about rights and social justice.

In parallel with notions about rights and social justice have been other developments in the last third of the twentieth century. There has been a decline in respect for authority, and particularly the kind of authority and power exercised by professionals and other experts. That declining respect has given rise to an increase in parental voice and power in education and latterly even to something that would have been unheard of even in the 1980s: a hearing of the child's voice. As these various voices have been heard, and as their speakers have gained in confidence, the equation of power has shifted from expert to user, from those who provide knowledge to those who need to use knowledge. The culture of 'doctor knows best' (or psychologist or teacher knows best) has diminished substantially.

This changing balance of power has arisen as a result both of self-questioning on the part of forward-thinking professionals and of questioning by users of the forms of authority and knowledge that are wielded by experts. More assertive parents have asked what benefits accrue from many of the diagnoses proffered by professionals. They have questioned at local and national levels the wisdom of segregated education for their children. In particular, the definitive and brutal statements that were sometimes made by medics about the prognosis for particular children in countless cases proved to be inaccurate. The exposure given to these in an open and litigious society has dented the authority of the professional source.

We have tried to compile in this book a spectrum of voices, from child to practitioner to academic, to reflect the range of contributions that have been made to this many-voiced and many-faceted debate about inclusion.

There are four parts to the book. In the first part we examine frameworks in which inclusive thought has developed – in rights, participation, social justice. The selection here, as elsewhere in the book, is idiosyncratic rather than exhaustive, though we have tried at all times to provide exemplary material for the points that we are making. The emphasis here at the beginning of the book is on inclusion based in justice as distinct from needs. The point we make at the outset is that the move to greater equality and participation recently is in fact part of a much more extended movement historically, from which there was only a brief deviation provided by the twentieth century experiment into special education. In making this point we have drawn from voices over a period of two centuries. We have taken extracts from Thomas Paine, R.H. Tawney and John Rawls, not because they had anything in particular to say about inclusion, but because they exemplify the long march of change from a discourse of authority to one of greater democracy, fraternity and equity.

The piece from Martin Luther King's 'I have a dream' speech is given as a symbol of the civil rights movement of the 1960s. People remember this speech as a marker of the changes that took place at that time, changes that occurred when the anger that had lain dormant about discrimination finally became expressed. That movement was primarily about race discrimination, but its success also led to expressions of injustice in other areas, notably the injustices created by the segregation of special schooling.

In the rest of the first part, we draw from a range of modern sources that locate inclusion in social justice. The excerpt from Roaf and Bines puts the ideas of those fundamental pieces in the context of education: the argument is made that the policies and practices of an education system should be based not on needs but on rights. Sharon Rustemier uses the United Nations Convention on the Rights of the Child as a cornerstone for her argument that inclusion is in danger of becoming merely a warm word for policy documents and political speeches. It has to be seen as more than this – as the polar opposite of exclusion. David Hevey in his piece calls, as a disabled person, for rights rather than charity.

The second part of the book marshals some arguments and evidence about segregation. After briefly looking at the groundbreaking work of Goffman, who wrote the seminal *Asylums* and *Stigma*, we turn to early discussion papers from the United States – those of Dunn and Christoplos and Renz from the late 1960s – and move on to more recent critical discussions, such as that from Sally Tomlinson, about the place and purpose of special education in the wider education system. Included also are syntheses of research about the effectiveness or otherwise of special pedagogy: from the US we include that of Anderson and Pellicer and, from Europe, Seamus Hegarty and colleagues. In two forward thinking pieces of work from the 1980s and 1990s, Tony Booth and Sam Carson discuss the need for participation and normalization, and special education's place in resisting these. In this part we also try to point to changes in the nature of inclusion as the mood shifted from the specific themes of mainstreaming to the broader range of issues involved in inclusion. Much of this shifting mood is reflected in the work and publications of CSIE, first established in 1982, from which we draw in this part along with other key publications. The pioneering work of the Canadians in the Hamilton and Waterloo Boards, and US administrator, Tom Hehir's, thoughts on 'Changing the way we think about kids with disabilities' are included. Here, a range of issues are tackled, from the pragmatics of financing inclusion to human rights to the metaphors used for 'explaining' children's difficulties at school.

In the third part, we focus on national and international legislation, on reports, policy documents and other official statements from the US, the UK and international organizations. These, of course, represent the response of politicians and policymakers to a changing mood – they do not initiate change. However, they are important because they cement in place the new mood, albeit more weakly than some would wish: they mark progress and (again, more tentatively than many would wish) prevent backsliding from that progress. Here we include, for example, extracts from important changes to legislation made on both sides of the Atlantic, as well as the UNESCO Salamanca Statement of 1994. Interesting as a contrast to the official documents drawn on in this part is the Institute for Public Policy Research's Alternative White Paper, which calls for an end to the exclusionary practice that they see exemplified in special education.

In the final part of the book we examine inclusion in action, pointing to places where inclusion has been made to happen. Inspired projects arose across the world from the work of imaginative educators whose creativity led to original, distinctive endeavour. And those projects seeded many more of their kind nationally and internationally. We give, for example, extracts from the account of how the staff of Bishopswood School were inspired by the UN Declaration of the Rights of Disabled People to change the way that their school operated to become part of the mainstream. And similarly, in Dave Walker's interview about the Somerset Inclusion Project, there is an account of the changing mindset that led the staff at his special school to close the school and convert it into an inclusion service. There are also accounts in this final part from individuals who have fought with their families for inclusion in the mainstream.

As we have already noted, there is no pretence here to have furnished an exhaustive history of inclusive education. Rather, we have tried to compile a set of tasters that give the context – the wider picture – within which inclusion has been framed. It is a picture of political change, research evidence and slow but steady advance in educational practice.

A final note. To aid continuity we have put references from each piece at the end of the book. Given that each piece has a certain integrity, we have not conflated all references into one list, as is the usual practice.

PART ONE

The context – rights, participation, social justice

1. Thomas Paine: *The Rights of Man*

The march toward equal rights for all – including the politically weak, the disenfranchised and the oppressed – has been a long and difficult one. Its conclusion in the civil rights movement of the 1960s and today's anti-discriminatory legislative environment represents the coming together of many streams of thought.

One of the first thinkers to challenge the authority and power of a limited, privileged class of people who strove to exclude and dominate – as opposed to include and value – was Thomas Paine. He published *African Slavery in America*, in the spring of 1775, very much against the spirit of the times, opposing the evils of slavery. The following year he formulated his ideas on American independence in his pamphlet *Common Sense*. In 1792 he published *The Rights of Man*, a publication principally directed to defending the French Revolution against attacks by Edmund Burke. But *The Rights of Man* was more than a defence of the French Revolution: it was an analysis of the roots of discontent in Europe, which Paine attributed to arbitrary government, poverty, illiteracy, unemployment and war.

The Rights of Man became a statement of the importance of central rights and in many ways it shaped thought over the next two centuries. More than this, though, it was an argument about malaise and its roots in injustice. It was a treatise to governments – and anyone else who would read it – on the running of a civilized society. Although it does not use today's vocabulary of inclusion, it contains the roots of modern thought about inclusion: about equality, respect and decent education for all.

Paine uses the *Declaration of the Rights of Man and of Citizens by the National Assembly of France* as the basis for his discussion of rights. Below is a brief section from *The Rights of Man* in which he makes commentary on these and the other 11 rights, noting that the first three provide the basis for all the others and that most of the others provide elucidation in some form for those basic rights.

It is in the sixth right that one finds the articulation of the notion of equality under the law that forms the basis for our thinking on rights today. The very last words of this, namely 'equally eligible to all honours, places, and employments, according to their different abilities, without any other distinction than that created by their virtues and talents' says something very important: that the law should offer a guarantee against discrimination and that people's life chances should not be restricted by irrelevant considerations. Paine argues that the only thing that is truly hereditary is the rights of man: 'The Rights of men in society, are neither devisable, nor transferable, nor annihilable, but descendable only.'

> 66   . . . the National Assembly doth recognize and declare, in the presence of the Supreme Being, and with the hope of his blessing and favour, the following sacred rights of men and of citizens:

One: men are born, and always continue, free and equal in respect of their rights. Civil distinctions, therefore, can be founded only on public utility.

Two: the end of all political associations is the preservation of the natural and imprescriptible rights of man; and these rights are liberty, property, security, and resistance of oppression.

Three: the nation is essentially the source of all sovereignty; nor can any individual, or any body of men, be entitled to any authority which is not expressly derived from it.

Four: political liberty consists in the power of doing whatever does not injure another. The exercise of the natural rights of every man, has no other limits than those which are necessary to secure to every other man the free exercise of the same rights; and these limits are determinable only by the law.

Five: the law ought to prohibit only actions hurtful to society. What is not prohibited by the law should not be hindered; nor should anyone be compelled to that which the law does not require.

Six: the law is an expression of the will of the community. All citizens have a right to concur, either personally or by their representatives, in its formation. It should be the same to all, whether it protects or punishes; and all being equal in its sight, are equally eligible to all honours, places, and employments, according to their different abilities, without any other distinction than that created by their virtues and talents.   **99**

(Paine 1999)

2. R.H. Tawney: *Equality*

The author of *Equality*, R.H. Tawney, was of enormous significance in the movement to social democracy in Britain.

The following piece from *Equality* was written in 1931 and is remarkably modern in its attitude to difference. In it, Tawney accepts that there are differences between people. It would be absurd to pretend otherwise. But he says that we should celebrate these differences, just as we try to find ways of neutralizing and suppressing elements of policy and organization that maintain the inequalities between people. He makes the point that discrimination of any kind – on grounds of gender, income, race or ability – is iniquitous in its effects on social life.

At the end of this passage Tawney stresses – just as we are stressing today – the origins of many kinds of difficulty in poverty, or as he calls it 'economic life'. He argues, just as the early pioneers of de-segregation argued, that the disadvantages people experience in education (or indeed any sphere of social life) are due not to constitutional difficulties, though sometimes this may be the case, but as often as not are caused by the social arrangements that society engineers.

66 Inequality and Social Structure

So to criticise inequality and to desire equality is not, as is sometimes suggested, to cherish the romantic illusion that men are equal in character and intelligence. It is to hold that, while their natural endowments differ profoundly, it is the mark of a civilised society to aim at eliminating such inequalities as have their source, not in individual differences, but in its own organization, and that individual differences, which are a source of social energy, are more likely to ripen and find expression if social inequalities are, as far as practicable, diminished. And the obstacle to the progress of equality is something simpler and more potent than finds expression in the familiar truism that men vary in their mental and moral, as well as in their physical characteristics, important and valuable though that truism is as a reminder that different individuals require different types of provision. It is the habit of mind which thinks it, not regrettable, but natural and desirable, that different sections of a community should be distinguished from each other by sharp differences of economic status, of environment, of education and culture and habit of life. It is the temper which regards with approval the social institutions and economic arrangements by which such differences are emphasized and enhanced, and feels distrust and apprehension at all attempts to diminish them.

The institutions and policies in which that temper has found expression are infinite in number. At one time it has coloured the relations between the sexes; at another, those between religions; at a third, those between members of different races. But in communities no longer divided by religion or race, and in which men and women are treated as political and economic equals, the divisions which remain are, nevertheless, not insignificant. The practical form which they most commonly assume – the most conspicuous external symptom of difference of economic status and social position – is, of course, a graduated system of social classes, and it is by softening or obliterating, not individual differences, but class gradations, that the historical movements directed towards diminishing inequality have attempted to attain their objective. It is, therefore, by considering the class system that light upon the problem of inequality is, in the first place at least, to be sought, and it is by their attitude to the relations between classes that the equalitarian temper and philosophy are distinguished from their opposite.

A society which values equality will attach a high degree of significance to differences of character and intelligence between different individuals, and a low degree of significance to economic and social differences between different groups. It will endeavour, in shaping its policy and organisation, to encourage the former and to neutralize and suppress the latter, and will regard it as vulgar and childish to emphasize them when, unfortunately, they still exist. A society which is in love with inequality will take such differences seriously, and will allow them to overflow from the regions, such as economic life, where they have their origin, and from

which it is difficult wholly to expel them, till they become a kind of morbid
obsession, colouring the whole world of social relations.

(Tawney [1931] 1964)

3. John Rawls: *A Theory of Justice*

It is easy to underestimate the influence of John Rawls's *A Theory of Justice* in
giving legitimacy – academic and political – to the popular currents of change
that occurred after the civil rights movements of the 1960s in the US and
elsewhere. The following sections of a piece by Martha Nussbaum sum up
Rawls's place in cementing thinking about rights and social justice that took
place in the 1970s and since. In particular, she stresses a central tenet of Rawls's
work, that '. . . the pursuit of a greater social good should not make us mar the
lives of individuals by abridging their basic rights and entitlements'.

> Rawls played a major role in reviving an interest in the substantive
> questions of political philosophy. What makes a society just? How is social
> justice connected to an individual's pursuit of the good life? . . . In 1971,
> when Rawls published *A Theory of Justice*, [his] ideas took hold through
> their own power, decisively shifting the climate of debate not only in
> philosophy but also in such fields as economics, law, and public policy.
> By now, these ideas are central starting points in many nations for dis-
> cussions of justice . . . Rawls's views are always presented abstractly and
> are often difficult for nonphilosophers to penetrate. But he has given new
> specificity and vigor to one of the most valuable legacies of the liberal
> political tradition: the idea that a person has a dignity and worth that
> social structures should not be permitted to violate. Thirty years after
> publication of *A Theory of Justice*, with all the discussion of rights and
> pluralism that has ensued, it is easy to forget that a whole generation of
> our political and moral philosophers had virtually stopped talking about
> that idea, and about how it can guide a . . . diverse society like our
> own . . .
>   The intuitive idea from which Rawls's theory starts is simple and pro-
> found: 'Each person possesses an inviolability founded on justice that
> even the welfare of society as a whole cannot override.' In other words,
> the pursuit of a greater social good should not make us mar the lives of
> individuals by abridging their basic rights and entitlements. In particular,
> Rawls is concerned with the many ways in which attributes that have
> no moral worth – like class, race, and sex – frequently deform people's
> prospects in life. Even if racism and sexism could be shown to maximize
> social utility, he says, they would still violate our basic sense of fairness . . .
> Starting from the basic idea of fairness, Rawls famously argues that all
> parties would insist on a very strong priority for basic liberties, because
> they would not want to risk something as important, say, as religious

freedom on the luck of where they might be placed in society. Then he argues, more controversially, that the parties would prefer a distribution of basic goods that would tolerate inequalities (because inequalities provide incentives to production) only when those inequalities raise the level of the least well off.   **99**

(Nussbaum 2001)

Rawls's text, as Nussbaum notes, is replete with cross references to many of the ideas he expounds in *A Theory of Justice* and this makes him difficult to read, as familiarity with the whole is necessary for understanding each part. To give a flavour of the text, here is an example in which he refers to fraternity, justice, democracy and meritocracy. At several points he mentions the *difference principle*. It is worth noting that the difference principle requires that inequalities in wealth and social position (which are inevitable) be arranged to benefit the worst off group in society – an important point to consider when thinking about opportunities in education, and how to maximize everyone's inclusion in education.

He concludes with the point that a sense of self-worth is important for all of society's members and that this need for self-worth should impose limits on the amount of inequality that a society should tolerate.

66 The ideal of fraternity is sometimes thought to involve ties of sentiment and feeling which it is unrealistic to expect between members of the wider society. And this is surely a further reason for its relative neglect in democratic theory. Many have felt that it has no proper place in political affairs. But if it is interpreted as incorporating the requirements of the difference principle, it is not an impracticable conception. It does seem that the institutions and policies which we most confidently think to be just satisfy its demands, at least in the sense that the inequalities permitted by them contribute to the well-being of the less favored. . . . On this interpretation, then, the principle of fraternity is a perfectly feasible standard. Once we accept it we can associate the traditional ideas of liberty, equality and fraternity with the democratic interpretation of the two principles of justice as follows: liberty corresponds to the first principle, equality to the idea of equality in the first principle together with equality of fair opportunity, and fraternity to the difference principle. In this way we have found a place for the conception of fraternity in the democratic interpretation of the two principles, and we see that it imposes a definite requirement on the basic structure of society. The other aspects of fraternity should not be forgotten, but the difference principle expresses its fundamental meaning from the standpoint of social justice.

Now it seems evident in the light of these observations that the democratic interpretation of the two principles will not lead to a meritocratic society. This form of social order follows the principle of careers open to talents and uses equality of opportunity as a way of releasing men's energies in the pursuit of economic prosperity and political dominion.

There exists a marked disparity between the upper and lower classes in both means of life and the rights and privileges of organizational authority. The culture of the poorer strata is impoverished while that of the governing and technocratic elite is securely based on the service of the national ends of power and wealth. Equality of opportunity means an equal chance to leave the less fortunate behind in the personal quest for influence and social position. Thus a meritocratic society is a danger for the other interpretations of the principles of justice but not for the democratic conception. For, as we have just seen, the difference principle transforms the aims of society in fundamental respects. This consequence is even more obvious once we note that we must when necessary take into account the essential primary good of self-respect and the fact that a well-ordered society is a social union of social unions . . . It follows that the confident sense of their own worth should be sought for the least favored and this limits the forms of hierarchy and the degrees of inequality that justice permits. Thus, for example, resources for education are not to be allotted solely or necessarily mainly according to their return as estimated in productive trained abilities, but also according to their worth in enriching the personal and social life of citizens, including here the less favored. As a society progresses the latter consideration becomes increasingly more important.

(Rawls 1972)

4. Martin Luther King: *I have a dream*

Martin Luther King's speech at the civil rights march before the Lincoln Memorial in August 1963 has a noble place in history for its call for the rights of black people to be recognized by a discriminatory, white America. Some progress has been made in the US since then, but like recognition of rights for disabled children and adults, there is still much to be achieved. King spoke powerfully of his country defaulting (for many years) on a constitutional promise of equality and said black people will 'never be satisfied' until they were afforded equal rights in all spheres.

The natural resonance that his famous speech has with issues surrounding segregation in education offers powerful insights and is worth revisiting time and again. The full text of his speech, *I have a dream* is given below.

> ❝   I am happy to join with you today in what will go down in history as the greatest demonstration for freedom in the history of our nation.
>
> Five score years ago, a great American, in whose symbolic shadow we stand today, signed the Emancipation Proclamation. This momentous decree came as a great beacon light of hope to millions of Negro slaves who had been seared in the flames of withering injustice. It came as a joyous daybreak to end the long night of their captivity.

But one hundred years later, the Negro still is not free; one hundred years later, the life of the Negro is still sadly crippled by the manacles of segregation and the chains of discrimination; one hundred years later, the Negro lives on a lonely island of poverty in the midst of a vast ocean of material prosperity; one hundred years later, the Negro is still languished in the corners of American society and finds himself in exile in his own land.

So we've come here today to dramatise a shameful condition. In a sense we've come to our nation's capital to cash a check. When the architects of our republic wrote the magnificent words of the Constitution and the Declaration of Independence, they were signing a promissory note to which every American was to fall heir. This note was the promise that all men, yes, black men as well as white men, would be guaranteed the unalienable rights of life, liberty, and the pursuit of happiness.

It is obvious today that America has defaulted on this promissory note in so far as her citizens of color are concerned. Instead of honoring this sacred obligation, America has given the Negro people a bad check; a check which has come back marked 'insufficient funds.' We refuse to believe that there are insufficient funds in the great vaults of opportunity of this nation. And so we've come to cash this check, a check that will give us upon demand the riches of freedom and the security of justice.

We have also come to this hallowed spot to remind America of the fierce urgency of now. This is no time to engage in the luxury of cooling off or to take the tranquilizing drug of gradualism. Now is the time to make real the promises of democracy; now is the time to rise from the dark and desolate valley of segregation to the sunlit path of racial justice; now is the time to lift our nation from the quicksands of racial injustice to the solid rock of brotherhood; now is the time to make justice a reality for all God's children. It would be fatal for the nation to overlook the urgency of the moment. This sweltering summer of the Negro's legitimate dis-content will not pass until there is an invigorating autumn of freedom and equality.

Nineteen sixty-three is not an end, but a beginning. And those who hope that the Negro needed to blow off steam and will now be content, will have a rude awakening if the nation returns to business as usual.

There will be neither rest nor tranquillity in America until the Negro is granted his citizenship rights. The whirlwinds of revolt will continue to shake the foundations of our nation until the bright day of justice emerges.

But there is something that I must say to my people who stand on the warm threshold which leads into the palace of justice. In the process of gaining our rightful place we must not be guilty of wrongful deeds.

Let us not seek to satisfy our thirst for freedom by drinking from the cup of bitterness and hatred. We must forever conduct our struggle on the high plane of dignity and discipline. We must not allow our creative pro-test to degenerate into physical violence. Again and again we must rise to the majestic heights of meeting physical force with soul force.

The marvellous new militancy which has engulfed the Negro community must not lead us to a distrust of all white people, for many of our white brothers, as evidenced by their presence here today, have come to realize that their destiny is tied up with our destiny and they have come to realize that their freedom is inextricably bound to our freedom. This offense we share mounted to storm the battlements of injustice must be carried forth by a biracial army. We cannot walk alone.

And as we walk, we must make the pledge that we shall always march ahead. We cannot turn back. There are those who are asking the devotees of civil rights, 'When will you be satisfied?'

We can never be satisfied as long as the Negro is the victim of the unspeakable horrors of police brutality.

We can never be satisfied as long as our bodies, heavy with fatigue of travel, cannot gain lodging in the motels of the highways and the hotels of the cities. We cannot be satisfied as long as the Negro's basic mobility is from a smaller ghetto to a larger one.

We can never be satisfied as long as our children are stripped of their selfhood and robbed of their dignity by signs stating 'for whites only.' We cannot be satisfied as long as a Negro in Mississippi cannot vote and a Negro in New York believes he has nothing for which to vote. No, we are not satisfied, and we will not be satisfied until justice rolls down like waters and righteousness like a mighty stream.

I am not unmindful that some of you come here out of excessive trials and tribulation. Some of you have come fresh from narrow jail cells. Some of you have come from areas where your quest for freedom left you battered by the storms of persecution and staggered by the winds of police brutality. You have been the veterans of creative suffering. Continue to work with the faith that unearned suffering is redemptive.

Go back to Mississippi; go back to Alabama; go back to South Carolina; go back to Georgia; go back to Louisiana; go back to the slums and ghettos of the northern cities, knowing that somehow this situation can, and will be changed. Let us not wallow in the valley of despair.

So I say to you, my friends, that even though we must face the difficulties of today and tomorrow, I still have a dream. It is a dream deeply rooted in the American dream that one day this nation will rise up and live out the true meaning of its creed – we hold these truths to be self-evident, that all men are created equal.

I have a dream that one day on the red hills of Georgia, sons of former slaves and sons of former slave-owners will be able to sit down together at the table of brotherhood.

I have a dream that one day, even the state of Mississippi, a state sweltering with the heat of injustice, sweltering with the heat of oppression, will be transformed into an oasis of freedom and justice.

I have a dream my four little children will one day live in a nation where they will not be judged by the color of their skin but by the content of their character. I have a dream today!

I have a dream that one day, down in Alabama, with its vicious racists, with its governor having his lips dripping with the words of interposition and nullification, that one day, right there in Alabama, little black boys and black girls will be able to join hands with little white boys and white girls as sisters and brothers. I have a dream today!

I have a dream that one day every valley shall be exalted, every hill and mountain shall be made low, the rough places shall be made plain, and the crooked places shall be made straight and the glory of the Lord will be revealed and all flesh shall see it together.

This is our hope. This is the faith that I go back to the South with.

With this faith we will be able to hew out of the mountain of despair a stone of hope. With this faith we will be able to transform the jangling discords of our nation into a beautiful symphony of brotherhood.

With this faith we will be able to work together, to pray together, to struggle together, to go to jail together, to stand up for freedom, together, knowing that we will be free one day. This will be the day, when all of God's children will be able to sing with new meaning – 'my country 'tis of thee; sweet land of liberty; of thee I sing; land, where my fathers died, land of the pilgrim's pride; from every mountain side, let freedom ring' – and if America is to be a great nation, this must become true.

So let freedom ring from the prodigious hilltops of New Hampshire.

Let freedom ring from the mighty mountains of New York.

Let freedom ring from the heightening Alleghenies of Pennsylvania.

Let freedom ring from the snow-capped Rockies of Colorado.

Let freedom ring from the curvaceous slopes of California.

But not only that.

Let freedom ring from Stone Mountain of Georgia.

Let freedom ring from Lookout Mountain of Tennessee.

Let freedom ring from every hill and molehill of Mississippi, from every mountainside, let Freedom ring.

And when we allow freedom to ring, when we let it ring from every village and hamlet, from every state and city, we will be able to speed up that day when all of God's children – black men and white men, Jews and Gentiles, Catholics and Protestants – will be able to join hands and to sing in the words of the old Negro spiritual, 'Free at last, free at last; thank God Almighty, we are free at last.'   **99**

(King 1963)

5. Caroline Roaf and Hazel Bines: *Needs, Rights and Opportunities*

In the excerpts given so far, we have focused on the slow historical march to improvements in rights, justice, fraternity and equality. We view considerations on these matters to be at the cornerstone of any deliberation on the shape of an education system. Yet in deliberations about special education they have often been buried under discussions about the efficacy of this or that system. In the following piece from Roaf and Bines there is an appeal for a fundamental re-examination of the priorities of the special education system and an argument that policy underpinning the shape of any education system should be rooted in rights.

In the UK, the emphasis in the special education system – especially in its processes of assessment – has tended to emphasize *need*. In some ways this has presented distinct advantages over the American approach, which has by contrast stressed *disability*. Where British educators talk about *special needs*, Americans would be more likely to talk of *learning disabilities*. This emphasis on needs has offered benefits over the American approach, placing more stress on the provider than on the child. If the talk is of need, the corollary is to think of ways of meeting that need. If we talk, by contrast, of disability then there can be the tendency for a certain passivity on the part of those in the education system: the child has a disability, so not much can be expected. There is, in other words, no concomitant expectation that one could do much about the disability. Disability implies treatment, in the medical way of viewing things, while need implies provision for that need from a varied pool of potential resources.

This was the reason for the UK Warnock Committee's emphasis on needs in its report in 1978. The assumption was that an emphasis on needs would bring an end to the categorization – blind, 'educationally subnormal', maladjusted, and so forth – that had characterized assessment and pedagogy in the period prior to the report.

However, what happened, as Roaf and Bines point out in the following piece, was that the term 'need' merely became a new category in itself: a new way of labelling. Many teachers might quietly draw the attention of visitors to their classrooms to the 'special needs child' in the corner, or to 'the special educational needs (SEN) group'. Moreover, the term was subject to abuse in the sense that it could be interpreted relativistically: difficulties that might be interpreted to constitute a special need in leafy Surbiton might not even be thought worthy of comment in inner-city Birmingham.

Roaf and Bines thus suggest that rights and opportunities are a better way of framing the education of children who are experiencing difficulties at school. In making this suggestion they move full circle back to the American way of viewing things. For the Americans – even though they have perhaps employed an unhelpfully deficit-oriented emphasis in the use of 'disability' – have also had, from the very beginnings of their critical discourse on special education, a strong emphasis on rights in education.

Emphasizing civil and other rights places the spotlight on equity, and the dignity that comes from such equal treatment. As Roaf and Bines say in the following piece, 'Lack of dignity and respect is too often associated with "having a need".'

It is also more likely to engender a more assertive stance from the consumers of the education system – reducing, as Roaf and Bines point out, professional power and paternalism. It is this emphasis on rights that has led to the growing number of advocacy groups that emerged over the last decade of the twentieth century, many of them pushing explicitly for mainstream education to educate children with a range of difficulties.

More than this though, this spotlight on rights has also shifted attention away solely from disability – from 'integration' and mainstreaming. It has shifted attention toward a broader interest in genuinely inclusive education systems – systems that seek to include all children, whatever the provenance of their difficulty at school, whether it be disability, poverty, gender or culture.

❝ The central conception of this chapter is that the concept of 'need' is inadequate on its own as a means of achieving the goals of education for those identified as having special needs. Instead, we argue that the addition of the discourse of equal opportunities and rights, with its emphasis on entitlement, would provide a more effective basis for policy and practice . . .

The current emphasis on needs may have obscured other aspects in the development of special education, such as the degree to which equality of opportunity has been a significant dimension of debate and policy . . .

The concept of needs
Despite the changes in definition of special educational need, it remains a very difficult and complex concept in practice. It has the appearance of simplicity and familiarity, yet its use in so many contexts, the fact that it appears to have both normative and non-normative meaning and that it is essentially concerned with values and priorities, should alert us to its complexity. Thus, the greatest care is required in evaluating needs, in prioritizing them and in being clear in whose interest they are being stated. This is especially true at the present time when we are already a long way from the days when it was only handicapped children who were perceived as having needs.

Firstly, the term *needs* is often used in relation to the development and learning of all children. Given their individuality and idiosyncrasy, defining what constitutes a *special* educational need in any particular case can be difficult. However, if special education is to be used as a basis for special resource allocation, the difference between special and other educational needs would seem to have to be acknowledged. Although the 1981 Act emphasizes the relationship between learning difficulty and special educational need, learning difficulty in the past has largely been used in relation to remedial provision. Since this has been somewhat separate from other special education, its more general use for all forms of special needs is ambiguous. In addition, although 'special educational needs' is now the generic term, the number of specific descriptive categories has not been reduced. Indeed the Warnock Report and 1981 Act, while attempting to remove differences between handicapped and non-handicapped students, did not take special education out of the realm of handicap. Instead, more students have been brought within its brief under the much broader and ill-defined category of learning difficulty, and further divisions have emerged, particularly between students who are subjects of Statements and those who are not.

Secondly, the relativism of needs as currently understood can lead to haphazard and unequal provision. 'Special educational need' is a legal and administrative term as well as an educational and descriptive one thus taking on different meanings according to the context in which it is used. Such relativism is also a feature of the legislative definitions within the 1981 Education Act, where need is defined in terms of the level of difficulty experienced by other children and the kind of educational provision available. Being considered to have a special educational need may, therefore, largely depend on which school is attended and in which locality, leading to considerable variations in assessment, placement and subsequent educational treatment. Because needs in themselves do not necessarily indicate or define teaching approaches, nor the extent of special provision, current conceptions of needs have been developed as enabling rather than prescriptive and very much depend on current conceptions of good practice. Although there may at present be an emphasis on necessary change in the curricula and schools, the concept of needs in itself gives no protection or assurance that such a definition of good practice will be sustained. Since special needs are seen to be relative to those of other children and are also relative to current knowledge and conceptions of good practice, there is always the danger that different definitions may prevail. Unless we are very particular about what constitutes need, and associated provision, we may thus deny both general equal educational opportunity and equal special educational opportunity (Brennan, 1981).

Thirdly, as indicated by this relativism, needs are a matter of professional and value judgment. The moral and political basis of such judgments are usually neglected because we still focus on the *receiver* – the individual or group with needs. Yet hidden within these conceptions of needs are social interests, for example, to make the disabled productive or control troublesome children, together with a range of assumptions about what is *normal* (Tomlinson, 1982). When we focus on needs and particularly when we take our assumptions about the nature of those needs for granted, we do not ask who has the power to define the needs of others. We do not enquire why it is professionals who mostly define needs, as opposed to parents or the students themselves. Nor do we fully explore the normative nature of our assumptions, for example, that they are grounded in conceptions of 'normal' cognitive development or behaviour whether such assumptions are informally operated, by teachers in the classroom, or more formally operated, by normative testing. We focus on what seem to be the genuine needs of the individual who lacks something and who have a need. However, we do not consider how needs may be generated by valuing certain aspects of development and attainment more than others. For example, if we did not value certain cognitive skills, would there be the needs currently identified as 'special' in schools? (Hargreaves, 1983).

Finally, the term 'needs' has now become a euphemism for labelling individuals as 'special'. This is partly due to its hidden implications and partly to limited change in traditional approaches and practice. The idea of having a difficulty suggests something can be done about it (or even that the cause may be the difficulty of the learning on offer). Similarly, handicap, particularly if we apply the distinction between impairment, disability and handicap (the last being societal in character) suggests some social context. Needs, however, tends to refocus on individuals as a bottomless pit of problems to be overcome or filled up. The concept of needs remains deficit-based, despite attempts to relate it to context, with an inbuilt tendency to slippage back towards individuals and their problems. It is not always easy, for example, to make the distinction between those who have learning difficulties of one kind or another, and may require special provision, and those who need special provision but do not have learning difficulties. The classic example is of those for whom English is not the first language, but there are others. Needs are largely now special and seen as such despite the potential radicalism of the approach with which they are currently associated, and are often little more than a new label for old practices and problems.

Opportunity and equality

Given that 'needs' is a problematic concept, 'opportunity' would seem to offer a better approach to special education. Firstly, there is a much more explicit focus on context: 'opportunity' raises questions of system rather than individual failure. When linked with equality, to make 'equality of opportunity', it also raises issues of discrimination and disadvantage. Equality of opportunity is also a widely known and understood rationale, given the importance of egalitarianism in educational policies until recently. Even in the current political climate, egalitarianism remains in our educational thinking. Therefore, it may be easier for the majority of teachers and policymakers to relate to opportunity rather than needs or at least to see the educational, social and political implications of requiring that equal opportunity be extended to those with impairments and difficulties. Notions of opportunity and equality are also relevant to mainstream settings in that they are comprehensive, in rhetoric if not reality, and thus we should be able to argue for improved and integrated special education using the comprehensive principle (Booth, 1983). By focusing on opportunity, it should also be possible to relate developments in special education to some of the developments in comprehensive schooling, which have attempted to focus on success rather than failure, for example, records of achievement, the core curriculum and mixed ability grouping, all of which have been part of the effort to provide access to a common schooling, rather than exclusion from a selective schooling.

In addition, a lot of work has been done on equality of opportunity in other areas, for example, class, gender, race, on which we could draw (Adams, 1988; Byrne, 1985; ILEA, 1985). We understand inequality as structural, institutional and interpersonal and have strategies to deal with each of these levels (Lynch, 1986; Straker-Welds, 1984). For example, we understand how discrimination, and therefore lack of opportunity, may be subtly or indeed explicitly reflected in aspects of schooling such as the curriculum and teaching materials and could use such understanding in relation to special education. Equal opportunity is also an effective touchstone for evaluating provision.

However, there are problems with opportunity, particularly when put forward *as equal opportunity*. Firstly, there has been much confusion generally between liberal (access) and radical (outcomes) versions of the equality debate (Evetts, 1973). It can also be difficult to achieve equality of opportunity without encountering contradictions such as the difficulty of balancing normalization with the need for positive discrimination and provision. Such difficulties may be even more pertinent to debates about special educational needs because physical and other impairments may not just mean overcoming structural disadvantage and discrimination but also providing compensatory measures. By contrast the equality debate in relation to class, gender and race supposes all groups to have the same basic qualities. When different resources, teaching and provision are required, this raises a central area of confusion for teachers for whom a 'difference blind' or 'normalization' approach is more familiar than a 'social justice' perspective to equality concerned with realization of potential.

It is important to be very clear as to what form of equality of opportunity is being argued. Basic issues of access and integration have still not been solved and many educational opportunities continue to be denied just through a lack of resources, such as access for the physically disabled. Achieving such access would in itself be a major gain in some instances. It would also seem to be beneficial to operate the more radical notion of opportunity, arguing for positive discrimination in terms of staffing or resources in order to ensure that children and young people experiencing impairment or other difficulties do get full benefit from ordinary education. It would also seem worthwhile to make the connections between disadvantage arising out of class, race or gender and disadvantage arising out of special needs as traditionally perceived. Nevertheless, equality of opportunity still seems to imply being dependent on the gift of others and on making the best of yourself, which not all young people can do.

Finally, using the equality of opportunity approach to developing special education rests on certain political and moral assumptions and beliefs which are not accepted by all. Thus, even though egalitarianism is embedded in educational thinking, elitism is just as powerful an ideology, and increasingly so. Equality of opportunity may not, therefore, be the most effective rationale for developing provision or curriculum.

Rights
Rights as a basis for developing special education policy and practice would seem to have a number of advantages. As Kirp (1983) has

suggested, comparing British and American special education policies and legislation, thinking about special education in terms of political and legal rights makes one reappraise resource allocation, relationships among the affected parties, the level and amount of dispute and the very conception of handicap. In respect to resource allocation, for example, the American structure of rights does not formally treat resource limits as constraining what can be provided. Whereas the British approach weighs the interests of special and ordinary children, the American orientation on rights places the burden of adjustment on the ordinary school. The greater disputes engendered by a rights approach, including increased litigation, may make for a more dynamic policy and lead school authorities to offer more than would otherwise have been provided. In respect to the disabled themselves, rights should encourage a stronger definition and assertion of self and interests, reducing professional power and paternalism. When rights legislation is explicitly linked with other civil rights, special education also becomes part of the larger struggle for equity. Race or gender dimensions of being 'special' can then also be raised.

Rights would also seem to encourage a more careful and objective distribution of resources. It avoids the dangers of relativism and localism. It can potentially identify and secure not only type and amount of provision but also placement, policy, practice and curriculum, for example the *least restrictive environment* as in the USA. 'Rights' would seem to strengthen the social justice element in opportunity to raise broader social as well as educational issues.

To regard children considered to have special educational needs as children whose rights are being infringed in some way would very substantially alter the status not only of children themselves, but also of special needs teachers and others who work on their behalf in their negotiations with the educational hierarchy. For Bandman (1973), rights 'enable us to stand with dignity, if necessary to demand what is our due without having to grovel, plead or beg'. Lack of dignity and respect is too often associated with 'having a need'. As Freeman (1987, p. 300) argues:

> Children have not been accorded either dignity or respect. They have been reified, denied the status of participants in the social system, labelled as a problem population, reduced to being seen as property. Too often justice for the young has been trumped by considerations of utility or, even worse, of convenience.

The emergence of children's rights as an important social and political issue is thus to be welcomed. However, as with needs and opportunity, there are difficult issues in the rights approach to be faced by educators. Currently, there is more concern to protect children or professional interests than to protect children's rights. Further, in order to develop rights we need to identify groups and must ask whether entitlement presumes categories. This may well seem contradictory to special needs teachers who have been exhorted to abandon categories. We also have to consider whether a rights approach can be flexible enough to accommodate individuals with particular configurations of needs and therefore rights. In addition, there is the issue of what should be the basis of rights and how they can best be implemented. If we use legislation, there is the potential problem of too much litigation. On the other hand, just focusing on political discussion and change may be too long-term. There is also the question of how to balance the rights of some against the rights of others, given finite resources, and whether a rights approach would mesh effectively into the tendency of British policy approaches to be enabling rather than prescriptive and legalistic . . .

Conclusion

The picture which is emerging, then, is essentially one of progressively developing ideas about community and the extent to which it is possible to bring about a state of affairs in which people value each other with something approaching equality of esteem and concern. This raises a number of questions. How, for example, is a balance to be achieved between rights and responsibilities? On what basis is the distinction to be made between needs which can be met and those which cannot? In the past attempts to resolve these problems stemmed from philanthropy and empathy for others but were characterized by the spasmodic and indiscriminate attention typically bestowed upon minority, disadvantaged and powerless groups by powerful groups. This approach also allowed too readily for damage limitation, with those in power not needing to be more generous, observant or humane than was convenient to them. These new perspectives advocated here would seem to provide a more secure framework in which to define needs and assert rights.

However, although we have stressed the problems and limitations associated with a philanthropic approach, certain aspects of it should not be abandoned entirely. Caring for anyone is important, as are notions of duty and responsibility, neither of them far from the language of rights. Egalitarian and equal opportunity approaches have widened this but can only be effective when coupled with a strong emphasis on rights and anti-discrimination and a developing understanding of the effect of interpersonal, institutional and structural prejudice and discrimination (Lynch, 1986).

It is significant that the debates and dilemmas which we have been discussing in relation to young people who, in the pre-Warnock days were regarded as handicapped, have also been seen in relation to race and gender. In connection with ethnic minorities, a needs-based perspective emphasizing assimilation and integration characterized the fifties and sixties within which the needs of the immigrant communities were those defined by the host community. In turn this was succeeded by a perspective emphasizing diversity. This was an improvement, conferring a greater sense of community and equality of opportunity but in a notably 'weak' form. It has had to be strengthened by policies emphasizing the active reduction of prejudice and unfair discrimination, through the courts, both national and European if necessary. The gender debate has been characterized by a broadly similar succession of perspectives.

These developments in relation to special education could do much to move provision and curriculum from traditional, deficit-based and paternalistic approaches towards approaches which would embrace and protect the interests of all minority groups. We need to be aware, however, that the language used in the discourse and debate to promote a sense of community, in which social justice prevails, is open to a range of interpretations and can be all too readily moulded to the political climate of the time. Needs, rights and opportunity are powerful words with different meanings for different interest groups. They will have to be further clarified before they can be used to best effect and the implications and processes of change be well monitored and evaluated to ensure desired outcomes are being achieved. The issues are difficult and may not all be resolved but without the discussion of the strengths and limitations of current and potential approaches which this book hopes to generate, gains which have been made in special education will remain precarious and vulnerable.   **99**

(Roaf and Bines 1989)

6. Sharon Rustemier: Social justice

There is always a difficulty in understanding social issues in the context of human rights, and this seems particularly to have been the case in education. The publication of a ground-breaking document from CSIE in November 2002 entitled *Social and Educational Justice: The Human Rights Framework for Inclusion* took the debate in this area further.

The report rejects the notion of 'inclusive special schools' and calls for all resources in special schools to be transferred to mainstream settings, which themselves should be restructured to increase their capacity to respond to student diversity in its entirety.

The report, written by Sharon Rustemier, said that the central problem with the development of inclusive education in the UK is the continuing philosophical, financial and legislative support for segregated special schools and it demonstrates how this segregation is internationally recognized as discriminatory and damaging to individuals and to society as a whole.

As well as violating children's rights to inclusive education, Rustemier says segregated schooling breaches all four principles underpinning the 1989 United Nations Convention on the Rights of the Child.

These principles are:

❝ 1. non-discrimination (Article 2) – all children should enjoy all rights without discrimination and on the basis of equality of opportunity;
2. the best interests of the child (Article 3);
3. the right to life, survival and development (Article 6) – development is meant in its broadest sense, including physical health but also mental, emotional, cognitive, social and cultural, and 'to the maximum extent possible'; and
4. the views of the child (Article 12) – children have the right to be heard and to have their views taken seriously in matters affecting them. ❞

In the introduction to the report, Rustemier argues that 'inclusion' has come to mean almost everything but the elimination of exclusion.

❝ There have been significant advances towards inclusion in the UK in recent years. The legal strengthening of the right to mainstream education for pupils with statements of 'special educational needs' and the introduction of disability discrimination, race relations and human rights laws, mark milestones in developing the capacity of mainstream schools to enable all children and young people to learn together.
The introduction of citizenship to the national curriculum, the intention to develop a 'human rights culture', and the attention to social inclusion and community cohesion represent a real concern with ending discrimination and promoting equal opportunities in education and in society. . . . [with] the increased employment of learning supporters in schools and attention to their training and status, and a new commitment by all Government departments to involve children and young people in policy-making, the scene seems set for inclusion to become a reality in mainstream schools. There has never been a better framework for social and educational justice for disabled young people.
However, fundamental obstacles remain to the development of restructured, genuinely inclusive schools. The adoption of the term 'inclusion' into common education language signifies in many instances a genuine desire to improve the experiences of all learners. At other times it seems a concept misunderstood or even deliberately distorted. The confusion masks a deeply contradictory education system in which efforts to increase inclusion are continually beset by initiatives which promote exclusion through legislation and policy.
The current education system excludes and segregates large numbers of children from mainstream education because of learning difficulty, disability, and behaviour, despite claiming to have inclusion as its goal. Philosophical, financial and legislative support of separate 'special' schools continues. New special schools and pupil referral units are being opened at the same time as legislation against disability discrimination in schools and increasing rights to mainstream education is enacted. There are special schools that paradoxically describe themselves as inclusive.
There is no intention to reduce many of the competitive exclusionary pressures on schools in England – league tables, national tests, increasing

specialisation, and selection by ability. Competition within and between schools is a heavy disincentive to investment in developing schools' responsiveness to a wide diversity of pupils, rather than focusing on those likely to achieve highly. Claims of a social model approach to disability and difficulty in learning are undermined by the continuing investment of buildings, careers and training in separate 'special' education and medical models of needs, as well as by the reluctance of mainstream schools to undertake the restructuring necessary to embrace all learners.

These deep contradictions between forces for inclusion and pressures for exclusion severely limit the impact of the inclusion reforms and outcomes.

While many more people now seem to be speaking the language of inclusion – social cohesion, community cohesion, racial integration, human rights, disability rights, rights to mainstream – what is happening in practice is much more muddled.

'Inclusion' has come to mean almost everything but the elimination of exclusion. It has become commonly accepted that there are limits as to who can be included in the mainstream – the exceptions usually being those with high level support needs and others currently in special schools, those presenting behaviour that teachers and others find challenging, and now asylum seeking children. Social inclusion is seen to be achievable through education which practices segregation. 'Human rights' has similarly come to be beset with exceptions, most notably disabled people, children, and especially disabled children. The creation of a human rights culture and the teaching of human rights, have come to be seen as unrelated to the recognition of all children's human rights in education.

If the opportunities for inclusion heralded by the recent legislative reforms are to be maximised, the basic tenets of inclusion need to be restated, and the continuing exclusion of some children and young people from mainstream to special schools and pupil referral units needs to be recognised as a form of institutionalised discrimination and a denial of human rights which has serious consequences for individuals and society.   **99**

The report concludes by pointing out the importance of building . . .

66   . . . on the positive steps towards inclusion that have been taken in recent years. In particular, the disability discrimination laws and the duty on schools and LEAs to plan for increased accessibility should significantly reduce the segregation and exclusion of disabled pupils from mainstream education. However, fully inclusive education – the elimination of discrimination and the equalisation of opportunities for all students – requires far more.

The central problem in the development of inclusive education in the UK is a culture that rests on the continuing philosophical, financial and legislative support of segregated schooling, which has its roots in education services first designed 120 years ago. Legislative shortcomings, a focus on availability and accessibility at the expense of acceptability and adaptability, and contradictory messages about the purposes of education create the conditions in which special schools continue to play a role, despite the stated commitment to social and educational inclusion. Their existence is rationalised by appeals to deeply held false beliefs about the impossibility of ever including all children in the mainstream, the supposedly 'huge expense' of full inclusion, and the sanctity of parental choice.

The central task in developing real inclusive education, then, must be the phased closure of special schools, the transfer of all resources to mainstream settings, and the restructuring of mainstream schools to increase their capacity to respond to student diversity in its entirety.

Logically, it is not difficult to challenge the belief systems which are used to rationalise segregated provision for some students. That some children cannot possibly be included in mainstream education is refuted by the many successful experiences of including disabled students with high level support needs and those presenting challenging behaviour, to the benefit of all learners. Continuing to pour resources into statutory assessment and statementing and segregated special schools has been demonstrated as a highly inefficient use of public money. Transferring these resources to mainstream settings would offset the costs of inclusion. A real commitment to the human rights of children would address the current elevation of parents' rights.

In practice, these obstacles are less easily overcome because the process requires changing hearts and minds. The human rights approach demands a fundamental conviction that all human beings are of absolutely equal worth, simply by virtue of being human. Without this conviction, it is possible for special schools to continue to be supported despite being detrimental to children's best interests, contrary to the development of social inclusion, highly discriminatory, and an economically and educationally inefficient use of public money. With this conviction, it is possible that the ensuing sense of outrage will be sufficient to demand an end to the systematic violation of children's human rights through segregation.

                                                                      (Rustemier 2002)

7. David Hevey: Images of difference

Difference can be seen in two ways. It can either be seen as a source of division, or it can be seen as a source of new energy, of diversity and variety. Images of people who are in some way different or disabled can therefore take two broad forms: those that stress division (even supposedly kindly and sympathetically) or those that celebrate diversity.

Images of disabled people have long taken the former shape: stressing the division between those people and other 'normal' people. They have presented difference of this kind as difference to be pitied, and as such they can be insulting to those different people. Even in the supposedly celebratory form they can be stereotyped and patronizing. So it was refreshing in 1992 when the photographer David Hevey, who is himself disabled, wrote *The Creatures Time Forgot*. Hevey examined the representation of disabled people in society, particularly in advertising, and showed that such images portrayed disabled people as 'creatures' in one of two realms: the first was the 'tragic-but-brave' objects of the photographic gaze and, the second, the happy, handicapped person in so-called 'positive imagery' of advertising.

Hevey argues that following developments in the social position of disabled people through a movement that demanded 'Rights not Charity', there is a 'crisis in traditional forms of disability imagery'. Through a hard-hitting text and powerful collection of his own photographs, alongside a selection of typical 'charity' pictures of disabled people, Hevey's pioneering contribution has helped society gradually move away from a 'medical, charity or impairment-fixated imagery towards a visual equivalent of Rights not Charity'. The following extract is taken from the introduction to his book.

❝ I have had several flashes on the road to Damascus. The first came when, as a 15 year-old schoolboy, my chaos was compounded by the delirious, furious advent of an epileptic seizure. I did not know what it was and had probably never heard of epilepsy. Flashing lights, like bonfire sparklers with rainbow colours, appeared in front of my eyes. As I attempted to apologise to my grammar-school master for this inconvenience, my vision was almost totally eclipsed by this and the other hallucinations I was witnessing. I staggered into the playground out of his sight and into what I thought was oblivion. For years I lived with this terror. At that period, the point about epilepsy was fear. It was, for me, the monotonous consistency of this terror and fear that made me 'an epileptic' all of the time, not just at the point of seizures. In fact, a curious alleviation of this fear came when I began to hallucinate and knew very well that I had about three minutes to get myself lying down and, even more daunting, settle down all those panicking around me. I very quickly realised that responsibility for my epilepsy had brought with it responsibility for other people's reactions: sometimes idiocy and ignorance, sometimes clear strength and support.

The second flash on this road to Damascus as a disabled person came when I encountered the disability movement. I had learnt to live with my private fear and to feel that I was the only one involved in this fight. I had internalised my oppression. As a working-class son of Irish immigrants, I had experienced other struggles but, in retrospect, I evidently saw epilepsy as my hidden cross. I cannot explain how significantly all this was turned around when I came into contact with the notion of the social model of disabilities, rather than the medical model which I had hitherto lived with. Over a matter of months, my discomfort with this secret beast of burden called epilepsy, and my festering hatred at the silencing of myself as a disabled person, 'because I didn't look it', completely changed. I think I went through an almost evangelical conversion as I realised that my disability was not, in fact, the epilepsy, but the toxic drugs with their denied side-effects; the medical regime with its blaming of the victim; the judgement through distance and silence of bus-stop crowds, bar-room crowds, and dinner-table friends; the fear; and, not least, the employment problems. All this was the oppression, not the epileptic seizure at which I was hardly (consciously) present.

As I worked to separate out the medical condition from the disability, I began to work on, even attack, the disabling areas. The first was the fifteen years which I had spent on toxic drugs. I am now working through a holistic health regime of homeopathy and cranial massage. No longer do I have to live with burning stomach pains caused by my toxic medication, no longer do I experience epilepsy as an area of shame and chaos. In coming out as a disabled person, the internalised phantoms have also come out: the 'hidden' medical condition is no longer hidden, at least by me.

My personal journey of private crisis, of the slow gaining of understanding of disability as an external oppression, and on into the disability movement, vitally informs my photographs. Although the photographic portraits tell a part of the story of those portrayed, the photographs also in part tell my story of transformation.
""

(Hevey 1992)

PART   TWO

Arguments and evidence against segregation – 1960s to today

8. Erving Goffman: *Asylums*

We begin this part with Erving Goffman's work, not because it had anything specifically to say about special education, but because in 1968 it marked the beginnings of a questioning of the automatic assumption that separation of a portion of the public to segregated institutions must be a good thing. As Goffman points out, such institutions often present themselves as the rational and humane solution to people's difficulties, but they in fact operate merely as society's 'storage dumps'.

Goffman's *Asylums* became the kind of classic text that moves outside its original academic audience to a much wider public. The book comprises a series of papers about people placed in what Goffman called 'total institutions' – that is to say, places that separate their inhabitants from the outside world with locked doors and high walls. These include mental hospitals, boarding schools and so on.

The papers compiled in *Asylums* were originally published in academic journals. Although this was the case, *Asylums* caught the public imagination because it presented for questioning many shibboleths about helping services and the people who worked in them. Ideas taken to be truths and professional practices and social institutions that were previously beyond question became, with Goffman's work, open to question. Were these institutions really all they were supposed to be? Did the staff in them always act in the best interests of the inhabitants? Although Goffman was not the first to ask these questions, he was one of the first to put them in language that was accessible and interesting to the lay reader.

In *Asylums* Goffman looks at the people in these institutions and seeks to interpret their experience rather than justifying the system that contained them.

The special school is not a *total institution* in the way that Goffman writes about asylums. However, many of the questions that he asks of such institutions are relevant to special schools, and one sees those questions echoed in several other pieces in this volume. For example, what is the purpose of the special school, and of special education more generally? The implication of Goffman's piece is that institutions such as these are constructed to serve the purpose of the wider system rather than the inhabitants of the institution, and one can draw from this insight the possibility that the special school system may exist primarily for the convenience of the mainstream system rather than for the purpose of helping or improving the lives of those who are directed to the special system.

In the second part of the piece extracted below, Goffman refers to the 'paper trail' that accompanies patients as they move through the system. This is given as an illustration of the process that comes to dominate an institution: defensive action designed to protect staff rather than ensuring that the needs of patients are met. Here the insight – appropriate also to today's education – comes from seeing the 'flip-side' of a procedure: from seeing how a slogan such as 'protection' can in fact come to mean something altogether different.

In today's education system one can see a similar process operating as procedures set in place notionally to protect a child – such as an Individual Education Plan (IEP) or a statement of special educational needs – can in practice turn out to be hollow, comprising merely vacuous language devised to meet the needs only of the system, not the child. Thus a statement of special educational need, for example, will be couched in such general language that it could mean anything that the sponsoring local authority wants it to mean.

It is for this reason – for the 'flip-side' insights that it provides – that *Asylums* became a classic. And it is in the questioning of authority, authority's knowledge and the provision emerging from authority's edicts incorporated in those insights that it has relevance for our understanding of special education.

&& Many total institutions most of the time seem to function merely as storage dumps for inmates, but, as previously suggested, they usually present themselves to the public as rational organizations designed consciously, through and through, as effective machines for producing a few officially avowed and officially approved ends. It was also suggested [earlier in *Asylums*] that one frequent official objective is the reformation of inmates in the direction of some ideal standard. This contradiction, between what the institution does and what its officials must say it does, forms the basic context of the staff's daily activity.

Within this context, perhaps the first thing to say about the staff is that their work, and hence their world, have uniquely to do with people. This *people-work* is not quite like personnel work or the work of those involved in service relationships; the staff, after all, have objects and products to work upon, not services, but these objects and products are people.

As material upon which to work, people can take on somewhat the same characteristics as inanimate objects. Surgeons prefer to operate on slender patients rather than fat ones, because with fat ones instruments get slippery, and there are the extra layers to cut through. Morticians in mental hospitals sometimes favour thin females over fat men, because heavy 'stiffs' are difficult to move and male stiffs must be dressed in jackets that are hard to pull over stiffened arms and fingers. Also, mismanagement of either animate or inanimate objects may leave tell-tale marks for supervisors to see. And just as an article being processed through an industrial plant must be followed by a paper shadow showing what has been done by whom, what is to be done, and who last had responsibility for it, so a human object moving, say, through a mental-hospital system must be followed by a chain of informative receipts detailing what has been done to and by the patient and who had most recent responsibility for him. Even the presence or absence of a particular patient at a given meal or for a given night may have to be recorded, so that cost accounting can be maintained and appropriate adjustments rendered in billing. In the inmate's career from admission suite to burial plot, many different kinds of staff will add their official note to his case file as he temporarily passes under their jurisdiction, and long after he has died physically his marked remains will survive as an actionable entity in the hospital's bureaucratic system.   **99**

(Goffman [1961] 1968)

9. L.M. Dunn: Special education – is much of it justifiable?

In this article Dunn made a prescient case for the radical restructuring not just for special education but for education in general. It's an article frequently referred to in the academic literature as one of the markers of the beginnings of de-segregative thought.

It has to be remembered that Dunn was writing in 1968, before the substantial discussion that has brought us to where we are today in our thinking about inclusion. Dunn argues his case boldly and bravely – a case that would have attracted a great deal of opposition and resentment at that time. For special education, as Sally Tomlinson makes clear in the passage later in this part, was (and still is) seen by public and politicians as a Good Thing, and publicly to question it raised perplexity and hostility.

Many of his words predate much of the debate that is now going on. He makes the point that much of the problem with so-called 'learning disabled' children is merely to do with poverty. He suggests that ' . . .we must stop labelling these deprived children as mentally retarded. Furthermore we must stop segregating them by placing them into our allegedly special programs.'

After the passage extracted here, Dunn goes on to outline a 'blueprint for change' in which he puts forward a far more clinical approach to assessment and teaching than many of us would now endorse, knowing what we now know about the very limited effectiveness of, for example, diagnostic-prescriptive teaching. Moreover, his call is only for a limited form of inclusion. However, Dunn's views preceded many of the changes that were subsequently talked about.

66   *In lieu of an abstract to this article, I would like to preface it by saying this is my swan song for now – as I leave special education and this country for probably the next two years. I have been honored to be a past president of The Council for Exceptional Children. I have loyally supported and promoted special classes for the educable mentally retarded for most of the last 20 years, but with growing disaffection. In my view, much of our past and present practices are morally and educationally wrong. We have been living at the mercy of general educators who have referred their problem children to us. And we have been generally ill prepared and ineffective in educating these children. Let us stop being pressured into continuing and expanding* *a special education program that we know now to be undesirable for many of the children we are dedicated to serve.*

A better education than special class placement is needed for socio-culturally deprived children with mild learning problems who have been labeled educable mentally retarded. Over the years, the status of these pupils who come from poverty, broken and inadequate homes, and low status ethnic groups has been a checkered one. In the early days, these children were simply excluded from school. Then, as Hollingworth (1923) pointed out, with the advent of compulsory attendance laws, the schools and these children 'were forced into a reluctant mutual recognition of each other.' This resulted in the establishment of self contained special schools and classes as a method of transferring these 'misfits' out of the regular grades. This practice continues to this day and, unless counter-forces are set in motion now, it will probably become even more prevalent in the immediate future due in large measure to increased racial integration and militant teacher organizations. For example, a local affiliate of the National Education Association demanded of a local school board recently that more special classes be provided for disruptive and slow learning children (Nashville *Tennessean*, December 18, 1967).

The number of special day classes for the retarded has been increasing by leaps and bounds. The most recent 1967–1968 statistics compiled by the US Office of Education now indicate that there are approximately 32,000 teachers of the retarded employed by local school systems – over one-third of all special educators in the nation. In my best judgment, about 60 to 80 percent of the pupils taught by these teachers are children from low status backgrounds – including AfroAmericans, American Indians, Mexicans, and Puerto Rican Americans; those from nonstandard English speaking, broken, disorganized, and inadequate homes; and children from other nonmiddle class environments. This expensive pro-liferation of self contained special schools and classes raises serious educational and civil rights issues which must be squarely faced. It is my thesis that we must stop labeling these deprived children as mentally retarded. Furthermore we must stop segregating them by placing them into our allegedly special programs.

The purpose of this article is twofold: first, to provide reasons for taking the position that a large proportion of this so called special education in its present form is obsolete and unjustifiable from the point of view of the pupils so placed; and second, to outline a blueprint for changing this major segment of education for exceptional children to make it more acceptable. We are not arguing that we do away with our special educa-tion programs for the moderately and severely retarded, for other types of more handicapped children, or for the multiply handicapped. The emphasis is on doing something better for slow learning children who live in slum conditions, although much of what is said should also have relevance for those children we are labeling emotionally disturbed, per-ceptually impaired, brain injured, and learning disordered. Furthermore, the emphasis of the article is on children, in that no attempt is made to suggest an adequate high school environment for adolescents still functioning as slow learners.

Reasons for change

Regular teachers and administrators have sincerely felt they were doing these pupils a favor by removing them from the pressures of an unrealistic and inappropriate program of studies. Special educators have also fully believed that the children involved would make greater progress in special schools and classes. However, the overwhelming evidence is that our present and past practices have their major justification in removing pressures on regular teachers and pupils, at the expense of the socio-culturally deprived slow learning pupils themselves. Some major arguments for this position are outlined below.

Homogeneous groupings tend to work to the disadvantage of the slow learners and underprivileged. Apparently such pupils learn much from being in the same class with children from white middle class homes. Also, teachers seem to concentrate on the slower children to bring them up to standard. This principle was dramatically applied in the Judge J. Skelly Wright decision in the District of Columbia concerning the track system. Judge Wright ordered that tracks be abolished, contending they discriminated against the racially and/or economically disadvantaged and therefore were in violation of the Fifth Amendment of the Constitution of the United States. One may object to the Judge's making educational decisions based on legal considerations. However, Passow (1967), upon the completion of a study of the same school system, reached the same conclusion concerning tracking. The recent national study by Coleman, et al. (1966), provides supporting evidence in finding that academically disadvantaged Negro children in racially segregated schools made less progress than those of comparable ability in integrated schools. Furthermore, racial integration appeared to deter school progress very little for Caucasian and more academically able students.

What are the implications of Judge Wright's rulings for special education? Clearly special schools and classes are a form of homogeneous grouping and tracking. This fact was demonstrated in September, 1967, when the District of Columbia (as a result of the Wright decision) abolished Track 5, into which had been routed the slowest learning pupils in the District of Columbia schools. These pupils and their teachers were returned to the regular classrooms. Complaints followed from the regular teachers that these children were taking an inordinate amount of their time. A few parents observed that their slow learning children were frustrated by the more academic program and were rejected by the other students. Thus, there are efforts afoot to develop a special education program in D.C. which cannot be labeled a track. Self contained special classes will probably not be tolerated under the present court ruling but perhaps itinerant and resource room programs would be. What if the Supreme Court ruled against tracks, and all self contained special classes across the nation which serve primarily ethnically and/or economically disadvantaged children were forced to close down? Make no mistake – this could happen! If I were a Negro from the slums or a disadvantaged parent who had heard of the Judge Wright decision and knew what I know now about special classes for the educable mentally retarded, other things being equal, I would then go to court before allowing the schools to label my child as 'mentally retarded' and place him in a 'self contained special school or class.' Thus there is the real possibility that additional court actions will be forthcoming.

The findings of studies on the efficacy of special classes for the educable mentally retarded constitute another argument for change. These results are well known (Kirk, 1964) and suggest consistently that retarded pupils make as much or more progress in the regular grades as they do in special education. Recent studies such as those by Hoelke (1966) and Smith and Kennedy (1967) continue to provide similar evidence. Johnson (1962) has summarized the situation well:

> It is indeed paradoxical that mentally handicapped children having teachers especially trained, having more money (per capita) spent on their education and being designed to provide for their unique needs, should be accomplishing the objectives of their education at the same or at a lower level than similar mentally handicapped children who have not had these advantages and have been forced to remain in the regular grades [p. 66].

Efficacy studies on special day classes for other mildly handicapped children, including the emotionally handicapped, reveal the same results. For example, Rubin, Senison, and Retwee (1966) found that disturbed children did as well in the regular grades as in special classes, concluding that there is little or no evidence that special class programing is generally beneficial to emotionally disturbed children as a specific method of intervention and correction. Evidence such as this is another reason to find better ways of serving children with mild learning disorders than placing them in self contained special schools and classes.

Our past and present diagnostic procedures comprise another reason for change. These procedures have probably been doing more harm than good in that they have resulted in disability labels and in that they have grouped children homogeneously in school on the basis of these labels. Generally, these diagnostic practices have been conducted by one of two procedures. In rare cases, the workup has been provided by a multidisciplinary team, usually consisting of physicians, social workers, psychologists, speech and hearing specialists, and occasionally educators. The avowed goal of this approach has been to look at the complete child, but the outcome has been merely to label him mentally retarded, perceptually impaired, emotionally disturbed, minimally brain injured, or some other such term depending on the predispositions, idiosyncrasies, and backgrounds of the team members. Too, the team usually has looked for causation, and diagnosis tends to stop when something has been found wrong with the child, when the why has either been found or conjectured, and when some justification has been found for recommending placement in a special education class.

In the second and more common case, the assessment of educational potential has been left to the school psychologist who generally administers – in an hour or so – a psychometric battery, at best consisting of individual tests of intelligence, achievement, and social and personal adjustment. Again the purpose has been to find out what is wrong with the child in order to label him and thus make him eligible for special education services. In large measure this has resulted in digging the educational graves of many racially and/or economically disadvantaged children by using a WISC or Binet IQ score to justify the label 'mentally retarded.' This term then becomes a destructive, self fulfilling prophecy.

What is the evidence against the continued use of these diagnostic practices and disability labels?

First, we must examine the effects of these disability labels on the attitudes and expectancies of teachers. Here we can extrapolate from studies by Rosenthal and Jacobson (1966) who set out to determine whether or not the expectancies of teachers influenced pupil progress. Working with elementary school teachers across the first six grades, they obtained pretest measures on pupils by using intelligence and achievement tests. A sample of pupils was randomly drawn and labeled 'rapid learners' with hidden potential. Teachers were told that these children would show unusual intellectual gains and school progress during the year. All pupils were retested late in the school year. Not all differences were statistically significant, but the gains of the children who had been arbitrarily labeled rapid learners were generally significantly greater than those of the other pupils, with especially dramatic changes in the first and second grades. To extrapolate from this study, we must expect that labeling a child 'handicapped' reduces the teacher's expectancy for him to succeed.

Second, we must examine the effects of these disability labels on the pupils themselves. Certainly none of these labels are badges of distinction. Separating a child from other children in his neighborhood – or removing him from the regular classroom for therapy or special class placement – probably has a serious debilitating effect upon his self image. Here again our research is limited but supportive of this contention. Goffman (1961) has described the stripping and mortification process that takes place when an individual is placed in a residential facility. Meyerowitz (1965) demonstrated that a group of educable mentally retarded pupils increased in feelings of self derogation after one year in special classes. More recent results indicate that special class placement, instead of helping such a pupil adjust to his neighborhood peers, actually hinders him (Meyerowitz, 1967). While much more research is needed, we cannot ignore the evidence that removing a handicapped child from the regular grades for special education probably contributes significantly to his feelings of inferiority and problems of acceptance.

Another reason self contained special classes are less justifiable today than in the past is that regular school programs are now better able to deal with individual differences in pupils. No longer is the choice just between a self contained special class and a self contained regular elementary classroom. Although the impact of the American Revolution in Education is just beginning to be felt and is still more an ideal than a reality, special education should begin moving now to fit into a changing general education program and to assist in achieving the program's goals. Because of increased support at the local, state, and federal level, four powerful forces are at work:

Changes in school organization. In place of self contained regular classrooms, there is increasingly more team teaching, ungraded primary departments, and flexible groupings. Radical departures in school organization are projected – educational parks in place of neighborhood schools, metropolitan school districts cutting across our inner cities and wealthy suburbs, and, perhaps most revolutionary of all, competing public school systems. Furthermore, and of great significance to those of us who have focused our careers on slow learning children, public kindergartens and nurseries are becoming more available for children of the poor.

Curricular changes. Instead of the standard diet of Look and Say readers, many new and exciting options for teaching reading are evolving. Contemporary mathematics programs teach in the primary grades concepts formerly reserved for high school. More programed textbooks and other materials are finding their way into the classroom. Ingenious procedures, such as those by Bereiter and Engelmann (1966), are being developed to teach oral language and reasoning to preschool disadvantaged children.

Changes in professional public school personnel. More ancillary personnel are now employed by the schools – i.e., psychologists, guidance workers, physical educators, remedial educators, teacher aides, and technicians. Furthermore, some teachers are functioning in different ways, serving as teacher coordinators, or cluster teachers who provide released time for other teachers to prepare lessons, etc. Too, regular classroom teachers are increasingly better trained to deal with individual differences – although much still remains to be done.

Hardware changes. Computerized teaching, teaching machines, feedback typewriters, ETV, videotapes, and other materials are making autoinstruction possible, as never before.

We must ask what the implications of this American Revolution in Education are for special educators. Mackie (1967), formerly of the US Office of Education, addressed herself to the question: 'Is the modern school changing sufficiently to provide [adequate services in general education] for large numbers of pupils who have functional mental retardation due to environmental factors [p.5]?' In her view, hundreds – perhaps even thousands – of so called retarded pupils may make satisfactory progress in schools with diversified programs of instruction and thus will never need placement in self contained special classes. With earlier, better, and more flexible regular school programs many of the children should not need to be relegated to the type of special education we have so often provided.

In my view, the above four reasons for change are cogent ones. Much of special education for the mildly retarded is becoming obsolete. Never in our history has there been a greater urgency to take stock and to search out new roles for a large number of today's special educators. **99**

(Dunn 1968)

10. F. Christoplos and P. Renz: *A critical examination of special education programs*

After the shock waves that followed the publication of Dunn's article on desegregation and increasing integration, there ensued a major discussion about the place and the consequences of special education – a discussion that became a ferment during the 1970s and 1980s.

Christoplos and Renz were among the first to enter into the public debate, with this well argued and well referenced paper in 1969. In it they take pains to widen the discussion about the lack of success of special education, noting that Dunn's paper focused specifically on children categorized as having mild learning difficulties. They note that given Dunn's specific focus '. . . it seems appropriate to reevaluate the purposes of *all types* [emphasis added] of segregated classes for exceptional children on a philosophical as well as an empirical basis.'

66 Special educators have often taken satisfaction and pride in the rapid expansion of special education programs ([Dunn], 1967; Mackie, 1965; NEA, 1967). Recently, however, this pride has been shaken by criticisms emanating from several sources, the most noted among them being Lloyd Dunn (1968), who prefaced an article questioning the justification of special education programs with a plea that special educators 'stop being pressured into continuing and expanding a special education program that we know now to be undesirable for many of the children we are dedicated to serve' (p. 5).

Dunn's article was concerned only with special classes for educable and mildly retarded children, and his conclusions were based predominantly on empirical evidence. With the validity of such classes being widely discussed, it seems appropriate to reevaluate the purposes of all types of segregated classes for exceptional children on a philosophical as well as an empirical basis. Such is the intent of this paper.

The most commonly stated goal of special education programs is meeting the needs of exceptional children whose needs cannot be adequately met in regular programs (Baker, 1959; Cruickshank and

Johnson, 1958; Dunn, 1963; Jordan, 1962; Kirk, 1962). The current pro-liferation of special education programs, however, cannot be explained on the basis of supporting evidence indicating progress toward such a goal.

Amorphous good intentions have often substituted for lack of more objective accomplishments. Throughout the substantial number of years special education programs have been in operation, research findings have consistently indicated no differences in performance between those placed in special classes and those placed in regular classes. We cannot ignore, therefore, the disquieting possibility that self-perpetuation may be a factor in the continuation and expansion of special education programs.

On the other hand, the complexity of the issues involved in identifying appropriate educational goals cannot be overlooked. Compulsory public school education in a heterogeneous society is a sensitive and emotionally charged assignment, especially when it is extended to include children who deviate widely from the norm. The schizophrenic dilemma of a society trying to reconcile goals of competition and cooperation, quality and equality has been pinpointed by Keppel (1966). Although he believes that quality is necessary for success in a competitive society, he cannot accept the concomitant idea that the teaching of cooperation, which is the foundation of a durable democracy, must suffer in consequence. An avoidance of clearly stated purposes allows educators to verbally support cooperation (and include most children in the educational system) then establish programs appropriate only for a segment of the population; those who are able to manage competition. Indeed, competition is emphasized, and conflicting philosophy and practice are maintained without modification of either. There can be little doubt that a clear establishment of the priority of cooperation, in practice as well as in philosophy, is critical for special education.

Competition has no place for individuals who, because of injury, illness, or congenital incompetence, are unable to produce ... Social co-operation, with value attached to individual pursuits, performance in line with ability, freedom from anxiety, and social as well as economic security for all, are goals which need to be actively sought (Trippe, 1959, p. 175).

Carlson (1964) further clarified the conflict between philosophy and practice which is so apparent today in education. He categorized organizations in terms of the relationship between the organization and its clients. Public schools are of the organizational type in which there is no control over admission of clients (students), and in which the clients, in turn, have no choice but to accept the service being offered (education) regardless of its quality. There is no problem of the school meeting criterion goals at the risk of being abandoned. Regardless of the quality of the service, students will be available and financing of the schools will be relatively secure. Carlson identified two adaptive responses on the part of the public school to the problem of lack of control over selection of students: segregation and preferential treatment. These adaptations are made not for the purpose of meeting the client's needs, but rather:

> to make the organization-client relationship more tolerable from the point of view of the organization. Through these mechanisms the organization is able to exercise a form of subtle internal selection and sorting of clients as it goes about rendering its service ... to those students for which the school is geared to supply the most adequate service. Together, these mechanisms facilitate the fulfill-ment of the goals to which the school commits itself (pp. 272–273).

The rapidly increasing number of special education classes ([Dunn], 1967; Mackie, 1965; NEA, 1967) indicates that the goals and services of general education are not appropriate for exceptional children. Their segregation into special classes allows educators to attend predominantly to those students for whom the general educational service is beneficial.

Special education programs were not initiated in response to the needs of exceptional children, but rather as an expedient measure to resist a perceived threat to existing goals for 'normal' children who were being more or less adequately served by regular school programs. Parent movements pressured public schools to accept hitherto excluded children (Reynolds, 1967b) and hence forced the schools to initiate special education programs so as to avoid disturbing the traditional establishment.

There has been no reliable evidence produced to indicate that dif-ferential benefits, either social or academic, accrue to regular students as a result of either the exclusion or inclusion of exceptional students in regular classes. However, even if differential effects were found favoring the former, a democratic philosophy would dictate that the most justifi-able course of action in dealing with exceptionality would be the altering of classroom practices whenever possible, rather than the segregation of the deviant individuals. The rapid growth of special classes, in the face of lack of either supporting evidence or acceptable democratic social philosophy, has but limited justification.

Within the logic of the above argument, exceptionality is defined by the nature of society, not by the nature of individuals. Exceptionality in education becomes *the condition of NOT meeting one or more critical general education goals which are of such importance to educators that failure to achieve them on the part of some students is intolerable to the educators and results in total or partial, single or group, segregation of these students.*

A brief review of some of the literature comparing effects of differential placement will serve to clarify the above definition. The problem of special classes may be seen as an extension of the problem of homogeneous versus heterogeneous grouping within regular classes or regular pro-grams. An excellent survey published by the U.S. Office of Education

(Franseth and Koury, 1966) found no clear support for either homo-geneous or heterogeneous grouping in terms of academic achievement or social/emotional adjustment. The only exceptions to the long line of null results were found when personality variables such as achievement motivation or anxiety formed the basis for grouping (Atkinson and O'Connor, 1963). Sears (1963), Flanders (1964), and Thelan (1967) have also suggested that differential effects may be found when groups are patterned on criteria other than ability *per se*, yet the strongest arguments for grouping the handicapped together have been based on ability.

In spite of the lack of evidence supporting the positive value of ability grouping, a consistent and periodic pressure continues for the establish-ment of ability grouped classes in the public schools. Teachers and par-ents prefer ability grouping (Franseth and Koury, 1966, p. 50). Social and personal values appear to be more critical factors than academic realities in explaining the preference for ability grouped classes.

The academic consequences of special class placement on educable mentally handicapped (EMH) children also have been found to be negligible (Bacher, 1965; Baldwin, 1958; Blatt, 1958; Carroll, 1967; Cassidy and Stanton, 1959; Diggs, 1964; Goldstein, Moss and Jordan, 1965; Kern and Pfaeffle, 1962; Mayer, 1966; Meyerowitz, 1962, 1967b; Porter and Milazzo, 1958; Stanton and Cassidy, 1964; Thurstone, 1959). At times, a slight advantage from regular class placement for academic skills and a slight advantage from special class placement for social/emotional-adjustment has been found. However, varying definitions of academic skills and social/emotional adjustment make questionable even these slight differences. In addition, the selective factors involved in determining placement of EMH children in special classes or their retention in regular classes are critical (Robinson and Robinson, 1965, p. 465).

One of the most impressive investigations of the comparative effects of special and regular classes, in which the student selection bias was care-fully controlled, was conducted by Goldstein, Moss and Jordan (1965). Blackman (1967) succinctly summarized this study and concluded:

> Goldstein, Moss, and Jordan (1965) controlled for methodological inadequacies which had characterized previous investigations and conducted what was perhaps the most definitive study to date of the efficacy of special class training for the educable mentally retarded with respect to intellectual development, academic achievement, and social and personal development . . . What emerges is the sobering generality that this methodologically sophisticated study of the efficacy of special classes for mentally retarded children blends into the long line of negative findings that have characterized this area of research for the past 30 years (p. 8).

The possibility of attitudinal effects on parents whose children have been given special class placement should not be minimized. Meyerowitz

(1967a) examined the attitudes and awareness *of parents* of EMH children in special classes and in regular classes. He found that parents of EMH children in special classes generally showed greater awareness of their child's retardation but tended to derogate and devalue their child to a greater degree than did parents of EMH children in regular classes. Meyerowitz cautioned that special classes may lead, in the long run, to increased maladaptive behavior.

It is difficult moreover, to find research on the effects *on the regular students* of the inclusion in regular classes of various kinds of exceptionalities. If, as the present argument suggests, such effects are the major concern of educators, such research is critically needed. Deliberate inclusion of exceptionalities so as to determine the academic and social effects on regular students demands the researcher's attention.

The research on special class placement for gifted children has produced results similar to those obtained for the handicapped (Balow and Curtin, 1965).

Since gifted children are usually smart enough to know how to avoid interfering with the school's unwritten social mores, there is little school pressure to isolate them. Efforts to make special provisions for gifted children usually emanate from pressure applied on school personnel by industrial and other non-school people, who wish to utilize the gifted upon completion of their schooling. These efforts are generally concerned with refining the quality or accelerating the rate of doling out the educational fare (Pressey, 1963) or with early school admission (Reynolds, 1967a).

Special programs for brain-injured children (with recognition of the proverbial teapot tempest over nomenclature) and emotionally disturbed children are clearly established for reasons of intolerable social behavior. But so-called special methods recommended for these children are likely to be equally beneficial (or equally ineffective) for normal children in regular classrooms.

Placing orthopedic, blind, deaf, or even trainable children in regular classrooms is not usually considered feasible. Yet their isolation has frequently been cited as producing adverse effects. Cutsforth (1962) has found that vocation adjustment for the blind is handicapped by institutionalization with its 'parental type supervision' and 'lack of opportunity to develop aggressive social attitudes' (p. 183). A similar criticism of all special classes in public schools would not be remiss. Pintner (1942) found that the more able students tended to leave special classes for the visually handicapped, while the less able remained. This may also imply that regular classes contribute to making the more able child *even more* able, whereas the special class has the reverse effect. Meyerson (1963) found similar results with children who had impaired hearing. He concluded that 'present evidence indicates that a child may be well adjusted regardless of the method by which he is taught, the way in which he communicates, or his place of residence' (p. 138).

Another case in point is a study done in Scotland by T.T.S. Ingram (1965) with 200 cerebral palsied patients from the cities of Dundee and Edinburgh, and from surrounding rural areas. School placement of these children had been determined by the type of school locally available, rather than through 'optimum placement.' Ingram compared the vocational and social adjustments of the rural patients, who were generally in a 'sink or swim' situation, with those of the urban pupils, who had 'specialized' programs.

The rural patients managed to hold a place in normal schools or they did not receive education. They either remained in touch with normal people or they became housebound. There were no clubs for the handicapped and no special buses to take them for picnics. *It can be seen that there were more children in open and niche employment in the small towns than in Dundee and Edinburgh* (italics added). It seems possible that this may have been because patients in the small towns were kept in touch with their families and with normal people throughout their childhood. Segregation was avoided (p. 11).

Ingram's argument is that special educators must consider the value for out-of-school life adjustment of what they are teaching exceptional children. Not only the purposelessness of much of the special class curriculum, but also the deleterious effects of the pressure to learn is at issue here. If clearly beneficial objectives, unique for a particular exceptionality, cannot be identified, then the exceptional group in question should not be segregated from normal society, to suffer the additional hardship of categorization in a demeaned minority group.

Even if children with obvious and severe physical exceptionalities are assumed to require highly specialized teaching, unique for each exceptionality (and this assumption is questionable), isolation in special classes is not thereby the only action feasible. Special helping teachers (itinerant or school-based), resource rooms, and other well-known educational manipulations are possible alternatives. *Anticipated interference with social intercourse resulting from regular class placement of exceptional children is an indefensible explanation for their placement in special classes.*

Considering the overall picture of research evidence, what guidelines can be proposed in planning for the exceptional child? First, it should be recognized that the adjustment of the exceptional child to the normal world is unlikely to occur unless he has frequent and familiar interaction with it. The risk that such interaction may contribute to a greater *maladjustment* of the exceptional child is undeniable, yet adequate adjustment is dependent on taking such risks. Care must be taken lest the discomfort and anxiety of the normal population at the possibility of having daily and close interaction with deviant individuals become the cause of restriction of such interaction. That segregation is for the good of the exceptional, rather than for the comfort of the normal population, may be a deluding rationalization.

Secondly, lack of intimate knowledge about, and experience with, deviants denies the *normal* individual opportunities for social learning which may have the broadest implications for the understanding of human differences (Doll, 1966). An example is Billings' (1963) study which highlights the problem of segregation as it affects *normal* children. She examined attitudes of non-crippled children toward crippled ones and found that after third grade the attitudes of the non-crippled toward the crippled became more unfavorable and that *students judged to be high in social and emotional adjustment had the most unfavorable attitudes toward crippled children!* Surely it is appropriate to ask, 'What price social adjustment in our public schools?' The positive effects of familiar intercourse with exceptionalities is exemplified by Bateman's (1962) study whereby sighted children who knew blind children were found to be more positive in their appraisals of blind children's abilities than were those who did not know any blind children.

The possibility that special education is a solution to the 'problem' of educators in achieving their own goal of social homogeneity, instead of educational goals for children, should not be ignored. Specifically identified educational goals for children can insure that such improper solutions do not occur. Amorphous goals allow for surreptitious manipulation of a variety of behaviors far removed from those ethically in the realm of educational concern. This problem is common to the education of all children, but is more blatant with handicapped children, whose greater dependency and vulnerability may facilitate a wider use of unjustifiable manipulations. Before an exceptional child is segregated from the regular classroom, those behaviors which he must master for re-entry into it need to be identified and, if possible, programmed into his education. Such an identification can elicit a more frequent and healthy analysis of *why* certain specified behaviors are desirable or mandatory and whether all those students not segregated exhibit the desirable (or omit the undesirable) behavior. Considering handicapped children in terms of behaviors rather than in terms of classified exceptionalities would inhibit the establishment of segregated classes for any minority based on anything other than specifically-delineated educational goals.

The exceptional as a minority group
The 1954 Supreme Court decision on segregation in public schools (Warren, 1954) assumes great significance when applied to exceptional children as well as to racial minorities. Consider the following excerpts in which the underlined words have been changed to make the text apply to exceptional children:

> Segregation of *regular and exceptional* children in public schools has a detrimental effect on the *exceptional* children. The impact is greater when it has the sanction of the law; for the policy of separating *the*

students is usually interpreted as denoting the inferiority of the *exceptional* group. A sense of inferiority affects the motivation of a child to learn. Segregation with the sanction of the law, therefore, has a tendency to retard the educational and mental development of *exceptional* children and to deprive them of some of the benefits they would receive in a *totally* integrated system . . . We conclude that in the field of public education the doctrine of 'separate but equal' has no place. Separate educational facilities are inherently unequal (pp. 10–11).

Considering educationally exceptional persons as a minority group is not new (Barker, 1948; Tenny, 1953; Wright, 1960). However, as in Jordan's discussion (1963), attempts have been made to differentiate between the benevolent attitudes shown toward some minorities (e.g., the handicapped) and the malicious attitudes shown toward others (e.g., Negroes). This is begging the question. As long as any type of individual is segregated, the majority group avoids familiar interaction with it, thus avoiding having to make changes in its own values. The previously-identified distinction between benevolence and maliciousness on the part of the majority appears to parallel the difference between high and low potential for independence and power on the part of the minorities. It is not difficult to feel more benevolent toward handicapped minorities, who are more vulnerable to majority manipulations, than toward a struggling and militant racial minority. But it appears equally difficult for a majority group member to associate with either minority!

Another social analogy to educational exceptionality is that of delinquent youth. Empey (1967) wrote about delinquency in ways which special educators may find disquietingly pertinent to their own problems. He noted that only within special programs are delinquents' attitudes being changed:

But somehow these changes are not translated to the community where the offender's adjustment is submitted to the ultimate test . . . Delinquency and crime, and reactions to them, are social products and are socially defined. Society, not individuals, defines rules, labels those who break rules, and prescribes ways for reacting to the labeled person. The labeling process is often a means of isolating offenders from, rather than integrating them in, effective participation in such major societal institutions as schools, businesses, unions, churches, and political organizations (pp. 4–5).

Empey also believes that the basis of programming decisions for the delinquent should be clear with specific identification of goals:

When there is no consensus on objectives, there is no logical means for choosing one approach over another, one kind of staff over another, one program component over another. It would not make sense to initiate an experimental effort unless objectives were made explicit and a set of priorities chosen (p. 81).

A final aspect of special education programs to be considered is the possibility that once segregation becomes institutionalized, it is most difficult to eliminate. Any initial steps toward educational segregation should therefore be cautious, judicious, and adequately supported by research before wide implementation or dissemination is initiated. The difficulty is magnified if current special education programs are administratively well-entrenched and continue to multiply, giving rise to the very real danger that the primary goal of special education may become self perpetuation. There are indications that this has already occurred to some degree.

In conclusion, we ought to point out that attitudes of fear and rejection are concomitants of unfamiliarity. Familiarization with deviation, via inclusion of deviants in regular classrooms should minimize undesirable attitudes on the part of the 'normal' population. So, too, should familiarization with the 'normal' world have beneficial effects on the deviants. Evidence of difficult interactions between deviant and normal individuals in an integrated situation should lead to medial manipulations of the environment before segregation is considered as an alternative. This approach would be consistent with the establishment of a general pattern of positive reaction to, and inclusion of, the strange or different. Such positive valuing of differences is consistent with Francis Keppel's (1966) urgent message that we must not lose sight of the cooperative basis that must underlie our competitive society. The replications go beyond special education and general education to our national goals of world-wide understanding, peace, and cooperation.   **99**

(Christoplos and Renz 1969)

11. R.A. Weatherley and M. Lipsky: Street-level bureaucrats

In this much quoted article, Weatherley and Lipsky study the introduction of a new law in Massachusetts ('Chapter 766') that required school systems to identify and meet children's special needs. Weatherley and Lipsky examine the consequences of this new legislation for practice on the ground – at 'street level'. In an in-depth study they look at the problems that emerge from the expectations that surround the new policy, especially where that policy is not accompanied by additional funds or major changes in the structure of financing. In many ways these problems are the ones still facing local authorities today in implementing inclusive policy, in both the US (see Hehir in this volume, p. 101) and in the UK (see *Audit Commission, 1992*): no new finance, and little fundamental restructuring of financial arrangements, but many new expectations.

The consequence, Weatherley and Lipsky found, has been compromise.

Coping systems such as rationing and the short-circuiting of procedures emerged. (It is as much the case today as it was then.) And in this particular study it was found that even the behaviour of professionals became unhelpful. In short, as the authors say, the professionals sought to secure their own environments. What they call 'street level bureaucrats' end up by 'routinizing procedures, modifying goals, rationing services, asserting priorities, and limiting or controlling clientele'. The further consequence is that the consumers of services – parents and children – become 'relatively insignificant'.

As a result, the 'policy' that is delivered is vastly different from the one the government with its legislation intended. What ultimately emerges is something that may have effects contrary to those intended. Much of the opposition of the teaching profession to inclusion comes from its realization that this is the case – that real world implementation is different from mandated or theoretical implementation. Constant guard has to be kept up about this, and in particular about the fact that adequate financial arrangements often do not accompany changes of the kind discussed here. It is important to note that the need for new money is not necessarily being talked about here, but rather the intelligent redirecting of existing money to new purposes and priorities. The problem has often been that in innovative inclusive enterprise money stays in the old system as expensive initiatives are demanded of the mainstream.

From the conclusion:

> **❝** In September 1974, Massachusetts school systems confronted challenges to their management capabilities and to their deployment of personnel. They were obliged by the commonwealth to identify all pupils with special education requirements, including those not previously so classified. Moreover, this responsibility extended to a population both younger and older than the population the schools had previously had to serve. The systems were charged with assessing the special needs of children through consultation with a variety of specialists and with the complete involvement of parents. And they were responsible for designing individualized programs appropriate to those needs, regardless of cost. They were expected to do this with virtually no authoritative assertion of priorities and without firm assurance that they would be entirely reimbursed by the state for increased expenditures. Administrators were caught between the requirements to comply with the law, which they took quite seriously although the state's initial monitoring effort was much weaker than had originally been indicated, and the certainty that their school committees would rebel against expenditures that led to increased taxes. While they had the support of parent groups and others actively concerned with special education, school administrators were dubious about this support because these groups tended to be unsympathetic to any approach that implied that a school system would do less than the law required.

Special education personnel thus experienced pressures to accomplish enormous tasks in a short period of time with no certainty of substantially greater resources. Many school systems had already been moving in the direction indicated by Chapter 766 [the Comprehensive Special Education Law of Massachusetts], but now they had to accomplish what had previously been a matter of voluntary educational policy. Under the circumstances, special education personnel had to cope with their new job requirements in ways that would permit an acceptable solution to what theoretically appeared to be impossible demands.

That the systems we studied processed hundreds of children while maintaining the levels of services they did provide is a tribute to the dedication of school personnel and to the coercive, if diffuse, effects of the law. However, in certain respects the new law, by dictating so much, actually dictated very little. Like police officers who are required to enforce so many regulations that they are effectively free to enforce the law selectively, or public welfare workers who cannot master encyclopedic and constantly changing eligibility requirements and so operate with a much smaller set of regulations, special education personnel had to contrive their own adjustments to the multiple demands they encountered.

While not, for the most part, motivated by a desire to compromise compliance, school personnel had to formulate policies that would balance the new demands against available resources. To this end, school systems, schools, and individuals devised the following variety of coping patterns.

They rationed the number of assessments performed. They neglected to conduct assessments; placed limits on the numbers that were held; and biased the scheduling of assessments in favor of children who were behavior problems, who were not likely to cost the systems money, or who met the needs of school personnel seeking to practice their individual specialties.

They rationed services by reducing the hours of assignment to specialists, by favoring group over individual treatment, and by using specialists-in-training rather than experienced personnel as instructors. They short-circuited bureaucratic requirements for completing forms and for following the procedures mandated and designed to protect the interests of parents. They minimized the potentially time-consuming problem of getting parents to go along with plans by securing prior agreements on recommendations and by fostering deference to professional authority.

In short, they sought to secure their work environment. As individuals, teachers referred (dumped) students who posed the greatest threat to classroom control or recruited those with whom they were trained to work. Collectively, they sought contractual agreements that the new law would not increase their overall responsibilities.

These responses are not unique to special education personnel, but are typical of the coping behaviors of street-level bureaucrats. **99**

From the introduction:

> 66 ... 'street-level bureaucrats,' as we have called them, interact directly with citizens in the course of their jobs and have substantial discretion in the execution of their work. For such public workers, personal and organizational resources are chronically and severely limited in relation to the tasks that they are asked to perform. The demand for their services will always be as great as their ability to supply these services. To accomplish their required tasks, street-level bureaucrats must find ways to accommodate the demands placed upon them and confront the reality of resource limitations. They typically do this by routinizing procedures, modifying goals, rationing services, asserting priorities, and limiting or controlling clientele. In other words, they develop practices that permit them in some way to process the work they are required to do. The work of street-level bureaucrats is inherently discretionary. Some influences that might be thought to provide behavioral guidance for them do not actually do much to dictate their behavior. For example, the work objectives for public-service employees are usually vague and contradictory. Moreover, it is difficult to establish or impose valid work-performance measures, and the consumers of services are relatively insignificant as a reference group. Thus street-level bureaucrats are constrained but not directed in their work.
>
> These accommodations and coping mechanisms that they are free to develop form patterns of behavior that become the government program that is 'delivered' to the public. In a significant sense, then, street-level bureaucrats *are the policymakers* in their respective work arenas. From this perspective, it follows that the study of implementation of policy formulated at the federal or state level requires a twin focus. One must trace the fate of the policy in traditional fashion, from its authoritative articulation through various administrative modifications, to discover the ways this policy affects the context of street-level decision making. At the same time, one must study street-level bureaucrats within their specific work context to discover how their decision making about clients is modified, if at all, by the newly articulated policy. This turns the usual study of implementation on its head. Now the lowest levels of the policy chain are regarded as the makers of policy, and the higher level of decision making is seen as circumscribing, albeit in important ways'; the lower level policymaking context. The relationship between the development and implementation of policy is of necessity problematic since, in a sense, the meaning of policy cannot be known until it is worked out in practice at the street level.
>
> (Weatherley and Lipsky 1977)

12. Gerv Leyden: Psychologists and segregation

The following excerpt, written by educational psychologist, Gerv Leyden in 1978, comes from *Reconstructing Educational Psychology*, a book that assumed great significance for educational psychologists in Britain at the end of the 1970s. The book summarized a general dissatisfaction with the use of tests by psychologists and it optimistically suggested a range of alternative activities for psychologists in schools (the 'giving psychology away' to which Leyden refers toward the end of the piece), other than mere ascertainment.

Like Weatherley and Lipsky in the paper quoted from in the preceding excerpt, Leyden's critical analysis concerns the people who do the work in special education, in this case psychologists. Leyden commented on the generally uncritical character of psychologists' work. He noted that educational psychologists seemed to be hallucinated by the technical qualities of tests, to the extent that they paid too little attention to what was actually happening to the children on whom the tests were conducted. As he put it:

> 66   Far more time was allocated to this exercise [testing for special education] than in asking questions about whether such children benefit from a separate form of education . . . The hours spent in 'routine ascertainment' were in inverse proportion to the fleeting evaluation of the merit of what was being done.   99

He points out that intelligence tests continued (and, sadly, the case is still true today) to promote the notion that an intelligence quotient (IQ) is a robust indicator of some fairly stable inherited capacity for thinking. In fact, it is one indicator amongst many of the intellectual history of the child, which in turn will have been determined by the child's life events. Again here it is striking how far points being made in the 1970s are still having to be made today – notably about the link between poverty and IQ and achievement, with poverty being the ignored (less psychological) factor in examining reasons for poor achievement at school. It is far more impressive, after all, to impute blame to a 'scientific' cause such as intelligence than to something woolly such as poverty or, even worse, culture. Note what Leyden says here: 'The link between educational failure and social or cultural factors had been well established as far back as Gordon's studies of canal boat children in the 1920s.' It was true and understood in the 1920s; it was true and understood in the 1970s – one wonders how often empirical evidence needs to be brought forward demonstrating the same thing before policymakers and public will believe it.

Leyden points to the lack of evidence of special schools' success and the paradox therein of their continuing existence. The continuing predilection of psychologists and the educational establishment to want to proceed with the segregative system, he suggests, is thereby hard to explain. His points are valid to this day.

He makes further important points about the role of the psychologist in perpetuating the process of special school placement, where educational psychologists were often unclear about who their client was. If it was the mainstream school or the local authority (what Leyden calls 'the covert client'), a removal of a troublesome child to a special school could often be ticked off as a 'success'.

❝ Bruner (1966), in reviewing the failure of educational psychology to produce a major contribution to educational practice identified the basic flaw: *'the task was not really one of application in any obvious sense, but of formulation'*. Individual psychometry or treatment had not only failed to produce effective answers but prevented the appropriate questions being asked, since they had diverted the psychologist into a separate set of activities that were virtually self-contained – they asked their own questions and provided their own answers.

The reaction against the psychometric movement has been covered earlier in this book. It is too comfortable to forget that psychology departments and training courses endorsed the practice, and that the laudable intention was to identify and remedy children's learning difficulties. However the application of tests on the scale that we witnessed in the fifties and sixties had unintended results. Both child and psychologist were diminished by the process. The child became translated into a set of scores or numbers. (I worked in one service where all case notes had been filed in IQ categories.) His indifference, his anger, his confusion, his expectations, his fear were important to the extent that they were perceived to influence scores. The psychologist in turn was limited to a technician's role. Yet test scores did not provide explanations – they required them. Nevertheless as psychologists we frequently complied in using psychometric techniques to answer questions not formulated on educational, psychological or scientific grounds. For instance, group test surveys of school populations were regularly carried out to identify children for individual special school ascertainment. Far more time was allocated to this exercise than in asking questions about whether such children benefit from a separate form of education, or in studying the influence of school organisation of teaching methods on the failure of some children to progress in school. Perhaps the 'flooding' produced by the considerable period we spent questioning children overcame any tendency to ask questions elsewhere.

Clearly we were perceived by others, by teachers, parents, children, administrators and psychiatrists as psychometrists. Equally clearly we also saw this to be our area of particular competence and often operated entirely within this restricted framework. The reaction against psychometry induced further anxiety in those psychologists whose legitimacy pivoted on that technique, and there was no shortage of allusions to babies and bath water. Thus test scores provided an agenda for discussion in which neither teacher nor psychologist felt threatened and the search for explanation by tacit agreement focused on the child's responses. Take that away, and where might it lead? Even Burden's (1973) recent indictment of current tests hedges at the point of implementing his own conclusions, and is tantalisingly vague about alternatives and how they might be introduced.

Fortunately it is impossible to follow any work with pupils, teachers or parents in schools without being made forcibly aware of the significance of school organisation, the internal social dynamics, the curriculum – and the status accorded to different parts of it, and even the extent to which the design of the buildings can impose its own pattern on the structure of the school day. Although the same traditional techniques were initially applied the perspective rapidly broadened to encompass not only an individual child but also other contributory factors from within the school itself. Once this point was reached, the sterility of the traditional approach became obvious and the process of reformulation inevitable. Suddenly it became permissible and necessary to exorcise other inherited shibboleths which influenced the way in which we were working . . .

The controversy in the 1960s about the value and implications of separate special education echoed the heredity/environment debate. Post-war, the ESN [Educationally Sub-Normal] category unwittingly was more akin to a medical/educational condition. As previously indicated, the official 2HP was headed 'Report on child examined for a disability of mind'. It concluded that the child 'is/is not' educationally subnormal with a caveat for those children 'unsuitable for education at school' and children requiring a special physical examination or treatment at a child guidance clinic. The hereditarian-constitutional argument held sway. The psychologist contributed little more than IQ or other test scores for the medical officer to include under the 2HP, although even here some doctors carried this out themselves.

Yet the link between educational failure and social or cultural factors had been well established as far back as Gordon's studies of canal boat children in the 1920s, and had been freshly emphasised by the Newsom and Plowden reports and by research studies into the effectiveness of compensatory programmes. Evaluation studies of special schooling proved disturbing. Williams and Gruber (1967) classified the environmental handicaps suffered by children in ESN schools and found reduced infant schooling (as with summer born children) to be an important school variable associated with educational failure. Certainly no evidence emerged that the children attending ESN schools were a homogeneous group, but in fact encompassed a broad range of social handicap and learning difficulties. The grouping was primarily administrative and gave no indication of need, nor did it prescribe programmes or methods of teaching. In view of the diversity of 'diagnosis', it is not surprising to find that research evidence of the value of special schooling is, at best, inconclusive. Tizard (1966), whilst acknowledging the limitations of most of the evaluation studies, was only able to identify one such investigation which indicated clear cut gains by children receiving special schooling – and this was in a special class. Numerous other studies found no actual gains, and evidence that some children did less well. More recent reviews of evaluation research on special schooling (Presland, 1970; Moseley, 1975; Morgan, 1977; Ghodsian and Calnan, 1977) have not been able to present conclusive evidence of its effectiveness on the criteria studied, although it is possible there may be improved personal and social adjustment within the school in some cases. However, there is a strong risk that the children may have a difficulty in integrating within the community and in adjusting to an adult role and job. Many of the studies can be criticised precisely on the grounds that these sort of difficulties led to the original placement in a special school, but this does not answer the criticism that there seems to be little positive evidence that schools have been successful in helping children to overcome their difficulties. That so little evidence exists, and that so much of it is inconclusive is not a criticism of the work of special schools, nor of teachers. It is a further sad demonstration that as educational psychologists we have tended to accept assumptions without testing them, and have not rigorously scrutinised our own work. The hours spent in 'routine ascertainment' were in inverse proportion to the fleeting evaluation of the merit of what was being done.

This position has uneasy ethical overtones for the psychologist in his work with individual children and parents. In the light of current evidence, how do we answer parents' anxieties or children's fear of stigma if special schooling is proposed? Nor do those occasions where parent and child express no reservation necessarily justify such a move. Miller (1973) represented the views of a number of psychologists.

> Separating children from their peers, labelling them as deficient, and inadequate, and denying their parents rights over choice of schooling is a fairly drastic procedure. In order for it to be justified, the evidence that children benefit from the process must be unequivocal, and obvious not only to the teachers and administrators, but to the parents and children themselves. This evidence appears to be lacking.

An appreciation of a child's educational development clearly involves a study of the interaction between the child and his school. Similarly, there is an inter-relationship between ESN(M) [Educationally Sub-Normal (Moderate)] schools and their feeder primary and secondary schools. The special schools have played an essentially passive role in receiving children referred to them, via the school and psychological service, as 'slow learners'. In practice the referral was often triggered by the child presenting management difficulties in the school, of which learning difficulties were only a part. Consequently special schools have been faced with a significant number of children presenting both learning and behaviour problems and this in turn has required the school to devise methods of coping with their additional needs. The school cannot proceed on the premise that its pupils are primarily experiencing learning difficulties and that emotional or social problems are little more common than in other schools. Furthermore, the actual existence of special schools influences the outlook and organisation of its feeders, particularly in respect of slow learning children. Faced with unresponsive and possibly 'difficult' pupils and the knowledge that a system of special schools exists it is not surprising that the latter are often seen as an answer. When acute educational failure can be resolved by transferring the failing pupil to a special school, a valuable feedback function may be lost. The original school may lose the incentive to examine the role of its own organisation and methods in contributing to what is seen simply as a child's failure. Nor does it encourage the school to consider ways in which additional resources of staff, equipment and guidance can combine to provide an appropriate learning and developmental climate for the child in his own school. Responsibility for the acutely failing child is transferred from the feeder to the special school. The psychologist acts merely as catalyst in this process, absolving himself even from the responsibility of evaluating the changes he has engineered.

One of the dangers of the institutional role of the educational psychologist is that the apparent client may be contaminated by the institutional client. Although the apparent client may be a child experiencing difficulties, the covert client is often the institution, be it school or authority. Removal of this 'problem' from the jurisdiction of the institution may be interpreted as success. Such a crude oversimplification clearly ignores some essential factors of the situation, such as individual successes achieved by special schools, difficulties of reallocating resources for an individual child at local level, and it also denies the genuine concern and skilled help demonstrated by individual teachers. Nevertheless, the psychologist has to take into account and understand the influence of institutional forces – particularly if they run counter to the needs of the child . . .

I have given some attention to the issue of special schooling because it seems to me that the psychologist's contribution to it offers some immediate lessons about our services and the way we work. Initially we contributed largely as psychometrists, as technicians, providing test scores for other people to use. It would be naive to assume that individuals did not circumvent this, but most of us did not make a full contribution as psychologists, and were not always able to control the way in which our findings were implemented. For instance, a recommendation for special education could be interpreted in various ways by the school, teacher, psychologist, adviser or medical officer. In cases where actual placement was decided by administrators there was no guarantee that the education provided would match the needs of the child as defined. More currently, 'giving psychology away' clearly requires a greater responsibility for the psychologist in being aware of the situation in which it is being used, in monitoring and perhaps controlling that usage. (And at that point it can hardly be called a gift!)

The dearth of research on the value of special school placement is a rebuke to the psychologists who initiated such recommendations, not to the teachers involved. Where services are too busy or overwhelmed to evaluate their recommendations then there are more dangers in continuing uncritically than in calling a halt for an appraisal of what is being achieved and what is being assumed. Unguided activity does not confer effectiveness and surely we no longer have to justify the need for services to create time for identifying objectives and goals, devising and evaluating methods of achieving them and permitting staff opportunities for developing their own professional skills.   **99**

(Leyden 1978)

13. Will Swann: *Psychology and Special Education*

In 1982 a storm blew up in the education world with the publication of an Open University (OU) text which questioned the wisdom of educational psychologists in their work. It is interesting to read it in tandem with the pieces by Goffman (8), Weatherley and Lipsky (11), Leyden (12) and Tomlinson (15) for a taste of the critical assessment of professionals' work that was occurring at the time. No longer were professionals with impressive strings of letters after their names to be treated as though their knowledge were sacrosanct.

Swann's OU text suggested that the actions of educational psychologists might not always be in the best interests of the children said to be their clients, and that psychology as a discipline was not necessarily the best place to find answers to those children's difficulties at school. Indeed, the structure of psychological knowledge, with its fondness for supposedly scientific methods and its liking therein for measurement and testing led its applied exponents (educational psychologists) almost inexorably to become the people who constructed as their principal purpose in life the use of tests. It was only a small step then for the education system's apparatchiks to use the 'scientific' information gained from tests in validating the distribution of children between special and mainstream schools.

The document came as one of 16 units (texts) from the team of writers, Tony Booth, Patricia Potts and Will Swann. It was part of a postgraduate teacher education course which formed a substantial and positive contribution to the early integration movement. It called for, amongst other things, an end to outdated, inappropriate and discriminatory segregation.

The unit entitled *Psychology and Special Education*, written by Will Swann, provoked a considerable storm that included a series of sometimes vitriolic letters to the *Bulletin* of the British Psychological Society (BPS) about the unit, though this paled when compared to the response by the Association of Educational Psychologists (AEP) who wrote to the OU's vice chancellor asking that the unit be withdrawn.

The team's fundamental questioning of many of the traditional and long-accepted patterns of assessing and segregating was a powerful force for change in many areas of the education service. In fact, the ideas put forward in this OU unit on educational psychology now look quite uncontroversial and offer a healthy and appropriate baseline from which to work in developing inclusion.

The unit was not withdrawn; instead the OU course team met with officers of the AEP and agreed to send to all OU students doing the course copies of all the correspondence in the BPS *Bulletin*, as well as inviting contributions from the AEP.

> ❝ Psychologists like to think of themselves as a species of scientific philanthropists. They hand out their knowledge and skills for the benefit and betterment of the tradesmen – educators. At the same time they maintain a dignity of bearing and a reasonable distance from the shop floor: they are better paid, more highly qualified, seldom work fixed hours, and

cleave to their own professional integrity and independence. At the apex of their own internal pyramid of prestige are the researchers, devotedly rooting out the truth about children, which they pass down to the practitioners, the educational psychologists. These merchants in knowledge understand the character of the tradesmen, and know best how to sell and despatch the goods: a parcel of child development research, a package of behaviourist technique, always of course bearing the label of origin and guarantee of quality – the reference.

Perhaps the mercantile metaphor is a little overdrawn, but a caricature would be unrecognisable if it didn't bear some similarity to the original. Ten or so years ago, most psychologists doing research on handicapped children did actually think that they could just hand down their discoveries to teachers to use. Now they tend to have a less simple view and it is more common to hear that dissemination of research involves working with teachers in workshops and in the classroom, or even doing research with them. But the belief that psychology is the discipline from which innovations and improvements in special education may be expected is as strong as ever it was.

For many special educators, the way to understand handicapped children and their education is through the terms and ideas of psychology. This is not surprising as it has become very pervasive and influential. In England there are three professors of special education, Professors Gulliford, Mittler and Wedell, all of whom are psychologists. Books and courses on special education are overwhelmingly psychological. Some 900 educational psychologists exercise considerable power within local education authorities. Curriculum developments look to psychology for their ideas. Psychologists influence what research is funded by the DES (Department for Education and Science), and, by and large, do it. Cyril Burt firmly established the psychologist's power-base and projected his subject into a place in the developing special education system, where it has remained quite secure since . . . This unit is a critical analysis of the role psychology has played in special education: I hope to prompt you to think about whether psychology deserves to be as secure as it is. I will not be concerned with the subject of psychology itself, nor will my criticisms be aimed directly at 'pure' psychology. My interest is in the use of psychology in special education.

Few psychologists would disagree that knowing what is or might be the case is not sufficient grounds for choosing a path of action. But often in special education, a path of action's moral basis is concealed behind a scientific explanation. Is it possible, for example, to solve the problem of a disruptive child on a purely scientific basis? I shall argue that psychology may give the impression that it is, but in fact, it is not . . .

My aim . . . is to show how psychology has been used in the recent past in special education, and to show that its use has been far removed from the neutral application of a science. In fact, the nature of the education system played a role in shaping the psychology applied to it . . .   **99**

(Swann 1982)

14. Tony Booth: *Integration and Participation in Comprehensive Schools*

Twenty years ago, in 1983, there were few people linking integration of disabled pupils with the overdue reform and development of comprehensive education in such a concise way as Tony Booth, who produced a landmark article in the journal, *Forum*.

Booth defines integration as '. . . the process of increasing the participation of children in comprehensive nursery, primary and secondary school'. It seems a simple enough phrasing but Booth went on to highlight the paradox in England at that time. The Labour government of the day . . .

> 66   . . . expressed the intention . . . to establish comprehensive secondary schools 'in which pupils over the whole ability range and with differing interests and backgrounds can be encouraged to mix with each other'. Yet it was issued at a time of unprecedented expansion of segregated provision particularly for children labelled as mildly educationally subnormal or maladjusted. Although the expansion of official segregated special education tailed off at the end of the seventies, the decade ended with a dramatic growth in the numbers of children in separate 'disruptive units'.   99

Integration, he says, most usually referred to the

> 66   bringing of handicapped children from segregated special schools into ordinary schools and since they are an excluded group it is appropriate that this should be so. But there are problems associated with such a restricted definition. Firstly it may imply that the job of involving handicapped children in the educational and social life of schools is finished once they are within the ordinary school building. Secondly it may be taken to mean that handicapped children have a greater right to participation and an appropriate education in ordinary schools than other children. Integration can be applied then not only to children thought of as handicapped but to all children who have needs and interests to which schools do not respond. The children who are sent to special schools and classes are there, for the most part, because ordinary schools have not adapted their curricula and forms of organisation to diverse needs, interests and talents. They pose the same challenge to the education system to become truly comprehensive as the amalgamation of grammar, secondary modern and technical schools.   99

Referring to his earlier chapter, 'Demystifying Integration' in *The Practice of Special Education* Booth reminds us that

> 66   The growth in segregation did not occur because it was the only possible way in which special education could be organised. The vast majority of

children currently segregated could be included within ordinary schools if the principle of integration were put into practice. Not all children would be in the ordinary classroom all of the time and for some a certain degree of centralisation of provision might be necessary or desirable but there could be few reasons why this centralisation of resources should occur outside ordinary schools. I am convinced by arguments that children whose first language is sign language have a need to be with other sign language users though I do not agree with those, including some deaf adults, who argue that this should be in segregated, usually residential, schools. The provision of special education could not require a separated school building unless the isolation of a group of similarly categorised children was seen as an essential feature of the education they were to receive.   99

When Margaret Thatcher, as Secretary of State for Education, appointed Mary Warnock, the ex-head of an independent, selective, single-sex school to head the committee of inquiry into special education in 1973, Booth argues it was 'hardly surprising that integration and comprehensive education were not linked within the Warnock report or that, as Mary Warnock put it, the integration issue in that report was "fudged deliberately" '.

By the time the 1981 Education Act came into force there had been decades of official government regulations and legislation defining handicapped children as being unable to cope with the 'normal curriculum' in mainstream schools. In his *Forum* piece Booth adds:

66   The assumption still is that ordinary schools can only be expected to supply one 'normal' form of education. But if we expect schools to cater routinely for children with diverse needs and interests then our whole approach to the notion of special needs should change. Special needs are those to which schools do not currently respond. The numbers of children with special needs varies from school to school not only because of the characteristics of pupils but because of the organisation and curriculum of the school.

Integration and the development of comprehensive education require a fresh starting point for schools rather than the uneasy amalgamation of separate systems. They both involve a client-centred approach to education which starts with the question: 'Whose school is it?'   99
                                                                        (Booth 1983)

15. Sally Tomlinson: *A Sociology of Special Education*

Sally Tomlinson's *A Sociology of Special Education* in 1982 was a landmark in the discussion of the field, for it addressed as problematic many taken-for-granted notions about special education. In her book, Tomlinson suggests that special education may not have developed straightforwardly as a humane enterprise. Rather, it may have developed to serve the larger system – that is to say the mainstream and those who worked in it – rather than the children in the special system.

Tomlinson here looks through a sociologist's eyes in theorizing on the development of special education, examining for example the *interests* at work in the system and how these play themselves out in the arrangements that have come to be adopted. She looks also at the likely function of the system in reproducing the existing social order.

Many of these ideas had not been considered seriously in relation to special education before the publication of Tomlinson's book, and *A Sociology of Special Education* helped to shape the intellectual climate in which special education was discussed. That climate – one of questioning and challenge, rather than of passive acceptance of the good done by special education – came increasingly to dominate the debate over the following two decades.

66 Why a sociology of special education?

In Britain, the way in which children are categorised out of ordinary or mainstream education and into special education is generally regarded as enlightened and advanced, and an instance of the obligation placed upon civilised society to care for its weaker members. Special education is permeated by an ideology of benevolent humanitarianism, which provides a moral framework within which professionals and practitioners work.

But it is important to recognise that the recognition, classification, provision for, or treatment of, children who have been at various times defined as defective, handicapped or as having special needs, may very well be enlightened and advanced, but it is also a social categorisation of weaker social groups.

All over the world, powerful social groups are in the process of categorising and classifying weaker social groups, and treating them unequally and differentially. The rationalisations and explanations which powerful groups offer for their actions differ from country to country and the ideologies supporting systems of categorisation differ. The notion that a variety of professional groups are solely engaged in 'doing good' to the children they refer, assess, place and teach in special education is something of a rationalisation. Professionals and practitioners have vested interests in the expansion and development of special education. They also have very real power to define and affect the lives and futures of the children they deal with. A crucial factor in special education is that, unlike other parts of the education system, the children concerned cannot speak for themselves, and despite the growth of parental pressure groups, parents still have little influence on special education processes. The clients of special education, children and their parents, have the least say and influence over what happens to them, and are subject to the most pressures, persuasions and coercion, of any group in the education system.

State special education is a sub-system of the wider normal education system. It has developed to cater for children who are categorised out of the ordinary education offered to the majority of children in the society. It is important to stress at the outset that in modern industrial societies, which increasingly demand qualifications and credentials acquired through the education system, to be categorised out of 'normal' education represents the ultimate in non-achievement in terms of ordinary educational goals. Occupational success, social mobility, privilege and advancement are currently legitimated by the education system; those who receive a 'special' rather than an ordinary education are, by and large, excluded from these things. The rationale for exclusion has been that children were defective, handicapped or, more recently, have special needs. The result of exclusion is that the majority of the children are destined for a 'special' career and life-style in terms of employability and self-sufficiency.

Special education has been steadily increasing in size and importance over the past hundred years, and it often has appeared to be in a permanently dynamic state of change. But education systems and their parts do not develop spontaneously, they do not mysteriously adapt to social requirements, change without intent, and they do not necessarily develop in order to benefit different groups of children. Education systems, as Archer has pointed out (Archer, 1979), develop their characteristics because of the goals pursued by the people who control them and who have vested interests in their development. They change because of debates, arguments and power struggles. Changes in the form, organisation and provision of special education are not the result of mysterious processes of evolution, nor are they benevolent adaptations to new social requirements. Change happens because certain people want it to happen and can impose their views and goals on others. Thus, changes in the law relating to special education, in statutory categories, in separate or integrated provision, in increased professional involvement, in special curricula, and so on, occur as a result of deliberate decisions by people who have power to make the decisions.

Similarly, special education did not develop because individuals or groups were inspired by benevolent humanitarianism to 'do good' to certain children.

The idea that the development of special education was solely a matter of 'doing good' and was civilised progress, can possibly be traced to eighteenth-century humanism and nineteenth-century Christian reformism. But humanitarianism can itself become an ideology, legitimating principles of social control within a society. For example, A.F. Tredgold, who published an influential textbook on *Mental Deficiency* in 1908, dedicated his book to 'all those of sound mind who are interested in the welfare of their less fortunate fellow creatures'. But Tredgold also served on a committee concerned with the sterilisation of defective people, and supported the idea of euthanasia for idiots and imbeciles.

The Charity Organisation Society, who took an interest in the defective and feeble-minded from the 1880s, urged social reform based on Christian principles of 'love, working through individual and social life' (Mowat, 1961). But they also urged that the feeble-minded be segregated in institutions and made to perform useful work.

This book attempts to bring sociological perspectives to bear upon those social processes, policies and practices which comprise special education. The processes of special education are very complex, as are most social processes. Theory and practice in special education are informed by a variety of disciplines and approaches, but, by and large, sociology is not one of them. Medical, psychological, educational, administrative and technical approaches all influence and inform special education, but the sociological input is currently very limited. Sociological perspectives should be able to help all those concerned with special education by making clearer what is happening and why it is happening, particularly the way in which people or groups exercise power and influence, and can shape and change special education . . .

New perspectives
Sociology, and particularly the sociology of education, has over the last ten years produced a variety of alternative perspectives, theories, approaches and methods which illuminate the educational arrangements made in our society. As Eggleston (1979) has pointed out:

> It is now possible to see the over-simplification of the earlier socio-logical view of the world as running smoothly, with agreed norms of behaviour, with institutions and individuals performing functions that maintained society and where even conflict was restricted to agreed areas.

It has become commonplace within sociology to note that sociologists have been freed from over-reliance on positivistic quantitative method-ologies, and that functionalist views of society have been augmented by a variety of conflict and interpretative approaches (Karabel and Halsey, 1977). The conflict approaches stem particularly from neo-Marxist writings, and the interpretative approaches have developed from, and alongside, phenomenological traditions. Thus the new perspectives which could be brought to bear are: first, those concerned with the nature of the historical development, and the economic, political and social climates in which special education developed, and how these developments contribute towards the reproduction of a given social order in society, and second, those relating to the social construction and maintenance of the world of special education and the interactions of the social participants.

From structural perspectives, questions could be raised about the whole development and purpose of special education in a class-stratified industrial society. Sociologists who used these perspectives would maintain that, since conflict is endemic in all social institutions, special education is no exception. There is conflict in a variety of situations in special education, not least within professions, between professionals, between parents and professionals in special schools, and between mainstream and special schooling; and power and coercion play a large part in resolving conflicts.

Conflict theories in education stem from the works of Marx and Weber, and while this is not the place to expand on their writings, it is important to stress the differences between their views, as they do provide the basis for the two major conflict approaches towards a study of social institutions and processes. While Marx was primarily interested in analysing social conflict in terms of class and labour-market, Weber showed that the domination of one group over another could occur in a variety of ways, and that a key concept in domination is authority. It is the acceptance of legitimate authority, as well as outright coercion, that ensures the compliance of some groups to others. This is an important notion in explaining why, for example, parents have come to accept professional judgment and opinion as to what 'is best' for their children. In a discussion of education Weber (1972) showed how group interests penetrate the education system and how dominant interest groups can shape the structures of education for their own purpose. Thus, from this perspective sociologists could analyse the development of special education and its changes in terms of the conflicts between government and practitioners, or between professional groups.

Neo-Marxist conflict perspectives in education centre on the notion that a given educational structure is the outcome of political and ideological struggles between social classes, that class interests are behind any given pattern of educational organisation and that it is not possible to understand the working of any part of the education system independently of the class structure. Two important contributors to neo-Marxist sociological theory are Bowles and Gintis (1977) who have theorised about the role of education in the reproduction of the social division of labour, and – importantly for analysis of special education – have attacked the role of IQ measurement in assessment processes. They regard IQ more as a mechanism for the legitimation of inequality than as saying much about an individual's intellectual capacity.

Similarly, the work of Bourdieu and Passeron (1977) is concerned with the function of the education system in legitimating and perpetuating a given social order, by making social hierarchies appear to be based on gifts or merits. They argue that while educational advancement is based on ostensibly fair testing, the system demands a cultural competence not possessed by many families in society. From this perspective it no longer seems surprising that the mildly mentally handicapped or the educationally subnormal in society are predominantly lower-class. The large amount of literature which simply presents this as a 'fact' (Stein and Susser, 1960; Williams and Gruber, 1967; Gulliford, 1971) and the *assumption* that the lower social classes have a natural tendency to be more educationally retarded can be challenged from this perspective.

It is from these kinds of historical conflict perspectives that questions can be asked about the needs of a society that has developed and expanded a whole sub-system of education called 'special'. It becomes possible to turn rhetoric about the 'special needs' of children around, and ask what are the needs and interests of particular groups in the society that have influenced the development of special education, and what kinds of conflicts lie behind new developments?

This book is particularly concerned to ask some of the following questions, which will provide a context for the discussions held in each chapter:

(a) In whose interests did special education actually develop? Do the social origins lie more in the interests of ordinary education?

(b) Why did complicated categories of handicap and processes of selection and assessment develop? How were these processes legitimated? And why, having developed mechanisms to exclude children, is a debate on integration into normal education now taking place?

(c) How is the system of administration of special education linked to the use of professional expertise? And are the vested interests of expanding groups of professionals and practitioners served by the discovery of more and more children with 'special needs'?

(d) What are the goals of special education and why is curriculum theory and practice in this area so undeveloped?

(e) Are some types of special schooling more a form of control for particular groups of children? Why have black children been over-placed in ESN-M schooling, and can the treatment of ethnic minority children in special education illuminate its goals and purposes?

(f) What are the purposes of proposed expansion in special education?

The variety of interpretative and phenomenological approaches in sociology is also available to ask questions about special education. Phenomenologists stress the way in which social reality is a creation of social participants, and that social categories and social knowledge are not given or natural, but are socially constructed – a product of conscious communications and action between people. They tend to be preoccupied with the micro-world, examining how people make and remake the social world by their own interpretations and actions (Berger and Luckmann, 1971). The application of phenomenological perspectives to education opened up new empirical possibilities, as researchers were able to 'take as problematic' things that had previously been taken for granted. The major preoccupations of the 'new' sociologists of education have tended to be the classroom and teacher-pupil interaction (Woods, 1979), the curriculum, and knowledge. It is surprising that so far sociologists have shown little interest in applying these perspectives to special education. Deviancy theory and labelling theory (Becker, 1963; Downes, 1966) would also seem to be perspectives from which those categorised as 'in need' of special education can be regarded as deviating from behaviour required in ordinary education. Becker considered that 'the deviant is the one to whom that label has successfully been applied' (Becker, 1963). Special education provides more problematic 'labels' than any other part of the education system, many of which, for historical reasons, carry a stigma of inferiority and low status, and studies from deviancy perspectives might prevent simplistic acceptance of categories and labels.

There are some studies which have been carried out from interpretative perspectives, but usually from the point of view of the handicapped in society generally, rather than specifically applied to special education. Scott, using Goffman's notion of stigma, discussed the treatment of the handicapped by professionals (Scott, 1970). Dexter, as early as 1958, questioned the 'social problem' approach to mental deficiency (Dexter, 1958) and Spectre and Kitsuse, in studying how social situations attained the status of social problem, examined the use of the category 'moron' in the USA (Spectre and Kitsuse, 1977). Barton, in a paper to the twenty-first anniversary conference of the British Society for Mental Sub-normality, applied Goffman's notion of 'total institution' to a study of the 'institutionalised mind' (Barton, 1973).

Given that we know very little about the workings and functions of all types of special schools, teachers, teacher-pupil interactions and negotiation, special school curriculum, the 'knowledge' that is deemed to be suitable for special schools, and the treatment and experiences of pupils and their parents – there are a variety of questions that could form the basis for research and study from interactionist perspectives. One question with which this book will concern itself particularly is: what are the experiences of pupils and teachers in special schools, given the negative emphasis of special schooling, which stress incapacity and inability, and how are parents treated in special education?

The new perspectives and approaches suggested here provide what is loosely called macro and micro analysis in sociology. But while it is useful, particularly in research, to differentiate between levels of analysis – classroom or clinic, school, community, society – in practice these levels are not distinct. Some of the more recent work in the sociology of education has been devoted to demonstrating just how classroom activities are related to wider social processes (Woods, 1980a and b).   **99**

(Tomlinson 1982)

16. Seamus Hegarty *et al.*: *Educating Pupils with Special Needs in the Ordinary School*

In 1981 the largest ever research study of integration in Britain was published with the conclusion that integration was working well and that there could be much more than was happening at that time.

This support for integration came from the National Foundation for Educational Research (NFER) after three years of investigations across a range of English and Welsh schools and LEAs and resulted in a 550 page report (plus a later follow-up report of 14 integration programmes in *Integration in Action*, 1982). The NFER study was a formative contribution to a burgeoning national debate about whether segregated disabled children could and should be educated in the mainstream. The NFER research team of Seamus Hegarty, Keith Pocklington and Dorothy Lucas had begun their work shortly after publication of the Warnock Report in 1978 (see 29) and 1981 was, of course, the year of the new Education Act that contained the first enacted duty on LEAs to integrate disabled children (see 30). It was also the year of a pioneering national day conference promoting integration as a welcome change in the education system, organized by the Advisory Centre for Education (ACE) and the former Spastics Society (now Scope).

The NFER study hit the education world with authoritative detail and examination of the issues surrounding the education of children with special needs. It forced LEAs, professionals, administrators and other academics to sit up and take notice that a profound social change had been occurring in local schools around the country and that more integration could happen if certain arrangements were in place. Sadly, the study hasn't been repeated or equalled in subsequent or more up to date investigations of inclusive education.

The opening pages of the NFER study set the scene:

> **❝** Integration has become a central focus of concern in special education in recent years. Despite the widespread advocacy of it, many educationists view the trend toward integration with some unease. Special school staff fear that the systems of support they have built up will be dismantled and pupils' special needs may go unmet, while many teachers working in ordinary schools feel that they lack the competence to educate these pupils. Debate on the matter has been bedevilled by lack of clarity. Integration is not simply a new form of provision, another option as it were. It is a process rather whereby the education offered by ordinary schools becomes more differentiated and geared to meeting a wider range of pupil needs. This process can take many forms and in any case is a dynamic one both at local level and more generally. Its effects are pervasive within the school and throughout the education system.

In their opening chapter the authors analysed the problem of integration for researchers saying:

- integration had become a catchword, laden with unanalysed assumptions;
- integration was used to mean different things, sometimes in a confusing way; and
- the understanding of special educational treatment linked with concepts of integration was misconceived in important ways.

The NFER team stated their traditional independence from any philosophical conviction that might support integration:

> 66 Integration has made great strides as a desirable educational goal in recent years. It is not simply a neutral description of provision but rather the connotation of a state of affairs we should all be striving toward. There are strong emotive overtones. Like motherhood and democracy, integration is a good thing and no right thinking person who cares for children could be against it.
>
> This is nonsense of course. Integration is a means, not an end in itself. Pupils with special needs do not need integration. What they need is education. Integrated placement may well turn out to be important in achieving educational goals or in facilitating certain aspects of development, and to that extent becomes important. The primary concern however must be with individual development, and other considerations such as where the education takes place have relevance only in relation to it. This is not to say that integration must wait on supporting evidence or even that one cannot have a presumption in favour of integration in the absence of such evidence. What it does say is that the case needs to be made. Integration is *not a self-evident goal and must be justified in a rational way* [authors' italics]. Whether this is done purely by reference to value judgements or empirical evidence is adduced as well, the essential criterion must be the development and well being of pupils.
>
> When this is overlooked and integration is seen as a goal in its own right, *all sorts of unfortunate consequences are possible* [authors' italics]. Pupils with special needs are automatically assumed to be better off in ordinary schools than in special schools. The imperfections of integration arrangements in the latter are seen as passing and incidental – if they are not totally ignored – even when the reality is one of disastrous educational provision. This produces a reaction that can be just as unreflective. People see that pupils' needs are going unmet in the ordinary school, attribute the blame to integration, and refuse to countenance any form of integration as a consequence. To do this is as incorrect as to take integration as one's goal. 99

By the end of the three-year study, the researchers reported in their concluding summary:

> 66 The resounding conclusion to emerge from this study is that integration is possible. Special educational needs can be met in the ordinary school, and to a far greater extent than is currently the practice. There are

many pupils in special schools at the moment who could be educated satisfactorily in ordinary schools, given the requisite commitment and resources. So far from damaging the ordinary school in any way, this process can add to its educational strength and enhance the provision made for all its pupils. The difficulties and drawbacks must not be minimised since that would be to sacrifice pupils' educational well-being on the altar of principle. If an ordinary school cannot accommodate given pupils without educational loss, then special schools may well continue to be the preferred placement. Such situations however pose a considerable challenge to both special schools and ordinary schools. As long as some pupils attend special schools when their peers with comparable special needs elsewhere receive satisfactory education in ordinary schools, there are grounds for disquiet.

(Hegarty *et al.* 1981)

17. ILEA: *Educational Opportunities for All?* (Fish Report)

The Fish Committee was set up by the then Inner London Education Authority to examine provision for special educational needs in London. Although the talk in their report, published in 1985, is of *special needs* and *integration*, the seeds of an inclusive philosophy can be seen emerging at that time, not least in the passage excerpted below. In it, the committee talk of reformulating the Authority's equal opportunities policy to include children with special educational needs.

The consequences of this are significant: if 'equal opportunities' as a notion can encompass special educational needs, then the latter can be thought of in the same way as all of those issues formerly embraced by equal opportunities policies. Here can be seen some of the first indications of a realization and acceptance that inclusion (though the word is not used here) is first and foremost about comprehensive education, equal participation and equal rights for all children. It is not just about what was formerly called 'special educational needs' or disability.

This recognition marked a fundamental shift in thinking, for only four years earlier the 1981 Education Act (about special educational needs) had excluded certain groups – such as those with English as a second language – from its remit and its orders. One has to stop to consider the significance of this exclusion, for why shouldn't children with English as a second language be considered to have special educational needs? Aren't they likely to have different needs from those of most children or, in other words, *special* needs? The only conclusion that one can come to is that 'special educational needs' was considered in the minds of the legislators and their advisers to be about a putative set of disabling conditions – disabling by virtue of some supposed physical or quasi-physical characteristic. If children whose first language is not

English cannot be seen to have special educational needs, then special needs must constitute some special category concerned solely with certain kinds of conditions that have particular mental or physical consequences for the child.

It is the *medical model* that drives such a view of children with difficulties: a model of something almost constitutional being wrong which needs to be diagnosed and treated. Medical models are fine in their place, when thinking about measles or chickenpox. But they are less helpful in the consideration of people and their relationship to the cultures and organizations in which they live and learn. When children fail to thrive in the educational cultures that they are forced by law to attend, they can fail for a bewildering array of factors – their anxiety, their culture being different from that of the school's predominant culture, poverty and so on. Restricting the meaning of *special educational needs* so that as far as possible methods of identification and assessment control out these 'contaminating' factors is profoundly to over-simplify children's difficulties at school. One of the very unfortunate consequences of such a way of looking at things was that in the official mind problems would tend to stay with the child rather than becoming in any way the school's.

With the advent of thought about inclusion came an acceptance that children's success and failure at school rested on an assortment of factors that were as much to do with the school's ability to adapt to children's differences and frailties as they were to the differences and frailties themselves. It was an acceptance of the comprehensive ideal in education. Seen as such, inclusive education is less concerned with the nature and status of children's supposed needs and becomes more concerned with the discovering of children's individuality and the celebration of their distinctiveness.

It is the acceptance of all of this – of the primacy of the comprehensive principle, and the absurdity of separating some kinds of needs (special needs) from other kinds of needs (special educational needs) – that gives rise to the recommendations of the Fish Committee extracted below.

66 Policy and Planning

3.16.7 The Authority has made clear its overall policies for equal opportunities with regard to race, sex and class. It has not yet made clear its intention with respect to the disabilities and significant difficulties, which children and young people being educated by the Authority may have. In the Committee's view this is of equal importance. **We recommend that the Authority take immediate steps to reformulate its equal opportunities policy to include children and young people who may have special educational needs.**

3.16.8 There are two aspects of this overall recommendation which give rise to questions. First, what is the Authority's policy for making special educational provision? Secondly, if the Authority strongly endorses the comprehensive principle, why has it no stated policy on the integration of children and young people with special educational needs in schools and colleges for all? It is necessary to separate two related aspects of these questions, the development of a policy of any kind and the specific question of a policy for integration. The first aspect relates to the currently fragmented pattern of responsibilities and provision. Part II provides the basic information available to the Committee and the issues related to different kinds of arrangement. As can be seen, policy development where it occurs is currently related to different aspects of the range of provision such as special schools, off-site centres and services for specific learning difficulties. It is also the concern of different administrative and professional groups. What is now needed is a unified and comprehensive approach to meeting special educational needs which is readily understood not only by professionals but also by governors, parents and the general public. The Committee, with its relatively limited time for consultation, recommends the framework within which such a policy should be developed. **We recommend that as an immediate priority the Authority develop, through consultation, a policy for the development of provision to meet special educational needs which covers the whole range of arrangements in schools, colleges, units, special schools and elsewhere.**

3.16.9   The major feature of that policy should be the Authority's approach to the issue of integration. At present this is very uncertain. More provision is being made for individuals and groups within nursery, primary and secondary schools and colleges but the percentage of the school population attending special schools has been increasing until very recently. This is an issue where aspirations and long term objectives need to be distinguished from practical considerations and short term objectives. The Committee is in no doubt about the principles involved namely, that the right place for children and young people with special educational needs to be educated is where they retain regular contact with all their contemporaries. If alternative or different provision is to be made elsewhere for the time being this should be because it is not possible fully to implement the comprehensive principle. **We recommend that the Authority adopt a policy which aims to meet all children and young people's special educational needs within nursery, primary and secondary schools and colleges.**

3.16.10   The Committee recognises that there will be circumstances in which this may not be practicable in the short term or even for a small number of children and young people in the longer term. **Therefore we recommend that whenever or wherever alternative or different provision is made outside nursery, primary and secondary schools and colleges this be closely linked with such schools and colleges and seen as supportive and supplementary to their work.**

3.16.11   A policy for special educational provision cannot be separated from other education policies because of the relative nature of special educational needs. Any major decisions about education for under fives, primary and secondary education and further and continuing education have implications for children and young people with disabilities and sig-

nificant difficulties. **We recommend that procedures be instituted to include special educational needs considerations in an integral way within all the Authority's policies for educational provision.**
3.16.12   A distinction has been made in Chapter 1 between special needs and special educational needs. The Committee recognizes the pressure on schools and colleges to provide for a variety of special needs including those which may arise from learning English as a second language, giftedness and social disadvantage. The initiatives to meet these special needs have much in common with meeting special educational needs. They include in-service education, advisory teaching services, support teaching in ordinary classrooms and withdrawal for specific purposes. The common elements in these demands on schools and colleges need to be recognized. Policies to meet them need to be considered as a whole. **We recommend that the Authority develop consistent and common policies with respect to additional and supportive provision to meet all special needs in schools and colleges including special educational needs.**
3.16.13   In formulating a strategy for implementing recommendations 3.16.8 and 3.16.9 the Authority will need to consult widely about the mechanisms to achieve it. In the short-term the needs of individuals will not be met by hasty and piecemeal implementation. Planning is essential and an incremental approach most likely to succeed. **We recommend that the Authority draw up plans for integration, in consultation with all concerned, to make provision within primary and secondary schools to meet the needs of those children and young people currently in separate provision. These plans should be set within a defined time scale.** 〞

(ILEA 1985)

18. Doug Biklen: *Achieving the Complete School*

The book from which the following piece by Doug Biklen is taken reports on two intensive studies, the first of 25 mainstreaming programmes in American schools and the other of 20 programmes that had developed promising practice from which others could learn. Coming after much of the groundwork discussion and legislation of the 1970s, the piece is interesting on a number of counts.

First, it makes a powerful argument that mainstreaming is an issue to be discussed and decided on a political basis – not one that can be decided on the basis of empirical findings of one kind or another, though the latter may, of course, contribute powerfully to any political debate. Drawing vivid metaphors, Biklen makes the case that one decides on the shape of policy on the basis of whether that policy is morally right. If it turns out to be difficult to enact the policy in practice, one doesn't discard it – one finds better forms of practice; the consequence of difficulty, in other words, is not to ignore the moral position and surrender to expediency.

Second, it gives a lucid explanation of the activity in the American law courts in 1971 that gave rights to education for all children – the very same year that an Education Act gave children in Britain the same rights. Prior to this date, some children had been deemed 'ineducable' in both the US and the UK.

Third, it chronicles the background to the landmark American legislation in Public Law 94–142 (1975) with its notion of the 'least restrictive environment' (see also 28 in Part III of this volume).

Fourth, it provides a brief history of parallel ideas about normalization that had been developing in Scandinavia in the 1960s and that had found resonance in the US with the discussion and debate there on mainstreaming.

Last, it is interesting for the methods employed in the study on which it reports; these are entirely qualitative, producing a rich archive of powerful evidence on good practice. Qualitative inquiry has gone out of favour in official circles in recent years for its supposed susceptibility to distortion in the absence of the supposed 'rigour' of large scale quantitative research. In the book from which this extract is taken, however, qualitative research can be seen at its best, showing in detailed form how and why certain models of practice succeed while others are less successful. In our extract here there is space only for Biklen's commentary, but the full volume is well worth visiting for a colourful set of accounts and analyses of mainstreaming in practice.

❝ Asking the question, 'Is mainstreaming a good idea?' is a bit like asking, 'Is Tuesday a good idea?' Both are wrong questions. It's not so much whether mainstreaming and Tuesday are good ideas as what we make of them. In the past three years we have visited more than one hundred schools across America. In more than two dozen we have observed school life and, particularly, mainstreaming intensively. As we could easily have predicted, we have seen good and bad mainstreaming. Just as we can look back on all the Tuesdays in our lives and say, 'There have been good ones and bad ones,' we can also see that mainstreaming can succeed, fail, or just muddle along. Therefore, to ask, 'Does it work?' is also to ask the wrong question.

Is mainstreaming a good idea?

For obvious reasons, it is hard to escape this 'wrong question.' Skeptics of mainstreaming, as well as many like ourselves who are sympathetic to it, want some 'evidence' upon which to base their beliefs. 'Will handicapped students learn better if integrated?' 'Will nondisabled students develop better attitudes about their disabled peers if they rub shoulders with them?' Or is mainstreaming just a fad? Will 'normal' students lose ground because more of the teacher's time will be devoted to the special students? In other words, what are the facts about mainstreaming? Is there some scientific evidence that mainstreaming makes good sense educationally and socially?

Unfortunately, science cannot offer a positive or negative answer on mainstreaming. An analogy may make the point clearer. At the time of the American Civil War, should Abraham Lincoln have asked to see the scientific evidence on the benefits of ending slavery? Should he have consulted 'the experts,' perhaps a sociologist, an economist, a political scientist? Of course not. True, Lincoln made compromises and delayed before issuing the Emancipation Proclamation; he believed the immorality of slavery needed to be weighed against other values (e.g., keeping the nation united), but he never lost sight of the basis upon which slavery should be evaluated.

Slavery is not now and was not then an issue for science. It is a moral issue. But, just for a moment, suppose that an economist had been able to demonstrate that blacks would suffer economically, as would the entire South, from emancipation. Would that justify keeping slavery? And suppose a political scientist had argued that blacks had no experience with democracy, they were not ready for it. Would that have justified extending slavery? Or imagine that a sociologist could have advised Lincoln against abolishing slavery on the grounds that it would destroy the basic social structure of southern plantations, towns, and cities. From a racist perspective, all of these arguments might have seemed 'true.' But could they really justify slavery? Of course not. Slavery has no justification.

Take another example, this time from education. We have ample evidence that it is difficult to educate autistic students, particularly those with severe autism. Students who do not read, who communicate little if at all verbally, who have problems in coordinating their hands and feet, who sometimes (even often) behave in seemingly bizarre ways (i.e., screaming, self-stimulatory behavior), and who frequently have very short attention spans try the talents of even very skilled teachers. Some experts have suggested that the difficulty of teaching such students through traditional methods, and the fact that they abuse themselves regularly, justify 'treating' them with aversive conditioning such as, for example, isolating them in locked rooms for short periods of time or even giving them electric shocks with cattle prods. Those who advocate shocks and isolation do so out of their conviction that 'nothing else works' or that 'nothing works as well.' Of course others, ourselves included, have amassed incontrovertible evidence that even the so-called most difficult can benefit from educational strategies that do not include aversive conditioning. But even more important, we believe that, irrespective of 'the evidence,' certain practices have no place in education. Using shocks, however 'safe' or 'effective,' is tantamount to assault and battery. It offends our sensibilities and dehumanizes those upon whom it is used. And so we reject such practices outright. For some things we need no evidence. The practice itself is simply not acceptable.

We approach the topic of mainstreaming similarly. The question of whether or not to promote mainstreaming is not essentially a question for science. It is a moral question. It is a goal, indeed a value, we decide to pursue or reject on the basis of what we want our society to look like.

What does mainstreaming mean?

The term *mainstreaming* defies simple definition. For some people it is a code word for 'dumping.' To these people, it means placing students with disabilities into regular classes and providing no support services, no teacher preparation, and no special assistance to nondisabled students on how to relate to their disabled peers. Others say mainstreaming means carefully integrating students with disabilities into regular schools and classes with the appropriate support services and planning. Our two studies suggest that mainstreaming means different things to different people and takes many forms. These forms are described later in this chapter in the section 'Will the Real Mainstreaming Please Stand Up?' . . .

For some people mainstreaming means complying with the law, either because they want to or feel they must. A study parallel to our own (Brightman and Sullivan, 1980) found that parents regard lawsuits and the federal special education law, the Right to Education for All Handicapped Children Act (Public Law 94–142, 1975), as something that empowers them to demand equal access to schooling for their children. Thus, many parents regard mainstreaming as a principal right, as a symbol of their children's worthiness. From others, particularly from administrators charged with implementing the law, we have heard, alternately, 'it's the law, we are obligated to mainstream students wherever appropriate,' or 'the law gives us the wedge we need to break down the age-old barriers to handicapped students and to get them out of privately operated handicapped centers, institutions, and school basements into the mainstream of school life where they belong.'

October 7, 1971, marked a watershed victory for children with disabilities. From that day, when a decision was handed down in the case formally titled the Pennsylvania Association for Retarded Citizens v. the Commonwealth of Pennsylvania (PARC v. Penn, 1971; see also, Dybwad, 1980), the right of handicapped children to education became part of most American educators' consciousness. For parents of students with disabilities, PARC vindicated years of struggle against the social injustice of school exclusion. The PARC case, like more than one hundred subsequent cases styled after it, embodied at least five claims that the court endorsed: (1) that students with disabilities, in this case retarded students, had systematically, and at great individual and social cost, been denied a public education; (2) that all students could benefit from an education (testimony of Blatt and Goldberg, reported in Lippman and Goldberg, 1973); (3) that under the constitutional right of equal protection and various state claims, all students were entitled to a free appropriate education at public expense; (4) that parents had a right to due process by which they might question particular classification and placement decisions for their children; and (5) that students with disabilities were entitled to receive their education in the least restrictive environment possible.

Each of the five findings stirred controversy. How much would all this cost? Would the nature of public schools change overnight? Who would teach those students who heretofore had not been admitted to school? But, in fact, all but one of the provisions was straightforward and easily interpreted into practice, albeit sometimes hesitantly. After all, evidence in the case proved that there had been a long tradition of non-service for the plaintiffs (see Task Force, 1969, and Children's Defense Fund, 1974, for evidence of the exclusion problem nationally). Further, nationally renowned educational experts had stated unequivocally that all children were educable. It followed that all children were entitled to an education. Anything less would violate standards of equality set forth in the U.S. Constitution. In view of the problems encountered by parents in securing educational programs, it made good sense for the courts to mandate parental due process rights with respect to classification and placement. But the final principle, the notion that each student was entitled to an education in 'the least restrictive environment' possible, began a debate that is far from over (Public Law 94–142, 1975). It is the mainstreaming debate. The court-approved consent decree read:

> It is the Commonwealth's obligation to place each mentally retarded child in a free, public program of education and training appropriate to the child's capacity, within the context of the general educational policy that, among the alternative programs of education and training required by statute to be available, placement in a regular public school is preferable to placement in a special public school class and placement in a public school class is preferable to placement in any other type of program of education and training.
>
> (PARC v. Penn, 1971)

Did this mean that all children, irrespective of the severity of their disabilities, would be mainstreamed? Did it mean that institutions as well as private and public segregated schools for disabled children only would go out of business? How should parents and educators interpret the concept? What criteria should they use?

Congress did not settle the controversy by legislating the 'least restrictive' principle nationally. Public Law 94–142 (1975) does not define the words 'least restrictive environment,' but the concept is implied:

> To the maximum extent appropriate, handicapped children, including children in public or private institutions or other care facilities, are educated with children who are not handicapped, and that special classes, separate schooling, or other removal of handicapped children from the regular educational environment occurs only when the nature or severity of the handicap is such that education in regular classes with the use of supplementary aids and services cannot be achieved satisfactorily.
>
> (20 U.S.C. 1412[51 [B])

All this means that mainstreaming has a legal basis but one that calls on practitioners, namely principals, teachers, and parents, to define it in practical terms. It is up to the schools to demonstrate what shape mainstreaming will take in future years.

'As normal as possible'

The word *mainstreaming* was coined in America. The concept received its first serious airing in 1962 when a special education professor, Maynard Reynolds (1962), called for 'a continuum of placements for children with handicaps.' There was a sense that segregation, particularly in the forms of separate classes, separate schools, and segregated institutions, had been overdone and was largely unnecessary, even unjustifiable (Dunn, 1968; Blatt, 1969). Yet, three years before Reynolds published his article on integration, a related concept known as 'Normalization' was taking shape in Scandinavia. Many people in America, including many whom we met in the course of our two studies, now regard mainstreaming as the educational equivalent of normalization.

Bank-Mikkelsen, a Dane, coined the term *normalization* in 1959. With the word *normalization* he characterized the policy of permitting people with disabilities opportunities to live in as normal a fashion as possible. America learned about the concept largely through the work of another Scandinavian, Bengt Nirje (Kugel and Wolfensberger, 1969). Wolfensberger has since extended the term's application to other disability groups. Nirje defined normalization as 'making available to the mentally retarded patterns and conditions of everyday life which are as close as possible to the norms and patterns of the mainstream of society.' More recently, Wolfensberger (1983) has suggested that the term *social role valorization* better captures the essence of this process than does normalization.

One of Nirje's favorite examples, to illustrate the concept of normalization, grew out of a conference held in Scandinavia while he was the executive director of the Swedish Association for Retarded Children. At the conference, retarded people were asked to make requests for policy changes that might affect their lives. Their requests were consistent with the normalization principle. People asked not to be given special preference in receiving housing referrals (there were housing shortages in Sweden). The retarded people also said that when taken into town they preferred not to be taken in large groups but rather to go in groups of two or three. And they asked that as adults they not be sent to special camps for the retarded only, but that they be given opportunities to take their vacations in the standard vacation resorts of Europe as nonretarded people do.

It was just a short step for American educators and disability rights advocates to apply the principle of normalization to education . . .   99

(Biklen 1985)

19. Tony Dessent: *Making the Ordinary School Special*

Tony Dessent's book *Making the Ordinary School Special*, published in 1987, provided a punctuation mark in thought about the development of special education services in the UK. In clear language and drawing upon hard evidence it made people stop and think about what was actually happening following the supposedly progressive changes suggested by Warnock that were in part effected by the 1981 Education Act.

In the following paper from *Children and Society* Dessent summarises elements of *Making the Ordinary School Special*. He points out a number of *myths* in the special education enterprise. The first is the *integration myth*, wherein 'integration' implies that the child – almost charitably – is being accommodated by the mainstream system. Dessent suggests that this myth can be dispelled by replacing the idea of integration with that of *non-segregation*. Here, Dessent anticipates contemporary inclusive thinking by widening the ambit of thought about 'special needs'. The latter notion, he says – by focusing on a supposed identifiable difference – encourages separation and segregation. We should aim to move away from this segregative mindset, he advises, and examine our primary goals in the education enterprise. One of these, he suggests, is the achievement of a truly comprehensive education system, and this cannot, of course, be reached while there is segregation in the system. There are also the *practical*, the *expertise* and the *training myths*. These myths all have at their core a belief that meeting needs is about teachers' knowledge. Dessent refutes this, noting that '. . . meeting special needs within mainstream schools involves, first and foremost, crucial questions and decisions concerning values and attitudes, rather than "how" questions related to the curriculum, teaching methods, etc'.

He goes on to raise a number of important matters for the ordinary school, in order for it to become 'special'. There are issues about how resources are best spent, about schools coming to see that they 'own' children with difficulties and accepting that 'failure' occurs: that there are bound to be better and worse achievers at school. Schools and administrators must not 'fudge' issues by taking the easy way out by simply employing more assessment agents or implementing more defensive bureaucratic procedures (and there are echoes in the latter of the points made by Weatherley and Lipsky in their American study reported in this volume, 11). Rather, there has to be an acceptance that if problems occur in the education of certain children, extra resources have accurately to target those children. Further, schools have to accept that they exist to provide for these children.

66 Meeting special needs in ordinary schools – some current mythology

The increased focus and interest within recent years upon meeting special needs within normal school environments has provided something of a breeding ground for the development of myths within this field. The first of these is the *integration myth*. This involves the view that integration should be the aim for children with special needs in order for them to be educated within a mainstream environment. This myth has been emphasised by the plethora of articles and research projects on integration schemes which have appeared. Questions are asked such as, 'How do we go about integrating children with moderate learning difficulties, or those with emotional behavioural difficulties?' In contrast, I would suggest that the pursuit of integration is largely inappropriate when considering the needs of the majority group of children with special needs – those with a range of learning, social and emotional difficulties. For this group of children, in particular, the aim must surely be that of *non-segregation* rather than integration. The term 'integration' implies that the children concerned are first separate, different and distinct in some fundamental ways. Integration, in fact, implies some prior conceptual or actual segregation of the children. Integration (or indeed segregation) is something which can then be offered to these children. Non-segregation implies a quite different framework of thinking. It implies that the focus of our efforts should be directed towards extending the idea of a comprehensive education system to include the widest possible range of children. This may entail a range of resourcing and supportive strategies to help the ordinary school system avoid the need to segregate children. The conceptual distinction between integration and non-segregation is not a pedantic one. It has profound and far reaching implications for the way in which LEA policy is developed.

A second, and particularly potent and widespread myth at the present time in the field of special educational needs, is the *practical myth*. According to this piece of mythology, coping with special needs in mainstream schools is essentially a practical/technical issue requiring, for example, changes in teaching methods and the delivery and content of the mainstream curriculum. The practical myth is closely related to the notion that there exists a distinct form of special expertise (the *expertise myth*), often linked to a knowledge of assessment methods and behavioural techniques in programme planning. Linked to the expertise myth is the view that all mainstream teachers need to be intensively trained in these methods before the integration of children with special needs can occur (the *training myth*).

The practical myth ignores the fact that meeting special needs within mainstream schools involves, first and foremost, crucial questions and decisions concerning values and attitudes, rather than 'how' questions related to the curriculum, teaching methods, etc. When staff attitudes, values and school ethos are consistent with meeting a wide range of individual needs, the necessary curriculum and organisational reforms will usually follow. Similarly, while training and in-service education is an important professional right for all teachers, care must be taken to avoid ordinary teachers being inadvertently 'deskilled' by approaches which perpetuate a myth of exclusive 'special educational' knowledge and expertise. Meeting children's special needs requires the skills and expertise possessed by all good teachers. The primary requirement for most ordinary teachers is not necessarily that they receive specialist training, but that they are given an increased opportunity to develop their skills with children with special needs within ordinary classrooms.

Making the ordinary school special – major issues

Perhaps one of the chief reasons behind the expansion of segregated special education provision since the 1944 Education Act relates to the relative simplicity of managing, resourcing and administering a separate special system. In contrast, the development of non-segregation policies is complex in terms of administration and management. Moreover, the financial implications of such policies are, as yet, unknown (but unlikely to be cheap), and may even defy any costing. Non-segregation policies involve attention being paid to a number of interlinked issues. Important amongst these issues are the following:

The 'resource' issue

Meeting special needs is an expensive financial enterprise. The evidence provided by a number of LEAs to the recent House of Commons Select Committee on the implementation of the 1981 Education Act, well illustrates the importance of finance and resources in special education. One LEA (Derbyshire) provided information which indicates that approximately seven percent of the Authority's educational expenditure was attributed to meeting the special needs of some 2.5 percent of the overall child population (House of Commons, 1987) . . .

In terms of non-segregation approaches, a three strand resource policy might be envisaged. The first would involve local education authorities making explicit in their staffing of all ordinary schools an element to provide for special educational needs. This would involve the operation of a positive discrimination principle in the distribution of resources. The second strand would involve differential resourcing related to social and demographic factors which have a known relationship to educational difficulties amongst children. Finally, an individual resourcing strategy would be required to take account of the unique and unpredictable needs of a small number of disabled pupils.

The result of resourcing policies of this kind would be a reduction in the number of pupils individually assessed and 'statemented' under the terms of the 1981 Act. Available resources would be focused upon increasing the provision normally available for children within ordinary schools rather than upon the resourcing of assessment procedures. The professional time which is currently being used in manning the, often mindless, bureaucracy involved in the assessment procedures could then be switched towards enhancing the staffing and resourcing of ordinary schools in order to meet needs.

The 'ownership' issue

Currently, the ordinary school system does not 'own' either the responsibility or the resources for meeting special educational needs. We exist with a dual system. We have special education teachers, advisers for special education, administrators who oversee special education. This special/normal division is reflected throughout the organisation of LEAs, within teacher training establishments, as well as within the organisation of Her Majesty's Inspectorate and the DES. If we are to help ordinary schools to become special, changes must occur in these structures. Progressively, and perhaps painfully, ownership and control of the special education system must pass to the ordinary structures of the ordinary school system . . .

The 'support' issue
The implementation of the 1981 Act has been followed in many LEAs by a significant increase in the number of educational psychologists and external advisory support teachers (Gipps and Goldstein, 1984). Such services can have an important part to play in supporting the development of provision for children with special needs in ordinary schools. However, there is a danger that such centralised services will be developed by local education authorities as an *alternative* to making adequate provision within ordinary schools for meeting special educational needs. The development of a large, centralised special needs' service is a cheap and administratively simple answer for LEAs confronted by an indefinable resourcing problem. Putting all their special resources for mainstream schools into a central team, out of the hands and control of ordinary schools, is the cheapest possible way of defining what resources should be made ordinarily available for meeting special needs in ordinary schools. Support and advice is then offered to schools which are often inadequately resourced and poorly organised to meet special needs. Such services can easily be caught in the trap of finding themselves offering advice to hard pressed teachers who lack the opportunity to implement the ideas presented. Ordinary schools do not primarily require an army of educational psychologists or advisory/peripatetic teachers to deliver their special expertise to growing numbers of individual children for whom the schools are inadequately resourced and/or organised. A rationale for support in special education can only develop within a context of resourcing and management which enables the headteacher and staff of the ordinary school to make appropriate responses to children with special educational needs.

The 'failure' issue
Most parents would like their children to be 'at least average' in terms of educational attainment and scholastic prowess. All good teachers want their pupils to succeed and to make optimal progress. In contrast, there will always – by definition – be children who are 'below average' and there will always be children who, relative to their peers, make limited, and sometimes imperceptible, educational progress. Living with these conflicts and realities is a central aspect of meeting special needs in ordinary schools. The teacher in the special school does not feel as

implicated in an individual child's difficulties as does the teacher in the mainstream school from whence the child came. Arrival in the special school validates the child as being the cause of the failure – not the teacher, not the curriculum, nor the teaching methods. Special school placement is a recognition that the child will fail and make limited learning progress. Helping teachers in ordinary schools to live with diversity and variation between children in learning and social behaviour; helping them to learn to live with the relative failure of some pupils in traditional educational skills, but to continue to feel responsible for the child's future learning, must be a central part of 'making the ordinary school special' . . .

The 'parent' issue
Interactive concepts of special educational need imply that special needs do not simply exist 'within children'. We are increasingly aware of the role played by school, curriculum, resourcing and attitudinal factors in determining whether or not a special need is said to exist. Home background, and the needs, skills and expectations of parents are also enormously powerful variables in determining special educational needs. This is particularly relevant when considering the majority group of children with special needs – those with learning difficulties and a range of social emotional difficulties. Many children arrive in special educational settings primarily because of family, domestic and parenting difficulties, rather than because of the strictly educational difficulties of the individual child . . .

   Making a positive response to the special needs of parents, as well as to the needs of children, is one of the major challenges faced by ordinary schools. This is an area of work which has undergone considerable development within the field of segregated special education. However, responding to parent needs has not always been seen as part and parcel of the job of teachers in ordinary schools. Work of this kind requires a blurring of distinctions between meeting educational and social needs. Some teachers will regard it as social work rather than teaching. Yet it seems unlikely that special needs can be effectively met unless teachers in ordinary schools are resourced and helped to extend their responsibilities beyond the classroom and into a concern for the whole child within the context of family and community.

The 'positive discrimination' issue
The principle of positive discrimination lies at the very heart of special education. It is perhaps the single most important issue in terms of the aim of 'making the ordinary school special'. Positive discrimination implies an acceptance that some children – those who are disabled or who are educationally disadvantaged in some way relative to their peers – should receive *more* in terms of resources, time, etc. Historically, the educational system's approach to conferring positive discrimination on children with special needs has depended upon segregational processes

and practices. Our largely segregated special education system can usefully be viewed as a system which attempts to ensure positive discrimination in the use of resources, teacher expertise, positive teaching approaches, etc. . . .

The positive discrimination issue demonstrates most clearly the importance of ethical, attitudinal and value orientations in the field of special education. The teacher who maintains that all children have 'special needs' may be expressing a value position based on the principle that all children have an equal right to available resources and teacher time and that no child has a right to more than their peers. Such a principle must ultimately be at odds with the idea of special education as a system of positive discrimination for particular individual children.

The issue of positive discrimination is the single most important challenge with which the ordinary school system is faced, simply because it impinges upon the personal and individual values of all those concerned with the teaching of children in our schools. While there can be almost universal acceptance of positive discrimination for a grossly disabled child, there is far less agreement once the principle is applied to children with learning and social/behavioural difficulties. Positive discrimination for this group is all the more controversial when it is realised that providing more for these children implies that other groups – 'average' or 'bright' children – will receive less.

Non-segregation policies will always be limited by the extent to which positive discrimination for children with special needs is accepted within mainstream education. The implications of positive discrimination across the continuum of need are far reaching. It will certainly involve the development of resourcing policies which increase the level of provision normally available to children with special needs. It will also need to be reflected in the career structures of teachers and the recruitment policies of LEAs, in policies on school buildings, and upon the way in which schools are monitored and appraised.

Conclusions

If ordinary schools are to become special and non-segregation policies are to be developed, then significant changes will need to occur within our educational system. To prepare for these changes, we need first to 'clear the ground' and to dispel some of the unhelpful myths which have developed in the field of special educational needs. The *integration myth*, the *expertise myth* and the *training myth* are examples of these. So too is the myth that meeting special educational needs in ordinary schools is essentially a *practical* issue. Special education is an area in which major ethical, economic and organisational questions can be easily fudged. Easy solutions to complex problems can be pounced upon and implemented. More awareness courses; more advisers; more educational psychologists; more assessments; more expertise; are all known examples. In isolation from decisions about broad aims and principles, each of these 'solutions' is likely to lead nowhere. Some of the major issues which both LEAs and schools will need to consider have been outlined in this paper. It has been suggested that at the heart of non-segregation policies lies a set of moral, ethical and value issues linked to the principle of positive discrimination for children with special needs. Positive discrimination policies will impinge on most, if not all, aspects of the educational system. However, ultimately and most importantly, positive discrimination must be reflected in the way in which teachers, ordinary schools and their local communities respond to individual children who are disadvantaged in some way. Children who may never meet our traditional expectations of success in education need to be treated as individuals of equal worth and value within our ordinary schools. This is ultimately what 'making the ordinary school special' must imply.

99

(Dessent 1987–88)

20. L. Anderson and L. Pellicer: *Synthesis of research on compensatory and remedial education*

Anderson and Pellicer here widen the debate about what is provided for children who are having difficulty at school. The issue concerns not only special education in special schools but also concerns that array of measures referred to here as 'compensatory and remedial education'. Like Weatherley and Lipsky (see 11 in this volume) before them, Anderson and Pellicer are concerned that special provision for these children in the mainstream school is far from satisfactory. Interestingly, for these authors 'in the mainstream' means more than just 'in the mainstream school'. It means – in 1990, when this paper was published – in the mainstream curriculum and all the mainstream processes of the mainstream school.

In a synthesis of research Anderson and Pellicer show that although very large amounts of money were being spent (and continue to be spent) on these special programmes, all sorts of problems emerge with their implementation: poor co-ordination with the mainstream programme; resentment from mainstream teachers; over-reliance on untrained classroom assistants to implement programmes (to the detriment of the students); reliance on unchallenging seatwork activity for identified children; insufficiently differentiated work for children whose curricular needs are different and low chances of 'escaping' from the programme.

In their recommendations Anderson and Pellicer emerge with one of the key findings of research over four decades: if legislators and administrators really want to encourage inclusion they have to find ways of enabling money to be attached to a particular child rather than to a programme or a school.

Often these programmes are offered as an alternative form of special provision (alternative to special school that is), yet experience shows that what children ultimately receive can combine the worst of both worlds: stigma made more prominent by physical presence in the environment of the mainstream school combined with an expensive, exclusionary and ineffective curriculum.

❝ Over the past quarter century, programs designed to provide quality education for children who are economically disadvantaged and educationally deficient have received substantial funding. The major federally-funded program of this type, Chapter 1, accounts for 20 percent of the U.S. Department of Education's total budget, or almost four billion dollars a year. Approximately one of every nine school-age children is enrolled in the Chapter 1 program (OERI 1987).

In recent years, individual states have begun to fund their own programs targeted toward students who fail to meet state achievement standards. In South Carolina, for example, at least one-fourth of the children enrolled in public schools are in state funded compensatory and remedial programs. Since 1985, the cost of the program in South Carolina has averaged over $55 million per year, a figure which represents approximately 20 percent of the total monies raised in support of the school reform legislation (Anderson et al. 1989).

Whether the money is supplied by federal, state, or local funds, large amounts of money are spent on the education of these children. But what do we know about the operation and effectiveness of these programs? Do the academic gains made by the children served in these programs justify the large expenditure of funds? Are changes needed in the programs to increase their effectiveness? These are the issues we will examine in this paper, basing our generalizations on the results of numerous studies conducted during the past 15 years . . .

Organization and administration
Integration of compensatory and remedial programs into the total school program is often lacking. In addition, administrative leadership for these programs within the school often does not exist or exists at some minimal level. Schools' compensatory and remedial programs typically exist in isolation (Johnston et al. 1985, OERI 1987). Regular classroom teachers hold less than positive attitudes toward compensatory and remedial programs partly because of a perceived lack of coordination with the regular school program and partly because of a perceived lack of difficulty of the content and material included in the compensatory and remedial programs (Anderson et al. 1989). Regular classroom teachers complain that the scheduling of compensatory and remedial programs takes precedence over the scheduling of regular classes (Rowan et al. 1986).

In addition, 'weak or absent' coordination of the Chapter 1 program with the regular program tends to impede student learning (OERI 1987). District administrators usually make decisions concerning the models to use to deliver educational services to compensatory and remedial students without the involvement or even the knowledge of school principals. As a consequence, principals may not have a 'clear understanding of the rationale for selecting particular remedial and compensatory models for their schools, much less an understanding of how to integrate these special programs within the regular school curriculum' (Anderson et al. 1989, p. 42).

The district administrators' decisions concerning the models to use often reflect their own preferences or the availability of resources (e.g., space, personnel) (OERI 1987, Anderson et al. 1989), rather than concerns for meeting the needs of students or evidence concerning the effectiveness of particular models. The models they choose usually remain quite stable from year to year (OERI 1987). Furthermore, in schools which operate both state-funded and federally-funded programs, the two programs generally use the same delivery model (Rowan et al. 1986).

Finally, in addition to the lack of coordination with the 'regular' program, there may be a problem with the coordination of these programs with other special programs. For example, Anderson et al. (1989) found less effective state-funded programs in those schools which housed both federally-funded and state-funded compensatory and remedial programs. Along with federal programs for the handicapped and state programs for gifted and talented students, compensatory and remedial programs may be contributing, to both a fragmentation of the school curriculum and an administrative nightmare for principals.

*Staffing decisions may be more im*portant *to program effectiveness than decisions concerning the delivery model.* There is increasing evidence that the delivery model chosen does not *by itself* affect the quality of the instruction provided (Rowan et al. 1986) or the effectiveness of the program (Anderson et al. 1989). Excellent instruction, as well as poor quality instruction, has been observed in all delivery models (Rowan et al. 1986, Anderson et al. 1989).

The selection of instructional staff, on the other hand, may be quite important in influencing the effectiveness of the model. Specifically, using aides in compensatory and remedial programs is particularly problematic because of their general lack of qualifications (OERI 1987) and training (Anderson and Reynolds 1990). Furthermore, aides vary greatly in the quality of instruction they provide to the students (Rowan et al. 1986). Finally, less effective programs rely more on aides than do more effective programs (Anderson et al. 1989).

The two reasons for using aides are: (1) they are less expensive than certified teachers, and (2) they are less likely to cause role conflict between instructional personnel within the classroom (OERI 1987). Like the choice of models, the choice of personnel to staff the models seems more pragmatic than educational.

Instruction and teaching

. . . *Students in compensatory and remedial programs spend large amounts of time engaged in seatwork activities, particularly those students at the upper levels.* Despite their smaller class or group sizes, students in compensatory and remedial programs (particularly those at the middle or junior high and high school levels) are seldom taught as a group (Rowan et al. 1986). Their teachers spend little class time actively or interactively teaching, where the teacher explains material to a group of students and students interact with the teacher and one another by asking questions and making comments. Instead, the students spend large amounts of time working by themselves at their seats on written assignments. During this time, teachers circulate among the students, monitor their work, and provide tutoring as necessary (OERI 1987, Anderson et al. 1989). And in elementary reading classes, students may work for extended periods of time *without* supervision as the teacher interacts with another reading group (Lee et al. 1986).

Students in compensatory and remedial programs have very high success rates (in terms of the percentage of correct responses to classroom questions and the percentage of correct answers or solutions to exercises included on worksheets or other written assignments). Unfortunately, however, the demands placed on these students by the academic content that is the basis for these questions and worksheets are often far lower than those typically included on the state or national tests they may have to pass to exit from the programs. Teachers of students enrolled in compensatory and remedial programs appear to be caught between the proverbial rock and a hard place. They want to target their instruction to the current levels at which their students are functioning. At the same time, however, they want to ensure that their students achieve those levels of learning they must achieve to do well on the end-of-year tests. Unfortunately, the data suggest that teachers teach to the students' present levels of academic functioning, rather than to the levels they will need to achieve to be successful in the future (Rowan et al. 1986, Anderson et al. 1989). As a consequence, many compensatory and remedial students appear to be very successful in the short term but remain largely unsuccessful over the long haul.

In general, expectations for students in compensatory and remedial programs are very low. In this regard, there is some evidence that these students would benefit greatly from increased expectations and demands. This generalization follows quite naturally from the previous one. Teachers of students in compensatory and remedial programs tend to perceive that their students live in 'intellectually deficient' home environments, lack self-esteem, are unable to work without supervision, and are 'slow learners' (Rowan et al. 1986). Furthermore, as we have mentioned, the assignments they give to students at the middle or junior high and high school levels are frequently below the level at which they are functioning, let alone the level at which they need to function in order to pass the test which is the basis for exiting the programs (Anderson et al. 1989). Finally, compensatory and remedial programs rarely teach the development of higher-order skills (Rowan et al. 1986). Rather, their emphasis is on the acquisition of basic facts and skills (Pogrow 1990).

Peterson (1989) suggests that when teachers hold higher expectations for remedial students' mathematics achievement (i.e., they teach algebra rather than review previously taught mechanical skills), the students actually do reach higher levels of achievement. Similarly, Anderson et al. (1989) concluded that giving middle or junior high school students more challenging assignments that result in a greater number of errors is more beneficial over the long term than giving them easier assignments on which they make fewer errors. Finally, Pogrow (1990) contends that emphasizing higher-order thinking skills (HOTS) 'can develop the natural intellectual potential of at-risk students in a way that dramatically improves their basic skills' (p. 397).

The effectiveness of compensatory and remedial programs

Compensatory and remedial programs are more effective for 'marginal' students (those closest to the standard set for program inclusion) and substantially less effective for the remainder of the students enrolled in these programs. Clearly two distinct groups of students are served by compensatory and remedial programs: the compensatory students (who have severe learning problems as a result of cumulative environmental and/or intellectual deficits) and the remedial students (who have less serious learning problems, problems associated with their inability or unwillingness to learn in regular classroom settings). Carter (1984) concluded that Chapter 1 has been effective for 'students who were only moderately disadvantaged, but it did not improve the relative achievement of the most disadvantaged part of the school population' (p. 7). As a consequence, Rowan et al. (1986) contend that the delivery models and assignments provided to 'marginal' remedial students vs. the compensatory students should be very different. Presently, they are not (Anderson et al. 1989).

   The majority of students enrolled in compensatory and remedial programs remain in or periodically return to those programs for the better part of their school lives. The percentage of students who remain in compensatory and remedial programs from one year to the next ranges from 40 percent to 75 percent (Carter 1984, Davidoff et al. 1989, Potter and Wall 1990). In addition, approximately one-half of those who exit the program at the end of any given year qualify for re-entry to the program at the next testing date (Davidoff et al. 1989). As a consequence, almost one-half of the students initially enrolled in a compensatory and remedial program spend more of their school years in the program than out of the program (Potter and Wall 1990) . . .

Recommendations for change

There are three recommendations for change that we believe to be of primary importance in ameliorating some of the shortcomings of remedial and compensatory education programs.

   Compensatory and remedial programs should be reconceptualized as educational programs rather than funding programs. The availability and allocation of sufficient funding for these programs is a necessary but not sufficient condition for their effectiveness. A number of researchers have documented a wide variety of approaches and strategies used in providing services to these students. As a consequence, there is no single identifiable educational program that we can reliably term 'compensatory and remedial.' Program input is the focus in the administration of these programs, not program implementation or outcomes. Thus, a student's *access* to a compensatory or remedial program is, in effect, of greater importance than his or her *exit* from it. In fact, many funding formulas actually reward school districts for having greater numbers of students in compensatory and remedial programs.

The use of the normal curve equivalent (NCE) metric in evaluating these programs should be reconsidered. An NCE gain of one unit (currently used as a standard in judging the success of federal and state programs in several states) requires that students, on the average, attain marginally higher test scores than they might have been expected to attain given their previous test scores. But for students to re-enter and achieve success in the regular school program they must attain substantially, not marginally, higher test scores. Program success should be equated with individual student success, not with the marginal success of students 'on the average.' Stated somewhat differently, compensatory and remedial programs should be judged successful only when large numbers of their students return to and remain in the academic mainstream.

Compensatory and remedial programs must be more completely integrated into the total school program. If the goals of these special programs are to be reached, they must achieve greater integration into the total school program. Several aspects of this needed integration must be addressed simultaneously.

Principals are the key players in integrating special programs into the total school program in individual schools. Presently, many building administrators are unfamiliar with compensatory and remedial programs and the students served by these programs. Principals must acquaint themselves with compensatory and remedial programs and actively involve themselves in important decisions about the programs. Teachers also have a role to play in cross-program coordination. Rowan and his colleagues (1986) concluded that informal coordination was an important factor in program integration. However, regular classroom teachers and special program teachers must develop mutual respect and must function as colleagues if informal coordination is to occur. In the words of Rowan and his colleagues: 'Schools that showed the tightest coupling between Chapter 1 and regular instruction were those in which staff endorsed a norm of collegiality and had developed shared beliefs about instruction' (p. 94) . . .

The quality of the education provided to compensatory and remedial students must be increased substantially. Once children are placed in compensatory and remedial programs, they usually remain in or return to those programs throughout their school careers. The evidence for this is so compelling that Anderson and his colleagues (1989) referred to these students as 'lifers,' while Pogrow (1990) termed them 'professional Chapter 1 students.' The specific reasons for this phenomenon are not completely clear, but there is ample reason to believe that the level and quality of instruction provided to these students are among the primary causes. (Anderson et al. 1990).

In order to improve the level and quality of instruction provided to compensatory and remedial students, we must first admit that smaller classes and greater individual student attention do not guarantee excellence in teaching or learning. The qualifications and training of those providing the services, the quality of the services provided (as opposed to whether the services have been provided), and the accomplishments of those receiving the services must be considered in determining program effectiveness . . .

Back to the mainstream
In 25 years, we have apparently learned very little as a result of our efforts to provide appropriate educational experiences for culturally and educationally deprived children. Our neediest students are enrolled in the neediest programs . . .

Throwing money at the problem in no way absolves policymakers and society in general of the responsibility for providing these students with a set of educational experiences that are both appropriate and effective. In the final analysis, successful programs can be realistically defined only in terms of individual student success. And the ultimate measure of success can only be the ability of large numbers of remedial and compensatory students to exit these special programs and return to and remain in the academic mainstream.   **99**

(Anderson and Pellicer 1990)

21. John O'Brien and Marsha Forest: *Action for Inclusion*

The question has often been asked 'When did the word *inclusion* first start being used in favour of integration or the earlier mainstreaming?' In July 1988 a group of 14 people from North America who were concerned about the slow progress of integration in education brainstormed around a table at Frontier College, Toronto, Canada, and came up with the concept of *inclusion* to formally describe better the process of placing children and adults with disabilities or learning difficulties in the mainstream. This group included educators, writers, parents and disabled adults who had first-hand experience of segregated education.

Switching their thinking from 'integration' to 'inclusion' at this legendary meeting was indeed a radical gesture and the use of the word *inclusion* caught on quickly across Canada and the US. It took a few years for *inclusion* to be accepted more readily in the UK and elsewhere. This group's discussions and subsequent actions formed a key turning point in the history of inclusive education.

Around the same time material was being gathered for a new book called *Action for Inclusion*. This seminal document from Inclusion Press in Toronto was published the following year in 1989 and had as its sub-title: *How to Improve Schools by Welcoming Children with Special Needs into Regular Classrooms*. It was written by John O'Brien and Marsha Forest, with contributions by Judith Snow, Jack Pearpoint and Dave Hasbury, all of whom were part of the July 1988 meeting. This book consolidated the ideas and early practice surrounding integration and then took readers on a major leap forward with practical suggestions for heads, teachers, parents, students and others – and introduced the notion of *inclusion* for all.

Interestingly the book reveals itself as being like a moth in a chrysalis – resonating with a new message on something great about to emerge; this is demonstrated by the duality of some of the text, using both the terms 'integration' and 'inclusion'. It opens with: 'Integration is our goal . . . Inclusion of those who have been left outside is the first step in integration . . . Some people think that you can speak of integration without inclusion. This seems a nonsense to us.'

The book begins with a bold philosophical statement, which with hindsight looks non-controversial. In 1989 this teachers' manual was indeed both innovative and radical.

> **66** Good schools get better when they include all the children in the school's neighbourhood. Good teachers grow stronger when they involve each child as a member of a class of active learners by offering each the individualised challenges and supports necessary for learning. Students develop more fully when they welcome people with different gifts and abilities into their lives and when all students feel secure that they will receive individualised help when they need it. Families get stronger when they join teachers and students to create classrooms that work for everyone.
>
> Inclusion is fundamental to learning about the world as it really is. Until each child belongs, efforts to achieve educational excellence build on sand. Daily relationships which disclose the myriad capacities and gifts of all people lay at the foundation of education. Inclusive schools build and nurture these essential relationships. **99**

(O'Brien and Forest 1989)

These were new and strong words in 1989. Four of the authors (O'Brien, Forest, Snow and Pearpoint) later teamed up with George Flynn, Director of Education for the Waterloo education authority near Toronto, and Herb Lovett, advocate, writer, campaigner and educational psychologist from Boston, to form part of a powerful series of annual residential inclusion conferences in the UK (1991–94). This Anglo-North American link-up in the early 1990s was instrumental in helping to develop UK thinking around inclusion in schools and other educational establishments.

22. Sam Carson: Normalization and portrayal of disabled people

In 1992 Sam Carson, an educational psychologist with Durham County Council, argued that there was a growing acceptance of the 'principle of normalisation' and its use as a critique of practices in the human services. Young people who experienced significant difficulties, he said, had needs in common with their regular peers, yet they were at risk of discrimination and disadvantage because of 'devaluing attitudes' and needed counteracting, compensatory support.

In his article, Carson demonstrates that this has 'major implications for . . . inclusion'. The reader will notice how often the word 'normalization' could be replaced by the word 'inclusion', in order to fit a current-day discussion. His shopping list of how normalization/inclusion would appear in detail in mainstream schools makes radical reading for 1992 and was ahead of its time. In the following extract Carson surveys the literature on negative portrayals of disabled people and goes on to list a variety of wounding experiences for young people when they are socially devalued.

66 Compensatory needs

People with significant difficulties or disabilities/handicaps have been consistently portrayed and perceived in stereotypical ways. They have been, and continue to be, associated with devaluing images of disease and sickness; pity and charity; eternal children; sub-human, and as a menace (Wolfensberger, 1972). This has led to people being treated on the basis of such perceived characteristics. They have often come to be negatively valued as people; and have been treated in devaluing ways. Throughout their childhoods, and into adulthood, they accumulate many negative experiences that have been called 'wounds' (Vanier, 1971). Services, reflecting the preoccupations and prejudices of society at large, perpetuate and institutionalise this. Bluntly stated, most current services are to some extent involved in 'tidying away' people seen as not very important, into life experiences which are felt to be good enough for them – but which would not be seen as good enough for more valued people.

There is a growing body of research which highlights: (i) the more that people are integrated then the greater their likely achievement and (ii) the damage done to young people in traditional segregated provisions is considerable. Evidence published by Brinker and Thorpe (1983), Wang and Birch (1984), Slavin and Madden (1986), Ferguson and Asch (1989) and others supports the former proposition. They suggest that the richness of interactions, experiences and opportunities available within mainstream schools – particularly those aspects related to the presence of able peers – are often underestimated, thereby permitting segregation; or are under-used when integration is attempted. Further recent research gives substance to how regular classrooms in ordinary schools can create a good learning environment for all – for example, by better utilising groups of pupils (Bennett and Cass, 1989) and by creating a culture of support and inclusion by pupils (Forest and Pearpoint, 1990).

The data regarding the accumulation of negative consequences for segregated pupils sustains the second proposition above: 'research . . . at the most charitable interpretation fails . . . to support the view that children benefit . . . educationally from special schools rather than ordinary schools' (Galloway and Goodwin, 1987).

Young people in segregated settings tend to have fewer non-handicapped friends (Reiter and Levi, 1980); have generally more restricted interpersonal relationships than other groups (Illyes and Erdosi, 1981); have starkly limited life styles (Redding, 1979); are unprepared for accessing mainstream leisure and work experiences (Bluhm, 1977); and develop stunted self concepts (Chapman, 1988). Perhaps the most telling evidence comes from personal testimony. O'Brien and Lyle (1985), Oliver (1989), and many others have tried to highlight the creation of disadvantage within society; and the sense of oppression and personal devaluation experienced by vulnerable people. Segregated schooling is a cornerstone of such societal structures. Schools and other services, which try to do the best for those who rely on them will need to actively counteract the vicious circles of devaluation and marginalisation that are described by O'Brien and Tyne (1981).

When young people are socially devalued, they are more likely to have a variety of devaluing or wounding experiences. Some of the experiences that children who are at risk of social devaluation have in common are:

1. Rejection – children who have been pushed out of ordinary settings, routines and relationships. Often seen as not belonging to their local community, but exclusion justified as being 'better off' away from ordinary experiences and opportunities. Compensation would involve actively seeking to welcome children with difficulties into ordinary settings.

2. Segregation – children who are seen as needing their own version of things; separate schools; separate transport; separate swimming pools; separate lives. Compensation would involve actively building integrative programmes and opportunities; and creating an expectation of their presence.

3. Congregation – children who are placed together because they have one thing in common – their disability-associated, devalued status. When children are always in groups of disabled children, they have inappropriate models. They have little chance of being seen in terms of their individuality or in terms of what they have in common with other able children. They do not get to do things for real. They have friendship gaps unlikely to be filled. Compensation would involve the dilution of a child's difficulties through daily association with competent peers who can support, model and befriend.

4. Discontinuity of life experiences – children can easily lose, or never form, important contacts and relationships with able peers in their neighbourhoods, schools and local community settings. They easily fall out of step with age-appropriate behaviours and experiences; and with the rhythms and routines of ordinary life. Compensation would involve actively supporting fragile contacts and relationships by creating socially integrative opportunities throughout childhood; and providing the help into, rather than away from, family and local schools.
5. Denial of true feelings – it is said that they do not understand as well as others do, so some treat them as if they do not feel things as others do. Compensation would involve challenging and rebuffing negative attitudes and creating positive associations and stories.
6. Blamed for the problems – children never being told they are nice to know; ever. Spending hours in time out, when they have not been taught acceptable behaviours. Daily experiences of criticism, being shouted at, threatened, belittled, nagged and insulted. Some children spend years under heavy medication. Others are regularly pinned in by furniture and tied up within their clothing. Children who are seen as 'expensive to keep'; seen in need of exceptional or incredible resources; possibly seen as better off dead. Children who have whole portions of their childhoods wasted. Compensation would involve significant shifts of service systems towards making mainstream schools and their local community settings more competent at supporting these children.

Children and young people who have wounding life experiences will need to have measures taken to avoid their recurrence. They will need to have compensatory support to make up for their loss of contacts and loss of place; and be consoled for their hurt.

Implications for education
The principle of normalisation will have major implications in practice for how schools might best help children and young people who have significant difficulties. How extra help is given will have, firstly, an impact on how pupils experience their difficulties. It will also influence how others view and treat these pupils; which in turn will affect how the pupils tackle and cope with their difficulties. The principle of normalisation challenges schools to ensure not only that each pupil receives the specialist help in an effective and functionally useful way, but further that the pupil's general educational needs are met and wounding side effects are avoided or minimised. Normalisation suggests that this may be done by using 'culturally-valued means'.

What would be 'culturally-valued' within school provision? Basically, this asks us to use as a yardstick those values which would be the preferred options for regular pupils *i.e.* the pupils seen as important and valued within a school. Extra help should be given in at least such an acceptable way to less favoured pupils.

Normalisation puts those who plan services on the horns of a dilemma. It is neglectful to leave children to flounder within the mainstream setting without adequate support; but it is impossible actually to meet a child's general needs within long-term segregated settings. Wounding experiences are much more likely to occur in the latter setting – though unsupported placement (dumping) in a mainstream school can also give rise to painful conditions, such as bullying, teasing, unrelieved academic failure, etc.

Normalisation seeks to use valued means by which to offer help. Thus, the help should be given in a valued setting – where others would wish to be; in conducive groupings – among those best suited for learning to occur and in the company of others with positive reputations; following purposeful activities in intensely taught programmes of study; and with care taken to remove negative labels/associations, while building positive reputations.

In more specific detail, this involves:

1. A *setting* where the pupil –

   - attends the same local school as their able peers
   - learns alongside their able peers throughout each day
   - receives help to integrate socially among their class group
   - has attractive and age-appropriate surroundings
   - gains a positive reputation.

2. *Groupings* whereby the pupil –

   - pursues activities in groups of suitable composition, *i.e.* in mixed ability groups for project work; with able peers for most of the day for the modelling of appropriate behaviour, socialisation and friendships; with peers of equivalent ability for specific skill practice
   - spends time away from the class only for specified, intensive work
   - receives individual tutoring from teacher or tutor on specific tasks
   - is represented as belonging to the class group and this school
   - avoids spending much time alongside other pupils at risk of social devaluation.

3. *Activities* whereby the pupil –

   - follows age-appropriate tasks and experiences
   - follows purposeful and functionally-identifiable curricula, which lead to participation in their school and local community

- receives effective instruction using established techniques for building skills
- receives specialist help to reduce or remove stigmatising mannerisms/behaviours
- receives intensive instruction and frequent practice at priority skills, such as classroom survival/coping skills *or* shared communication skills
- receives extra support to participate in peer group activities
- has ensured access to the full variety of peer group experiences
- follows activities identified as image-enhancing and confidence building.

4. *Arrangements* whereby the pupil –

- has stigmatising labels and language removed
- has a positive profile among their peers built up
- is spoken to and about in respectful ways
- is involved, as far as possible, in making choices and decisions
- has an age-appropriate image deliberately sought and has inappropriately childish dress, reading materials, associations, etc., avoided.

These examples of valued means within schools are not intended to be exhaustive. Rather they are a quick checklist pointing towards a more 'normalisation-friendly' special needs provision. In the past, some schools have shown excellence in one area at the expense of others. A coherent and planned approach is needed, which manages a dynamic balance between the four areas outlined here, leading to a high quality education for each child with special educational needs. By accepting the principle of normalisation as a yardstick, educational psychologists may considerably influence policy, planning and provision within educational services for the better.

(Carson 1992)

23. Seamus Hegarty: *Reviewing the literature on integration*

The following piece represents an abbreviation of a paper published by Seamus Hegarty in 1993 following a major study commissioned by the Organisation for Economic Cooperation and Development (OECD). This drew on an international literature, having been conducted by leading experts in five countries.

The talk in the report is of integration rather than inclusion, reflecting both the vocabulary still predominantly used at the time and the report's basis in categories of disability. As such, it provides an excellent summary of the state of play internationally at the beginning of the 1990s. It makes the point that most countries had enacted laws that mandated a move away from special education but points out that progress had been uneven despite the legislation. Hegarty therefore goes on to ask whether there might be intractable barriers to integration happening.

In the article, Hegarty makes important methodological points about the difficulties of comparing special education with integration. He concludes his discussion on this point with the comment that if the empirical case is difficult if not impossible to prove (for a variety of reasons that he elaborates), the 'moral argument', as he calls it, in favour of integration becomes stronger. Failing to find a clear-cut advantage for segregation or integration (partly because of the methodological problems of comparing non-comparable groups), he concludes: 'While [the inadequacy of comparative research] means that any inferences drawn must be tentative, the absence of a clear-cut balance of advantage supports integration.'

Hegarty seems to be arguing that unless evidence relating to children's progress and happiness at school is unequivocally *un*supportive of inclusion, then the principles we have used to guide the current trend toward inclusive education should continue.

66 Integration at a crossroads

Integration has been a key topic in special education for twenty-five years now. The growing realization that many children and young people were in special schools when they did not need to be and the discovery that ordinary schools really could cater for a wider range of student needs gave strong impetus to the integration movement. Outside of certain countries which retained a major role for special schools, it came to be taken for granted that the proper place of education for students with disabilities was the ordinary school and that special schools should be used only as a last resort.

Of course, practice fell some way short of this. In practically every country large numbers of children continued to be educated in a segregated way, whether in separate special schools or in separate classes in ordinary schools. This gap between rhetoric and reality can be attributed to various factors – the pedagogical limitations of many ordinary schools, the imperatives of a national curriculum, lack of commitment on the part of key participants, the magnitude of the task, the inertia in education systems, resource allocation mechanisms, vested interests – but it should not be allowed to take away from the enormous attitudinal changes that have taken place . . .

Beginning in the 1960s and gathering momentum through the 1970s, the integration movement wrought a sea-change in attitudes. This is both expressed in and furthered by major pieces of legislation. Italy, Denmark, the United Kingdom and the United States, for example, all enacted laws mandating a move away from segregated education. Hundreds of research projects were carried out comparing the relative effects of segregated and integrated education or, more helpfully, investigating the factors related to successful integration. A great deal of excellent practice developed where ordinary schools effected curricular and organizational reforms that enabled students with a wide range of special needs to become fully part of the school's learning community and have their educational needs met within it.

Progress has been uneven, however, both within countries and, quite startlingly so, if one looks across countries. This is undoubtedly due in part to the difficulties in bringing about system changes, as suggested above. It is for consideration at least whether there are not other, more intractable barriers and that integration may be unable to develop beyond a certain level or, alternatively, that ordinary schools can only go a certain distance in accommodating students with special needs. It may be that the aspirations of yesteryear were set too high and that we have to accept that there are limits to integration.

Clearly, it is opportune to take stock. One element of doing so is to review the numerous studies that have been conducted into integration. The present enterprise therefore is designed to shed light on experience to date and help inform future developments.

The literature

The literature consulted for the purpose of carrying out these reviews includes empirical studies, evaluation reports, critical writings and other reviews conducted previously. It draws on a wide range of sources – American, Australian, British, German and Swedish, in particular, but with many other countries represented as well . . .

The reviews presented here exhibit a number of strengths. First, their comprehensive nature is to be noted. There have been various reviews previously but it is relatively uncommon for such reviews to draw in any extensive way on material outside one country or education system. To this extent these reviews should help to break down the insularity which constricts practice in so many countries and to make the special education community more aware of broader strands of thinking. Second, the reviews addressed a number of common issues. Reviewers were not obliged to follow a set pattern, but certain topics such as efficacy and attitudes recurred throughout. Third, the reviews are analytical. They do not confine themselves to describing and summarizing relevant studies; they also subject them to critical analysis. This level of analysis is essential if studies are to build on each other and genuinely extend our understanding of the issues. Fourth, close account has been taken of disability-specific factors. While the interactive notion of special educational needs stresses that students' learning difficulties do not derive simply from their disabilities or other factors within the individual, there are nevertheless specific considerations relating to different disabilities, particularly sensory impairments, which must not be ignored. The structure chosen for the review maximizes the likelihood that such factors are given due consideration . . .

Some key issues

The reviews focus attention on a large number of issues related to integration. In doing so they highlight the complexity of the phenomenon. Three key issues are singled out for brief elaboration here: the relative efficacy of integrated and segregated provision; the characteristics of effective integration programmes; and attitudinal factors bearing on integration.

Most of the reviews looked at the efficacy of integration in the terms of academic achievement and various aspects of social and emotional development. It is understandable that they should do so since there has been such great interest in establishing which is better, integration or segregation, and numerous studies have addressed the issue by comparing groups of students along different aspects of development or achievement. As with previous reviews of this kind, the conclusions were tentative at best and generally inconclusive.

Thus, Williams summarizes his discussion on the academic achievements of integrated and segregated students with moderate learning difficulties by arguing that 'although the balance of advantage seems to lie in favour of mainstreaming, the safer conclusion is the same as that for social effects: no consistent evidence for a clear difference'. Stukát found a mixed picture regarding the self-concepts of physically handicapped students: those in integrated placements tended to have lower physical self-concepts than their counterparts in segregated settings, presumably because the former were made more aware of their physical limitations in everyday interactions, but tended to have higher general self-esteem. Kyle infers from his review that 'taken superficially, it would seem that deaf children perform better in integrated settings but the lack of control and the apparent urge to believe such results for political reasons, caution against such acceptance'.

The fact that research has failed to establish a clear-cut advantage in either direction should not occasion too much surprise. On the face of it, there are two sharply contrasting experimental situations, integration and segregation, and examining the differential impact of each should be straightforward. In reality, however, integration and segregation are not sharply defined and integration, in particular, can take numerous forms, some of them overlapping with forms of provision that might be deemed segregation. Moreover, organizational structures vary so much between and in some cases within countries that easy comparisons between subsets of provision, such as are entailed in special educational provision, are simply not possible. Thus, even when the significant variable of disability is controlled out, as would appear to be the case in these reviews, it should not surprise anybody that the comparative enterprise does not issue in clear-cut findings.

In point of fact, however, the disability variable is thoroughly confounded in many of the underlying studies, with the result that they provide a poor basis for generalization. Most reviewers draw attention to the definition problem in their area. This raises particular difficulties in the cases of learning disabilities, where Walberg charts the ambiguities of measurement and classification, and emotional and behavioural difficulties, where Chazan draws attention to the confusing range of terminology in use. Conti-Ramsden highlights the 'international consensus on the fact that children who have difficulties with language and communication form a hugely heterogeneous group'.

There is a further, technical reason why the findings of comparative studies should not be given too much weight. These studies are based for the most part on the use of controlled groups matched in respect of certain key variables. Commonly, the matching variables do not extend beyond age, sex and IQ. This is the core of the difficulty: there are many factors besides these that bear on students' responses to an educational programme – prior learning experience, motivation, relationship to the teacher, home background – and matching that does not take account of them is likely to be incomplete. The corollary of this is that the body of research comparing integration and segregation has a limited validity. Relief rather than disappointment might be a more appropriate response to the tentative outcomes of the research enterprise since this makes it less likely that policy will be driven by flawed evidence!

There is another consideration, however, of major import. Integration and segregation are not simple alternatives, and the absence of a decisive verdict from the research reviews must be seen in a new light as a consequence. The case for integration does not depend solely on empirical claims regarding its superior efficacy; there are also substantial moral arguments. If the verdict in the empirical case is open, the moral argument in favour of integration becomes all the stronger. Put differently, the case for developing segregated provision depends on the deficiencies of ordinary schools: if certain students are not being educated satisfactorily in ordinary schools, it makes sense to make alternative, segregated provision *provided that* the alternative is better. If in the event the segregated provision proves to be no better, it is difficult to justify maintaining it.

The upshot of all this is that the research reviews provide some guarded support for integration. Comparative studies relating to academic achievement and social development are subject to considerable technical limitations – limitations which are magnified when one seeks to generalize across studies in widely differing contexts. While this means that any inferences drawn must be tentative, the absence of a clear-cut balance of advantage supports integration. There has to be a presumption in favour of integration and, in the absence of decisive countervailing evidence, it must be regarded as a central principle governing provision.

Characteristics of effective integration programmes

If integration is established as the option of choice, one of the most useful functions of research is to identify the characteristics of effective provision with a view to improving integrated practice. As Stukát puts it, the need is to gain 'insight into the social and educational processes that take place under various conditions'. In certain areas, notably specific language impairments, there is a dearth of the requisite research, but in others there is a substantial body of research to draw upon.

Williams reviews the characteristics of effective integration programmes for students with moderate learning difficulties under three headings: the curriculum; team teaching; and support personnel. Guaranteeing access to the curriculum is seen to rely critically on differentiation – of objectives, of materials and, especially, of teaching approach. Team teaching or support for teaching can be an effective alternative to withdrawing students from lessons for specific help provided outside the classroom. Various refinements of team teaching are described. The evidence regarding support personnel (other than teachers) is inconclusive: their presence is generally held to be efficacious but research studies offer little confirmatory evidence.

In a trenchant critique of research and practice relating to learning disabilities, Walberg argues that programmes based on learning disabilities concepts and diagnoses have little demonstrable effect. However, research has identified a range of practices that do enhance the education of students with learning disabilities: instruction based on student achievement needs; materials and procedures that allow students to proceed at their own pace; additional time for students who need it; increased student responsibility for their own learning; and co-operation among students in achieving learning goals.

Appelhans provides further support for the importance of support teaching and collaboration between class teachers and specialists in the education of students with visual impairment. Strikingly, it is suggested in this context that specific knowledge and experience of the visually handicapped may be less important for success than the quality of the relationship between adults and students. Appelhans emphasizes the importance of the adaptability of the ordinary school in securing successful integration. Drawing particularly on German research, he itemizes the following as key features within the school: differentiated learning goals; methodological and didactic modifications; changes in the social form of lessons; and a positive attitude towards handicapped people on the part of teachers.

Attitudes

Attitudinal factors are likely to have a major impact on integration, and several reviewers discuss them explicitly. There are various groups whose attitudes are relevant – teachers, parents, the students with the disabilities themselves and other students. Determining the attitudes of a given group is difficult not merely because of the general problem of measuring attitudes but also because of the differential experience of disability individuals will have had.

The general picture across categories of disability is mixed but negative attitudes predominate, particularly in the case of teachers and other students who have had limited prior experience of disability (cf. Jenkinson, Stukát and Williams). Parents' attitudes tend to be coloured by their experience of their own child's schooling. Parents of children with the most severe handicapping conditions tend to be most anxious about integrated placements. Thus, Jenkinson found that parents of children with severe learning difficulties who were in special schools 'generally held negative views about the potential integration of their children into regular schools', expressing concerns over isolation, abuse and poor quality education. Relatively few studies into the attitudes of students with disabilities were reported.

There is a certain amount of evidence that negative attitudes can be turned round and positive social interactions facilitated. At the most basic level, more contact can bring about improved attitudes. This is documented by Jenkinson, Stukát and Williams, though Kyle and Conti-Ramsden draw attention to the particular interaction difficulties of deaf students and those with specific language impairments respectively. Various studies have investigated the process of attitude change in relation to disabilities; the evidence is that structured programmes can yield positive outcomes but the area is not sufficiently well understood yet.

Looking ahead

Integration is in the end a matter of school reform. It entails creating schools that respond to students' individual differences within a common framework. The areas for action are the same as for any other reform of schooling: curriculum, academic organization, pedagogy, staffing levels and deployment, resourcing, parental involvement and professional development . . .

Reviews of research such as presented here provide a very proper focus on the needs of individuals. Educating a student with visual impairment is not the same as educating a student with emotional and behavioural difficulties, and integration poses very different questions in the two cases. By illuminating these differences and keeping them in view, such reviews can guide whole-school reform and help to ensure that planning and curriculum provision are firmly based on the needs of individual students.   **99**

(Hegarty 1993)

24. Tom Hehir: *Changing the way we think about kids with disabilities*

In this discussion, Tom Hehir, who at the time of the discussion (1996) was director of the Office of Special Education Programs in the US Department of Education, puts some powerful arguments for inclusion. He makes the point that not only are outcomes better for children designated as 'special' when they attend mainstream schools, but also the schools become better places when they are open to all. As he puts it: 'When people do inclusion right . . . the whole school becomes a better place. We've found that in all 50 states [of the US].'

He also makes important points about financing systems needing to be correct before inclusion can really happen: '. . . finance systems that were set up to support the development of special schools and segregated programs have become an obstacle to providing kids with the supports and aids they need to be successful in general education.' The same is true in the UK, where there are – just as in the US – issues about the possibility of success without a serious shift of resources taking place. The question is how to liberate the substantial resources locked into a continuing special school system. It is worth dwelling on this for a moment to see the mechanical nature of the issue. The issue – and it is clearly an international issue – is that with the current system of funding of special schools by numbers of places (rather than numbers of children), the fixed costs of still-existing special schools do not diminish when a child moves out to the mainstream. Thus there is no liberation of resources to make inclusion of the moved child satisfactory. This problem is well documented in the UK by the Audit Commission (1992). Here, while six figure sums of money go to pay for children at some residential special schools, those sums do not accompany those children if they move back to the mainstream. Nor are they available as a resource when the mainstream school is in the process of referring a child in the first place: there is no offering of choices such as: 'This child will go to a residential special school that will cost £100,000 per year. Alternatively, the £100,000 is available to spend on inclusive support in your school.'

This is precisely the issue that Hehir raises in this piece. He points out that despite legislative commitment to inclusion in many states, money does not follow children as they move to inclusive placements. The solution, he suggests, is for states to review and change their special education financing formulae, as Dessent (1987) suggested more than a decade ago for the UK.

Financing is a key instrument in enabling the move to inclusion. Despite its importance little work has been done to explicate its impact in this area.

The impact of finance, though, is at once more subtle and more powerful than a simple focus on the formulae of resource distribution would reveal. Students of economics study a process called 'cost externalization'. It is a term used by economists to describe a process wherein manufacturers and producers shunt their costs of production elsewhere. The costs which they might incur in producing goods or services are thereby paid by someone else. The freight-carrier, for example, uses lorry transport because it is cheaper than rail transport. But the costs imposed by making that choice – in diesel fumes that cause asthma, which has to be treated, or in vibration damage to buildings which have to be repaired, or in amenities or environment destroyed or despoiled for the construction of new roads – are not incurred by the freight-carrier. They are not incurred because it is possible, given weak regulatory mechanisms, to move them to others: it is possible to *externalize* the cost.

A suggestion that is now raised more frequently is that commercial organizations should pay the price – literally – for using processes and practices that are inappropriate or anti-social. Businesses must be obliged to take account of the hidden costs of their less acceptable practices – costs of restricted opportunity for employees, of pollution of the environment and so on. At the moment, they create damage for which they do not have to pay. The lessons learned from this analysis are surely valid also in schools. The social costs of segregation, many disabled people have argued, are high: the cost of exclusion and segregation is the alienation of people who would otherwise have been able and willing to take a much fuller part in society. Yet high-excluding schools and high-segregating LEAs have not had to bear these costs of social exclusion.

The final point Hehir makes is about rights. As he puts it: 'We are talking about kids' rights. Kids with disabilities have a right to be educated in the least restrictive environment. The very idea of "debating" rights is inappropriate. We don't debate rights in this country.'

> ❝ Tom Hehir was formerly associate superintendent in the Chicago Public Schools, Director of Special Education for the Boston Public Schools and a special education teacher at Keefe Tech in Framingham, Massachusetts. He was interviewed for the *Harvard Education Letter* (HEL) by Edward Miller
>
> HEL: How has special education changed over the past few years?
>
> Hehir: We have made tremendous progress in the way we think about disability. Disabled people are no longer viewed as the objects of charity, but as a distinct minority who have been historically subject to discrimination and have now gained full civil rights through the passage of the Americans with Disabilities Act. The ADA seeks nothing less than full participation and integration of disabled people in all aspects of American society.
>
> Children with disabilities should be educated as much as is appropriate with their nondisabled peers. That has been a requirement of federal law for the last 19 years – that children with disabilities not be removed from regular education in the first place unless they cannot be successfully educated in an integrated environment with appropriate support.
>
> At the same time, we have increasingly seen that kids with significant developmental disabilities like mental retardation, physical disabilities, and autism who we had thought needed to be in separate programs – can be successfully educated in general education settings. The outcomes are better for those kids if they are educated alongside their nondisabled peers.
>
> HEL: Why has inclusion become such a volatile issue?
>
> Hehir: A lot of the hoopla about inclusion has to do with kids with significant disabilities. But that's a very few kids. Most kids' disabilities are mild – about 75 to 80 percent of those served in this program. But people have this notion that there are hordes of kids who are significantly disabled.

Much of the controversy over inclusion is about the idea of it, not the practice of it. Where inclusion is done well, you don't find teachers or parents adamantly against it. But when people do it poorly – just decide that all the kids are going into regular classes and don't give the teachers or the kids support – you have the reaction against it. And people *should* react against that. It's not what the law provides for.

When people do inclusion right – which means involve and give training to the teachers, give the kids support in the integrated environment, involve general ed and special ed parents from the beginning, and make adjustments as the program is implemented – the whole school becomes a better place. We've found that in all 50 states.

The Department of Education has supported model demonstration projects over the last eight years, and we have found that one of the main factors in successful inclusion is the support of the principal and the administration.

HEL: Why do some administrators see special education as a special interest group that is getting too large a share of limited resources?

Hehir: We spend $32 billion a year on special education. For most school districts, special ed and Chapter 1 are the major support systems. If you view everything as a zero-sum game – in other words, what special ed gets, regular ed loses – it doesn't get you anywhere. The fact is, kids with disabilities are protected by laws. The reason they are protected and may appear to be a special interest group with organized advocacy behind them is that these kids have not been educated well by our system, or, until recently, educated at all.

It's important to recognize that when Public Law 94–142 [the Education for All Handicapped Children Act] was passed there were 750,000 disabled kids who were not being educated in public schools. They were in institutions or in private schools at their parents' expense, or they were out of school completely.

When the law was first passed, one of our policy objectives was to get kids out of institutions. At that time most people believed that kids with significant disabilities needed special schools or special programs. So finance systems were set up in many states with the goal of getting kids out of institutions and into public school programs. And it worked. Seventy percent fewer mentally retarded kids are in institutions today than when the law was passed.

Now, as more people are demonstrating that kids with significant disabilities can be appropriately educated in integrated settings and as more parents push for that for their own children, state finance systems that were set up to support the development of special schools and segregated programs have become an obstacle to providing kids with the supports and aids they need to be successful in general education. In many states that money does not follow the child when he moves into an integrated program. It's a situation set up for failure.

HEL: How is your office attacking the problem?

Hehir: If we find that a state's finance system is impeding the implementation of the law, which requires a free and appropriate public education in the least restrictive environment, then we say the system has to change.

Right now more than 35 states are looking at changing their special ed financing formulas.

We want to see finance systems that are, as much as possible, placement neutral. Some states have them: Massachusetts, Vermont, Pennsylvania. But other states like New York, New Jersey, and California do not. Parents can go to court to force the issue. But why should parents have to go to court to get what the law already provides?

HEL: What other initiatives is the Office of Special Education Programs pursuing?

Hehir: We need to focus far more on the results of the education system: whether or not kids, when they leave school, are capable of getting decent jobs and are able to live independently in the community.

Kids with disabilities currently drop out of school at twice the rate of other kids. There is a significantly greater unemployment rate for disabled adults than for nondisabled adults. Special education has focused an awful lot on process. Now we need to do much more long-range planning and look at what kinds of interventions produce the best results, whether they are in an inclusive environment or not.

Another initiative is improving services for kids with severe emotional disturbance. They have experienced by far the worst results from the education system. They have a 50 percent drop-out rate and very high incarceration and institutionalization rates after they leave school. Few get appropriate services in school counseling, for example, or behavior management plans.

HEL: Does the inclusion model still hold for these children?

Hehir: It's wrong to frame it as 'the inclusion model.' The philosophy holds in the sense that we need to provide these kids with the relevant support. Often what we've done with children with emotional disturbances is put them in containment programs. We have not provided them or their families with mental health services.

There isn't one model that works with all kids. But the assumption should be, for these as well as other kids, that you serve them as much as possible within the general education setting. Sometimes it's just not appropriate. The law calls for a 'free and appropriate public education.' That 'appropriate' is extremely important.

For instance, you can accommodate a blind student very easily by providing readers and someone to guide the kid from one classroom to the next. But most blind kids have a much lower probability of successful outcomes as adults if they don't learn Braille. And if you don't teach that kid orientation and mobility skills – how to get around by himself using a cane or a dog or whatever, not depending on other people – then you are not providing an appropriate education.

There's no one program that works for kids with serious emotional disturbance. The model that doesn't work is containment. Too often, these kids are devalued and put in classrooms with other kids like them. People have called that 'special education.' That isn't what they need. They need mental health services, behavior management, and an individualized program. The principle of least restrictive environment should be applied to them as well.

HEL: Isn't the research on inclusion actually inconclusive?

Hehir: We just finished the National Longitudinal Transition Study, a long-term look at 8,000 kids with disabilities who were in high schools in the middle 1980s. And yes, frankly, the results are mixed. The picture that emerges is quite complex in terms of integration.

These were really pre-inclusion kids. In other words, the kids in that study who were in regular education settings were served under traditional mainstream models. They either made it in regular education or they were put in traditional separate or pull-out special education programs.

There's no evidence in that study that justifies segregation, and there is significant evidence that justifies integration, especially for kids with physical disabilities. After correcting for variables such as race, income, sex, and even IQ, we found that those with physical disabilities who are integrated, as compared to those who are segregated, were 43 percent more likely to be employed upon leaving school. Also, we found that kids who were integrated into vocationally oriented curricula had much better outcomes than those who did not have that opportunity.

A large number of kids in the study with mild learning disabilities failed to make it in regular education. Many of those kids received very little support. A lot of them ended up dropping out.

But the study showed that kids who received support in the form of tutoring and counseling did significantly better than those who did not. Unfortunately, most of the kids who were integrated did not receive that kind of support in an integrated environment. That's contrary to the principles of inclusion.

Most of the kids in the study with mental retardation were segregated. So it's very difficult to draw conclusions about them. The group that we can really see differences in are kids with physical disabilities.

HEL: What are the implications of these findings for teachers and schools?

Hehir: The findings reinforce the need for supports to follow the kids into the general education classrooms. Instead of the child going to a special education teacher, the special ed teacher goes into the general education class. Instead of going to a pullout program or resource room, the child stays with his peers and the support services come to him – the special ed teacher, paraprofessional, or speech, occupational, or physical therapist.

We know that there is tremendous diversity in every classroom. Disability is just one form of diversity. We have to restructure the classroom environment to handle that diversity. We are finding in many inclusionary programs that special education, when integrated into the regular classroom, can help the overall classroom structure to handle the diversity that we know is there.

The O'Hearn School in Dorchester, Massachusetts, is an example. The special education teachers and the general education teachers work together. Every kid in that school is on an individualized program – bright kids, kids who are more advanced intellectually whether they're disabled or not, kids who have significant mental retardation. That used to be a school that nobody wanted their kids in. Now parents try very hard to get their kids into it – general ed parents as well as parents of kids with disabilities.

HEL: Isn't there a danger in inclusive classrooms that the curriculum will be 'dumbed down' and that bright kids won't be challenged?

Hehir: That fear is legitimate if we teach every child the same thing at the same time. But if classes have more resources and supports – more than one teacher at different times of the day, for example – then kids can move at their own pace.

My nephew is in first grade in an inclusive school and he is not disabled. He's always picked up quantitative concepts very well, and he's doing third-grade math. But for a good part of the day he works with the special ed teacher in his classroom and with a child who's having a lot of difficulty with math. Everyone benefits from this kind of individualized program.

Our schools have had low expectations for a lot of kids, not just those with disabilities. Look at Down syndrome, for instance. In the fifties and sixties, parents of newborn Down syndrome kids were told to forget them and put them in institutions. When we evaluated those kids in those settings, we found they were severely retarded.

Look at those same kids today. Most of them who have stayed at home, who have received good early intervention services, and who increasingly are being educated in integrated and inclusive environments, are testing much higher on standardized measures like IQ. Most kids with Down syndrome still are mentally retarded, but relatively few of them test in the severe range; most test in the mild to moderate range. Increasingly we see kids with Down syndrome reading and doing other academic work people didn't believe they could do.

The keynote address at our last conference was given by Chris Burke, an actor who has Down syndrome. Now, if you had said 30 years ago that the federal government was going to have a keynote given by what people referred to then as a 'Mongoloid,' which of course is a racist term, people would have thought you were off the wall.

Down syndrome hasn't changed. What has changed is our view of Down syndrome, and the opportunities that we provide for growth for these children. That's an example of what we should be doing with all kids. We should be holding the bar much higher and providing them with the learning opportunities to get over the bar. Often we decide very early on who's going to be the winners and the losers, based on our concept of 'aptitude,' and we provide them with very different opportunities.

HEL: Isn't separate sometimes better for kids with disabilities?

Hehir: Disabled people do see a need at certain times in their lives to be with other disabled people. Integration can be very stressful, particularly if the environment is hostile. But the issue is choice – having the opportunity to be integrated.

It's important to recognize that any one form of education is not appropriate for all kids with disabilities. The law requires an individualized plan for each kid based on his needs. That's what is really appropriate.

HEL: Is the inclusion debate really about civil rights, not just education?

Hehir: I have a lot of problems with the word 'debate.' We are talking about kids' rights. Kids with disabilities have a right to be educated in the least restrictive environment. The very idea of 'debating' rights is inappropriate. We don't debate rights in this country.

Children with disabilities have a right to an appropriate education. For large numbers of kids, particularly those with developmental disabilities, the only option in many places has been a segregated program. That has to change.   **99**

(Miller 1996)

25. Gary Thomas and Andrew Loxley: Medical models and metaphors

Changes have been possible in thinking about inclusive education in large part because of changes in the way that 'difficulty' is conceptualized. There is less willingness now to locate the difficulties that children experience at school *in* the children themselves – whether the 'in-ness' is about their social background, supposed intellectual ability, disability, gender, race or something else.

Explanations that reside in these factors arise again and again – both in academic and staff-room discourse – but always are inadequate because they are simplistic. When thinking this way, success or failure at school is not seen as governed by complex social, cultural and intellectual interactions but rather by one-dimensional factors such as disability. The thinking is in a *deficit* or *medical* model wherein something is seen to have gone wrong – and is to be put right. Much of the discussion in the previous pieces implicitly centres on the paucity of this kind of reasoning for children's difficulties at school.

When 'explanations' like this are offered for children's difficulties at school such explanations tacitly rest in models and metaphors, as Thomas and Loxley point out in this piece. And these models and metaphors, by focusing on children and their problems, distract attention from the complexities of context. The 'explanations' – way off the mark – lead teachers, policymakers and researchers into wild goose chases and dead ends.

> ❝ The emphasis [in special education] has been on finding solutions: a special way of teaching, or a new method of behaviour management. That the solutions often appear so transitory or illusory is as much down to the kinds of questions we ask about 'failure' as the methods we use to answer those questions. As clinical psychologist David Smail (1993: 8) puts it in the context of what he calls 'unhappiness': 'To proffer solutions for problems we are barely beginning to understand does nobody any service'. The problem, as Clark *et al.* (1998) indicate, is about naïve assumptions of linearity – from this cause to that outcome. In the world of education things are rarely that simple. In short, caution is needed when considering many of the issues which may be of interest in special education. This isn't to say that questions shouldn't be asked. But wherever simple relationships are sought – of the variety, 'What's wrong with this child?' – many obstacles bar the way to an answer. Where questions of this kind are posed, the focus is being directed to the child and his or her mind, and several problems emerge from this kind of focus.
>
> First, there are problems which emerge from what has variously been called a medical, within-child, or deficit model – a model of putative diagnosis and treatment. Medical models of disorder are fine in their place, when thinking about measles or chickenpox. But they are less helpful in the consideration of people and their relationship to the organisations in which they live and work. Here, where the interplay between individual and organisation is more subtle and multi-faceted the medical model breaks down (Thomas, 1992). Other, related, problems emerge from the supposed location of the problem in the person, as Szasz (1972) and Laing (1965) have pointed out.

But second, there are questions which special educators and educational psychologists have been less ready to ask. Perhaps 'questions' is too strong a word: doubts about the status of knowledge is perhaps nearer the mark. As the philosopher of mind Gilbert Ryle (1990) has pointed out, much of our thinking about mind is based on metaphor, and that metaphor can be profoundly misleading. As he notes, what the metaphorical consideration of mental processes involves is the presentation of facts belonging to one category in the idioms appropriate to another. In our case in special education, failures in learning are often presented in the language and idioms of capacity. Children's lack of ability to do certain things at school is discussed in the language of buckets and other instruments of capacity measurement. Children are said, for example, to lack intelligence, to have weak sequential memory or (more commonly nowadays) poor phonological awareness. A child may lack a 'proper moral sense' (a real example given to one of the authors when working as an educational psychologist). As we point out in chapter 4, the results derived from such metaphorical assays achieve narrative plausibility, but little else. The problem is that once such metaphor exists it is difficult to displace it, especially when all the paraphernalia of experimental endeavour comes to surround and bolster it. The impressive vocabulary and statistical impedimenta of psychometrics cements in place edifices of explanation which rest in little more than analogy. This kind of analogy, far from being helpful as some analogy unequivocally is, leads to what Ryle calls 'myth' and this myth leads researchers and practitioners down many a cul-de-sac.   **99**

(Thomas and Loxley 2001)

26. CSIE: *Reasons against segregated schooling*

In 2003 inclusive education was at a crossroads and schools and LEAs faced a choice of continuing to develop the capacity of the mainstream to include all learners, or to follow a route then being proposed by the government, as well as most LEAs and schools, to limit inclusion and retain segregated special schooling for some pupils in perpetuity.

The CSIE (Centre for Studies on Inclusive Education) published a paper putting forward the reasons against segregated schooling and said that evidence of the damage caused by segregation continued to accumulate.

The paper, which has an extensive reference list attached to it (to be found in full on page 201), made a number of points including the following:

66 • There is no compelling body of evidence that segregated 'special' education programmes have significant benefits for students.
   • Segregated 'special' schooling has been associated with: impoverished social experiences, abilities and outcomes; reduced academic experiences in terms of curriculum provision, outcomes, examination

opportunities and accreditation; lower student aspirations and teacher expectations; high absence rates; difficulty re-integrating into the mainstream; poverty in adulthood; poor preparation for adult life.

- Negative consequences for segregated pupils identified in the research also include: depression, abuse, lack of autonomy and choice, dependency, lack of self-esteem and status, alienation, isolation, fewer friends, more restrictive inter-personal relationships, bullying and limited life styles.
- The discrimination inherent in segregated schooling offends the human dignity of the child and is capable of undermining or even destroying the capacity of the child to benefit from educational opportunities.
- The existence of segregated 'special' schools stifles creativity of mainstream schools about how to respond to diversity and weakens their responsibilities to include all learners. It undermines efforts to develop inclusive education by draining resources from mainstream, which in turn sets back the development of inclusive communities.
- The existence of 'special' schools contributes to insecurity and fear of rejection by those in the mainstream.
- Retaining segregated 'special' schools is out of step with the [UK] Government's learning disability policy, *Valuing People*, which has set a target for closing the remaining 21 long-stay segregated 'mental handicap' hospitals by 2004.
- Segregated schooling appeases the human tendency to negatively label and isolate those perceived as different. It gives legal re-enforcement and consolidation to a deeply embedded, self-fulfilling, social process of devaluing and distancing others on the basis of appearance and ability in order to consolidate a sense of normality and status.
- Segregated schooling perpetuates discrimination, devaluation, stigmatisation, stereotyping, prejudice, and isolation – the very conditions which disabled adults identify as among the biggest barriers to respect, participation and a full life.
- Segregated schooling does not lead to inclusion.   **"**

(CSIE 2003)

27. Mike Oliver: *Does special education have a role to play in the 21st century?*

Oliver argues in this article from 1995 that such has been the extent of failure of special education that nothing short of a complete deconstruction of the whole system will be enough to ensure appropriate, inclusive education.

Oliver states that it is only *reconstruction* that will guarantee 'the emergence of an enterprise that will be enabling, liberating and integrative for everyone'.

66   Special education: a history of failure

In most countries in the world throughout most of the twentieth century, the education of disabled children has been provided on a separate, segregated and special basis. The history of this provision has been one of abject failure, whatever criteria we use to judge it. If we say the purpose of such provision is to provide an equivalent education to that of non-disabled children, it has failed. If we say its purpose is to provide a basis for the full integration and participation into society of disabled children when they become adults, it has failed. If we say that its purpose is to provide a special form of education to meet the special needs of disabled children, again it has failed.

I do not make these claims lightly nor do I intend to use this failure as an opportunity to 'bash' those responsible for the system. The failure has been disastrous for all of us. It has been disastrous for all of us who pay taxes to support a system which socialises children into long-term dependency. It has been disastrous for those children who have been so socialised in that they have lived, and are living, impoverished and restricted lives. It has been disastrous for many committed and imaginative professionals who have devoted their professional lives to a system which has, ultimately, kept most of their children out of society rather than integrated them into it.

A deconstruction of the whole system

Such has been the extent of this failure that nothing short of a complete deconstruction of the whole enterprise of special education will suffice to ensure that its reconstruction in the twenty-first century will see the emergence of an enterprise that will be enabling, liberating and integrative for us all. What I have to say is a first step in this journey; a journey in which we all, disabled people, professionals, policymakers and citizens must embark. If the prospect of such a journey seems a long and daunting one, then we would do well to remember the words of Chairman Mao when he said that 'the longest journey begins with the first step'.

This failure has prompted reviews of the special education system in many parts of the world. In Britain there was the Warnock Report (DES 1978); in Ireland there has been the recent publication of the report of the Special Education Review Committee (1993). There is much in common in these reports and they share the same basic assumption: that it is the existing system that needs to be improved. For many years I had much sympathy with that assumption. Indeed I even served on such a major review myself and signed the published report (ILEA 1985).

I no longer believe that such 'tinkering', however radical and no matter what motives it is driven by, is enough to remedy the massive failures of special education that we have witnessed in the past hundred years. I will go further and suggest that nothing short of a radical deconstruction

of special education and the reconstruction of education in totality will be
enough, even if such a journey takes us another hundred years.   **99**

Oliver goes on to say that central to moving from integration to inclusion is
a deconstruction of school and teacher responses to special children.

66   Deconstructing school and teacher responses
Current educational wisdom suggests that schools must change in
order to accommodate children with special needs. The kinds of changes
necessary relate to the establishment of special needs departments, the
provision of support services both internal and external to the school,
the development of whole school policies and the implementation of
education authority-wide integration policies. These organisational
changes need to be planned in advance and properly resourced with a
clear vision of the aims and objectives necessary to achieve integration.
  As far as teachers are concerned, it is usually assumed that teachers
need to acquire extra knowledge and different skills in order to facilitate
the process of integration. Changes in teacher education at both initial
and in-service levels have tended to reinforce this. The problem is, of
course, beyond the additions in knowledge and skills that any professional working in a new area would be expected to provide, it is hard to
specify what this new knowledge or these new skills might be.

Reconstructing school and teacher responses
This implies fundamental changes which go beyond the organisational
and the professional. Reconstruction on the basis of rights to inclusion
suggests that there must be changes in the ethos of the school which
must mean that the school becomes a welcoming environment for
all children; [also] that there is no questioning of the rights of any to be
there and that organisational changes are part of an acceptance and
understanding of the fact that the purpose of schools is to educate all
children, not merely those who meet an increasingly narrowing band
of selection criteria, whether those selection criteria are imposed by
governments, professional groups or schools themselves.
  In addition, the arguments usually advanced against integration until
teachers have been properly trained can be seen as rationalisations to
preserve the status quo rather than genuine concerns about the inabilities
of teachers to cope with a whole range of new demands. In my view,
teaching is teaching regardless of the range or needs of pupils, and an
essential prerequisite of inclusion is the acquisition of a commitment on
the part of all teachers to work with all children, regardless of their needs.
Only when teachers acquire this commitment can inclusion truly be
achieved.

Deconstructing the curriculum
It is not just school organisation and professional practice that needs to be
deconstructed and reconstructed but the curriculum also, as this lies at

the heart of the educational enterprise. In terms of the curriculum in respect of reforming special education, the usual intention is to try to ensure that children with special needs have access to exactly the same curriculum as everyone else and that curriculum delivery must change in order to ensure this access.

The problem with this is that it focuses on delivery rather than content. Nowhere is the issue of what is taught about disability considered for any children, whether they have special needs or not. Despite controversy, it is generally acknowledged that curriculum materials have, up to now, been sexist or racist in their content. And indeed, considerable progress has been made in developing non-sexist and non-racist curriculum materials, despite attempts by right wing critics to ridicule the project.

With one notable exception (Rieser and Mason, 1990), there has been no acknowledgement that disablism actually exists, let alone admit the fact that the curriculum is full of disablist materials; images of disability are almost always presented in negative stereotypes, assessment procedures are based upon narrow academic criteria and judgements about children's progress are usually based upon ethnocentric and disablist assumptions about normal child development.

Reconstructing the curriculum

Reconstruction inevitably means that the ideology of 'normality' which underpins the curriculum and which, in its current version, preaches the acceptance and tolerance of children with special needs, will have to be abandoned. This view suggests that these people who are different have to be accepted and tolerated for after all, the different have come to accept and tolerate their difference so why shouldn't everyone else.

Such a view is underpinned by personal tragedy theory in terms of disability and deficit theory in educational terms. Tragedies and deficits are unfortunate chance happenings and these poor individuals should not be made to suffer further through rejection and stigmatisation; hence they should be accepted and tolerated.

It must be replaced with a view which challenges the very notion of normality in education and in society generally and argues that it does not exist (Oliver, 1988). Normality is a construct imposed on a reality where there is only difference. This new view is underpinned by an entirely different philosophy, what might be called the politics of personal identity. This demands that difference not be merely tolerated and accepted but that it is positively valued and celebrated.

Such a reconstruction of the curriculum implies nothing less than a total reconstruction of the whole enterprise of education; a task which we must begin with urgency if we are going to provide education for societies in the twenty-first century which will be organised around the idea of difference; a radical departure from twentieth century societies which have been organised around the idea of normality.

Translating moral commitment to political rights

What is needed as far as education is concerned, is a moral commitment to the inclusion of all children into a single education system as part of a wider commitment to the inclusion of all disabled people into society. Translating this moral commitment into political rights is something that can only be achieved by supporting disabled people and the parents of children with special needs as they struggle to empower themselves.

Support for these struggles may stem from a moral commitment but it must be properly resourced in terms of both money and other services, including those provided by professionals of all kinds. The history of the twentieth century for disabled people has been one of exclusion. The twenty-first century will see the struggle of disabled people for inclusion go from strength to strength. In such a struggle, special, segregated education has no role to play. **99**

(Oliver 1995)

PART THREE

Legislation, reports, statements

28. Public Law 94–142

Partly because of the civil rights movement, discussed in Part I of this book, the United States was ahead of the UK in its legislative provision about special education. Thus in 1975, six years before similar legislation was enacted in Britain, legislation came into place mandating mainstreaming where appropriate. Public Law (PL) 94–142 was a federal law that required states to provide 'a free, appropriate public education for every child between the ages of 3 and 21 . . . regardless of how, or how seriously, he may be handicapped'. PL 94–142 was the first law clearly to define the rights of disabled children to free appropriate public education. Before this legislation American states could exclude certain children from education because they were deemed ineducable.

Because of its requirement that students were placed in the *least restrictive environment* (LRE) PL 94–142 is sometimes taken to be the first ever statutory endorsement of mainstreaming. The requirement for the LRE meant placing the student in the most 'ordinary', natural or 'non-special' setting possible.

The law also required school systems to include parents when meeting about children or making decisions about their education. PL 94–142 mandated an individualized education programme (IEP) for every student with a disability. The IEP had to include short and long-term goals for the student, as well as to ensure that the necessary services were made available to the student.

PL 94–142 also required that students with disabilities were given non-discriminatory tests – tests that took into consideration the native language of the student and the effects of any disability.

The Individuals with Disabilities Education Act of 1990 (IDEA), Public Law 101–476, amended PL 94–142.

See *Mainstreaming in Massachusetts* (41) in Part IV of this volume for information on ways in which PL 94–142 was put into practice.

29. Warnock Report

The Warnock Committee looked at special education in England, Scotland and Wales and its Report (DES 1978) followed the largest ever investigation into this area of education in these countries. There is no doubt that the Report had a major influence on the national thinking of how special education should change and its many recommendations led to substantial improvements in the educational and social lives of children and young people with disabilities or learning difficulties. One of its most beneficial contributions was its support for the parent voice, declaring as it did the importance of parents' knowledge and understanding of their child and calling for parents to be seen as equal partners with professionals in the educational process.

The Report put the discussion about integration on the national agenda. Chapter 7, entitled Special Education in Ordinary Schools, began thus:

> **❝** In this chapter we move to the central contemporary issue in special education which has been earnestly debated far beyond the frontiers of the education service. The principle of educating handicapped and non-handicapped children together, which is described as 'integration' in this country and 'mainstreaming' in the United States of America, and is recognised as part of a much wider movement of 'normalisation' in Scandinavia and Canada, is the particular expression of a widely held and still growing conviction that, so far as is humanly possibly, handicapped people should share the opportunities for self-fulfilment enjoyed by other people. **❞**

The Warnock Committee also reported on the notion of three types of integration which they had seen, that revealed their limited conviction to integration. The three types were: *locational* where special units or classes existed in ordinary schools where little real integration took place; *social* where children in a special unit would eat or play with their mainstream peers; and *functional* where the relevant children were in regular classes and other activities either part- or full-time. The report firmly endorsed the validity of the three types and with hindsight it can be seen how limiting and damaging that endorsement turned out to be: it permitted and encouraged the continuation of a segregated framework and increased the odds against an effective development of integration.

The Warnock Committee did not take a strong stand in favour of integration, despite the popular belief that it was Warnock that brought in the idea of integration and strongly promoted it. This is not the case. While the Committee brought integration into the national consciousness, it sat on the fence regarding whether or not it was a good idea to integrate. Warnock's message about the wisdom or rightness of integration was ambiguous, to say the least. Many people believe today that inclusion in this country would be much further advanced than it is if the Committee had not taken such a cautious stand on the issue.

Why was the Warnock Committee so reluctant to give a strong endorsement of integration? There seem to be several reasons: one is that the Committee was probably over-influenced by an able-bodied, medical model perspective of the history of special education (portrayed clearly in Chapter 2 of the Report) and the enormous lobbying by those interested in preserving and maintaining the status quo. The Committee received this lobbying as evidence during the five years it sat. A look at the list in Appendix 1 of local authorities, organizations and professional bodies consulted by Warnock reveals the vast majority of them to be associated with separate special education; people, authorities and organizations that had (and many of whom still have) enormous investment in the perpetuation of separate special schools – investment that included buildings, career structures and philosophical commitment.

The fact that ignorance and fear of disability by most of mainstream society continued to be a direct by-product of ongoing segregation, did not appear to occur to the members of the Committee.

The awareness and understanding that we now have of the social model of disability against the medical model, was simply not around in the mid to late 1970s. Nearly 25 years later it would be inconceivable to imagine a national committee investigating the running of this part of the education service and not referring to the medical model or the formal, discriminatory procedures of identification, selection, fewer educational and social choices and subsequent isolation of pupils away from the mainstream, which many disabled adults now accurately describe as an oppressive part of their own educational experience.

The majority of those organizations that still play an important role in the provision of special education in the UK continue to refuse to adopt the social model of disability and still see disability and learning difficulty as deficits within an individual, which, if at all possible, should be 'fixed'. This stance by the major disability organizations in British society is echoed by their refusal over the years to sign up to the CSIE *Inclusion Charter* (see 38).

In their collective awareness the Warnock Committee did not want to change too much in relation to the existence of special schools, hence their pronouncement in the opening of Chapter 8 that they were 'in no doubt whatever that special schools will continue to feature prominently in the range of provision for children with special educational needs'. This view was supported by the 'weight of evidence' submitted to them including the Report's affirmation that the former Inner London Education Authority had told the Committee that 'in many respects, the special school represents a highly developed technique of positive discrimination'. The Report went on to give its warmest endorsement of this view and thus to set the philosophical tone: 'We believe that such discrimination will always be required to give some children with special educational needs the benefit of special facilities, teaching methods or expertise (or a combination of these) which cannot reasonably be provided in ordinary schools.'

Chapter 8 in the Warnock report gave the clearest message for ongoing support of special schools, and in retrospect there can be no doubt that the largely segregationist philosophy underpinning Warnock is partly to blame for slow progress in integration, and now inclusion, across the country. This chapter concludes:

> ❝ For special schools the future holds both challenge and opportunity . . . whilst there will probably be some decrease in the number of special schools, we see a *secure future* [emphasis added] for them as the main providers of special education for severely and multiply handicapped children in increasingly close collaboration with ordinary schools. ❞

Warnock also expected special schools to be the

> ❝ . . . pioneers of new and more effective ways of satisfying children's special needs [and] . . . sustainers of the quality of special education in ordinary schools through the mediation of their indispensable knowledge and expertise. These are vital tasks which carry the prospect of purpose and fulfilment. ❞
>
> (Department of Education and Science 1978)

There is another reason why Warnock held back in its support for integration and that is the evidence that the Committee gathered from overseas, particular the United States, *supporting* integration (mainstreaming); it seems the Committee could have been frightened away from the prospect of a movement towards greater integration (inclusion) based on a human rights platform – the popular notion of rights, of course, having no place at all in British legislation at that time. The Warnock Committee had full knowledge of US Public Law 94–142 (see 28) which stipulated that all handicapped children had be educated to the maximum extent in the least restrictive environment – that is to say, the most 'normal' environment possible.

Research by the Centre for Studies on Inclusive Education (CSIE) in 1985 showed that Committee members visited Massachusetts where the local state legislation, Chapter 766, went even further than the federal law in its promotion of integration and gave far-reaching and progressive rights to disabled students aged 14 years plus (as well as to parents). Chapter 766 also laid down time lines for assessments, production of a child's IEP (individual education plan) and appeals. In spite of visits to the United States by Committee members, neither the Warnock Report nor the subsequent English law, the 1981 Education Act, made any reference to these. Authorities in Massachusetts expressed to CSIE in 1985 their disbelief, for example, that the British government had introduced new legislation in this field without built-in time lines or basic rights for students and parents (see also *Mainstreaming in Massachusetts* in 41).

30. Education Acts 1944–2001

Education Act 1944

It could be said that the legal context for integration and inclusive education in England and Wales began with the Education Act 1944 where Section 33(2) stipulated that those children with severe disabilities were to be educated in special schools wherever possible, and which also *permitted* the education of those with less serious disabilities in the mainstream. Medical examination and intelligence testing had been used widely since the early 1900s and went on to be used more widely to help determine which mentally handicapped children might have special education; inevitably the procedure perpetuated the notion of the separateness of these children and led to the placement in special schools for all but a tiny minority.

Education Act 1970

A key piece of legislation in the development of special education was the Education (Handicapped Children) Act 1970 which brought the last small group of children, hitherto described as ineducable, into the education fold. The 1970 Act ended the arrangements for 'classifying children suffering from a disability of mind as children unsuitable for education at school'. It also took away the power of health authorities to provide training for 'children who suffer from a disability of mind', and from the date of its implementation in 1971 some 24,000 children from junior training centres and special care units across England along with 8,000 in 100 hospitals were entitled to special education.

This was a hugely significant gesture by parliament toward the last small minority of the population who for generation after generation had been denied access to even a basic education. From 1971, for the first time in history, 100 per cent of school age children were entitled to an education.

However, the children were immediately labelled 'severely educationally sub-normal (ESN[S])' and received their education at one of the 400 new special schools, formed as a result of this law. Although all of these children received their education in segregated settings for many years afterwards it was a very important part in the legislative jigsaw for them to have a basic right to be *within* education and not health, thus allowing later improvements in educational opportunities and more recently for some, the transfer to – and inclusion in – the mainstream.

Education Act 1976

The first opportunity for a clear duty for LEAs to integrate handicapped children in England and Wales came with the Education Act 1976 (Section 10), but it was never implemented. It had the status of coming into force on 'a day to be decided by the Secretary of State'. The Section required LEAs to arrange for the special education of all disabled children and young people to be given in county and voluntary schools, except where it was impracticable, incompatible with the efficient instruction in the schools or if it involved unreasonable public expenditure. When this law was passed in 1976, the Warnock Committee (see 29) was still investigating special education and Section 10 was never implemented because by this time it was almost certainly clear to government ministers and officials that a new, more far-reaching law was imminent from the work being done by the Committee.

Education Act 1981

The law that came out of the 1978 Warnock Report was the Education Act 1981 (implemented on 1 April 1983) in which Section 2 laid down the first ever duty for LEAs to ensure that children with 'special educational needs' were educated in ordinary schools, provided the views of the child's parents had been taken into account and that integration was compatible with:

1. the child receiving the special educational provision that he or she required;
2. the provision of efficient education for the children with whom he would be educated; and
3. the efficient use of resources.

The origin of the three provisos, which have been at the centre of the debate about progress with integration and inclusion over the past 20 years, clearly came from Section 10 of the 1976 Act. Had these provisos not been in the 1981 Act, or had they been worded in a less prescriptive manner, it is quite clear that authorities, their professionals and their officers, as well as individual schools, would have had to be far more positive toward parents' requests for their children to be included in ordinary schools.

Because of Section 2, the 1981 Act's instruction to integrate was weak. Both the Warnock Committee and government officials drafting this law were aware of better laws and regulations regarding integration on the international stage (see 41), yet they chose to bring into operation a set of rules and procedures that created only tentative and largely negative approaches to integration by schools and LEAs, and continually undermined the new and developing concept and practice of education in the mainstream for disabled pupils.

In many thousands of cases of the assessment and placement of disabled children, LEAs simply had to choose just one of the three provisos in Section 2 (see above) in order to sabotage a parent's desire for their child to be included in ordinary school. Time after time across England and Wales (and in Scotland where there was similar but separate legislation), many thousands of parents and their advocates had their wishes for an integrated education for their child thwarted by the segregationist tendencies of the vast majority of those in charge of running the 1981 Act's complex and bureaucratic procedures. It was a relatively easy matter for education officers and professionals simply to confirm the traditional special school route and placement for most children assessed as needing special education.

The injustice felt by parents, children and young people and their advocates was enormous, and the worst part about the use of Section 2 by LEA officers, professionals and by ordinary schools wishing to continue the exclusion of this group of local children, was the dishonesty of its operation. The dishonesty was in the possibility to use the Section to camouflage discrimination by those in positions of authority, who (while the law remained as weak as it was) were under no legal duty to move towards integration and inclusion if they did not want to. If local authorities wished to save themselves time and money by remaining with the status quo (and most did), they were at liberty to do so, given the loopholes provided by Section 2 of the 1981 Act.

Another major part of the 1981 Act that worked against integration and against parents was the so-called 'appeals procedure'. This was so inept and discriminatory that it is embarrassing to look back and think that such an unfair system could have been established by a modern democracy, apparently to give the consumer a proper hearing against grievance. For the most part the 1981 Act's appeals machinery was a sham, being virtually controlled by LEAs who in effect investigated themselves and found in favour of their proposed special school placements in the vast majority of cases. It offered little real democratic process of appeal for parents, their children or their advocates.

There was a similarly disappointing outcome at the national appeal level. Section 8 of the 1981 Act had permitted parents a legal right of appeal to the Secretary of State if they were not satisfied with the outcome of their local appeal. However, government officers insisted to advocates and parents that the appeal should be seen as an 'informal hearing', rather than as a legally based, formal appeal. Only a small minority of parental appeals against special school placements in favour of ordinary schools were ever successful at local or national levels.

A national survey in 1985 by CSIE gave a flavour of how LEAs in England were interpreting the 1981 Act and what they told – and did *not* tell – parents. *Caught in the Act* (CSIE 1986) found that in their literature to parents explaining the law covering assessments, statements and school placement, only 11 per cent of all English education authorities referred to the duty to integrate children with special needs in ordinary schools. Only one third of LEAs told parents they had a right to be fully consulted by the authority, while just 14 per cent referred to parents as partners in the assessment process. In these and many other areas of LEA information for parents, the government intended all figures to be 100 per cent.

Education Act 1993

It took over ten years, until the arrival of the 1993 Education Act (implemented in September 1994), before amending legislation gave the appeal process for parents the beginnings of any sense of democratic respectability. This came with the Act's accompanying Special Educational Needs Tribunal and was a step in the right direction. However, it is important to recall that even though the main legislation covering integration had been in force for ten years by this point, the government still refused to remove the provisos inhibiting integrated placements.

The central duty to integrate was maintained in the 1993 Education Act. In addition, the views of a child's parents, which in the 1981 Act had only to be taken account of, were strengthened in the 1993 Act to the status of a condition, which said children should be included in the mainstream, as long as parents were in agreement. This resulted in four provisos.

Disability Discrimination Act 1995

When this new law was passed, it was memorable for not referring to inclusion or to access to education, prompting a major debate about the government's continuing tolerance of discrimination against disabled children and young people (see SENDA p 126).

Education Act 1996

In 1996 a major consolidating piece of legislation was introduced and Section 314 contains the duty to integrate. As with earlier occasions, the 1996 Act was another failure by government to strengthen the duty to integrate when it left all four provisos in the law, despite a variety of amendments in parliament.

Special Educational Needs and Disability Act (SENDA) 2001

In 2001 the Labour government finally responded to pressure from a growing lobby to delete two of the provisos in Section 314 and passed SENDA 2001, which now amends the 1996 Act.

The two *deleted* provisos, which had been in law since 1981, were:

1. that the child can receive the special education he or she requires; and
2. that there is an efficient use of resources.

From 2001 the duty to educate disabled children in ordinary schools is now governed by the following two provisos:

1. that it is in accordance with the parent's wishes; and
2. that it does not affect the efficient education of other children.

SENDA 2001 also brought in new duties for LEAs to make arrangements for resolving disagreements that parents might have with schools or LEAs, without affecting parents' right of appeal to the tribunal. The tribunal appeals were also tightened up by the Act, for example, by bringing in time limits on the implementation of decisions.

SENDA, Part 2, amending the 1995 Disability Discrimination Act came into force in September 2002 and covered access to education for students and prospective students. It makes it unlawful for schools to discriminate against a disabled person in admission arrangements, provision of education and associated services or by exclusions. LEAs must also plan to increase accessibility for disabled pupils in terms of curriculum, the physical environment and information.

It will be some years before any government tackles the remaining limits on inclusion, which means that some children and their parents still face formal discrimination and do not have the basic right to inclusive education.

31. European Convention on Human Rights

It is ironic that in the same year as the United Nations finalized and published its Convention on the Rights of the Child in 1989 – with its firm support for inclusion – the European Commission of Human Rights in Strasbourg rejected appeals by four British families to have their disabled children included in ordinary schools. All four families appealed against special schools placements given by their English LEAs which were confirmed by the then Department for Education and Science.

The case of the four families was the first such education appeal from the UK to go to Strasbourg.

The decision of the Commission in October 1989 makes fascinating reading for many reasons, not least the Commission members' assumption that a policy of educating disabled children in ordinary schools 'cannot apply to all handicapped children' and their blunt rejection that parental desire for non-segregated education could have anything to do with 'philosophical convictions'. With this conclusion the Commission revealed its firm support for a thoroughly discriminatory approach toward settling such cases, and its belief that integration policies can apply to some disabled children but not to others. The Commission declined to suggest where the line should be drawn.

The four families, who were supported by CSIE throughout the UK and European processes of appeal, submitted their cases under four separate Articles of the European Convention for the Protection of Human Rights and Fundamental Freedoms. These were:

1. the right to be educated in accordance with philosophical beliefs (Article 2 of the First Protocol);
2. the right to have a speedy and fair determination of a matter of civil law (Article 6);
3. the right to respect for family life (Article 8); and
4. the right not to be discriminated against (Article 14).

In rejecting the parents' arguments, the Commission based their response within a medical, rather than social, model of disability and it appears that none of the 13 members of the Commission had any real knowledge or understanding of the arguments in favour of including disabled children in ordinary schools. They were therefore destined to come to such conclusions as: '. . . Sarah [changed name] had a severe developmental delay requiring a very small protective teaching group which *could not* [emphasis added] be provided in a normal school.'

The families argued that segregated education was an infringement of their right to respect for family life, but the Commission dismissed this too, saying that two days a week of part-time education in an ordinary school was acceptable.

Of course, the Commission was responding to British law of the day (the 1981 Education Act) and, unbelievably by today's standards, concluded that there was nothing unreasonable in the one year delay taken by the Secretary of State to review the assessment of each child under Section 8 of the 1981 Act, prior to the appeal. The Commission found that the review procedure before the Secretary of State was 'not a determination . . . of civic rights and obligations'. Since then the 1981 Act has been updated and it would now be illegal for the Secretary of State to take a year to review a family's case.

For these four families, from Rugby and Hereford, the decision was particularly disappointing because, at that time, the European Commission had shown itself to be quite progressive in its judgements in other areas (such as corporal punishment); but these 13 members sitting under Ms. C.A. Norgaard (President) and Mr. H.C. Kruger (Secretary), with Sir Basil Hall and Mrs. G.H. Thune from the UK, were determined not to see the appeals as having anything to do with discrimination against disabled children, human rights or injustice, or with the improvement in the educational and social experiences of disabled children and young people.

32. UNESCO: *The Salamanca Statement*

The broad changes in thinking that marked the change from the end of the 1980s to the beginning of the 1990s are demonstrated nowhere more clearly than in the Salamanca Statement.

There can be few reports from the United Nations Educational, Scientific and Cultural Organization (UNESCO) in the field of 'special educational needs' that received as much prominence as the ground-breaking 1994 Salamanca Statement and its accompanying Framework for Action. It has been adopted and quoted in every imaginable quarter, from the UK Government's 1997 Green Paper, *Excellence for All*, to numerous local education authority policy documents, to voluntary organizations, to trade unions and to local schools.

This report called for inclusion to be the norm. It was agreed by representatives of 92 governments and 25 international organizations, all of whom formed the World Conference on Special Education held in Salamanca, Spain in 1994.

UNESCO's Statement was unequivocal in asking the international community to endorse the approach of inclusive schooling when it said: 'We call upon all Governments and urge them to adopt as a matter of law or policy the principle of inclusive education, enrolling all children in regular schools, unless there are compelling reasons for doing otherwise.' All children 'must' have access to mainstream schools; it then added one of the most strident calls for systemic and philosophical change in education services anywhere, in one of the most widely quoted paragraphs of the education world of the 1990s:

❝ Regular schools with this inclusive orientation are the most effective means of combating discriminatory attitudes, creating welcoming communities, building an inclusive society and achieving education for all. Moreover, they provide an effective education to the majority of children and improve the efficiency and ultimately the cost-effectiveness of the entire education system. ❞

(UNESCO 1994)

Salamanca then called on all governments to undertake a variety of actions to try to achieve this outcome, including giving the 'highest policy and budgetary priority' to improve education services so that all children could be included, regardless of differences or difficulties. Countries with few or no special schools were encouraged to establish inclusive ordinary schools in order to educate disabled children, and not to build new special schools. The timing of the report – 1994 – was fortuitous and it went on to influence large sectors of the educational world internationally.

It seemed that in 1994 and shortly afterwards, schools, local authorities, parent groups and voluntary organizations were ready and eager to read the Salamanca Statement and to proclaim their support for it; here was an august body – UNESCO – taking a radical stand on education. It seemed people wanted to hear the message and they accepted it. The new labour government in the UK gave it support in the Green Paper, *Excellence for All Children: Meeting Special Educational Needs* (see 35).

The Salamanca Statement became popular at a local level in the UK because all could understand its supportive message in favour of inclusion. It was one of a number of major international documents, which according to Alison Wertheimer (1997) affirmed the principle of inclusive education and the importance of moving towards schools for all. Wertheimer quoted the Salamanca Statement as visualizing 'institutions which include everybody, celebrate differences, support learning and respond to individual needs'.

According to Wertheimer, the Salamanca Statement supported a 'human rights perspective' because it stated that 'inclusion and participation are essential to human dignity and the enjoyment and exercise of human rights'. Wertheimer added: 'Both this Statement and the (1989) UN Convention on the Rights of the Child give clear international authority to the issue of inclusion as one of human rights.'

33. UN Convention on the Rights of the Child

The rights of disabled children to be educated in the mainstream are spelled out in Article 23 of the Convention which reminds politicians and education decision makers that a child with a disability should not be excluded or discriminated against. It calls for a child to be educated in a manner that will allow the child to achieve the 'fullest possible social integration and individual development'. But it says that this right must be interpreted along with Article 2, which says that all rights in the Convention shall apply to all children without discrimination – and it specifically mentions disability in this light. In other words, Article 23 is strongly supported by Article 2.

34. UNESCO: *Inclusive Education on the Agenda*

In a later paper from UNESCO, *Inclusive Education on the Agenda*, the long-standing background discrimination against disabled children and young people was eloquently summarized:

> 66 Disabled children have throughout history been denied access to education, family life, adequate health care, play and work opportunities and the right to participate in mainstream life. In most, if not all countries, disadvantaged children and young people remain excluded from or marginalised within the education systems. The traditional pattern for most national education systems has been to divide education into regular and special provision in ways that are usually to the disadvantage of those with disabilities or learning difficulties. 99
>
> (UNESCO 1998)

The paper added that inclusive education had evolved as a movement to challenge exclusionary policies and practices and had gained ground over the past decade to become a 'favoured adopted approach' in addressing the needs of all students in regular schools and classrooms. International initiatives, according to UNESCO, added up to a consensus that 'all children have the right to be educated together, regardless of their disability or learning difficulty, and that inclusion makes good educational and social sense'.

35. DfEE: Green Paper

Publication of the UK government's Green Paper on special educational needs, *Excellence for All Children*, in October 1997, just a few months after a landslide general election victory, caused considerable excitement and optimism in the education world, particularly amongst those favouring a move toward greater inclusion. The 100 page consultation document covered an impressive framework for gradual change including sections on policy, parents, support, inclusion, planning, developing skills, interagency cooperation and dealing with emotional and behavioural difficulties. The foreword by David Blunkett, Secretary of State, came as a blast of fresh air:

> 66 Schools have to prepare for all children . . . That is a strong reason for educating all children with special educational needs, as far as possible, with their peers. Where all children are included as equal partners in the school community, the benefits are felt by all. That is why we are committed to comprehensive and enforceable civil rights for disabled people. 99

The chapter on inclusion opened with clear support for change:

66 The ultimate purpose of special education needs provision is to enable young people to flourish in adult life. There are therefore strong educational, as well as social and moral grounds for educating children with special educational needs with their peers. 99

(DfEE 1997)

It went on to support UNESCO's 1994 Salamanca Statement and Framework for Action. In this context the Green Paper spoke of the 'progressive extension of the capacity of mainstream schools to provide for children with a wide range of needs'. The chapter went on to offer a number of practical steps to promote greater inclusion in mainstream schools for children with special educational needs, and elsewhere there were many references to the benefits and wisdom of inclusion.

However, alongside this prospect for a challenging programme, the government made it clear that special schools still had a role to play within this new so-called inclusion scenario; a number of special schools would remain in perpetuity for a small population of children whose special educational needs apparently could never be met in the mainstream. The new government's approach to inclusion, said the Green Paper, would be 'practical, not dogmatic'. It contained a number of contradictory statements concerning inclusion and segregation. It gave strong support to mainstream schools becoming inclusive schools, but it said at the same time 'Parents will continue to have the right to express a preference for a special school where they consider this appropriate to their child's needs'.

And it added, 'We recognise the continuing need for special schools to provide . . . for a very small proportion of pupils whose needs cannot be fully met within the mainstream sector'. It contemplated the amalgamation of some special schools to create larger segregated institutions; it spoke of special school staff working more closely with mainstream staff, and it concluded there were 'exciting opportunities for special schools' as they increasingly provided a varied pattern of support for children with special educational needs.

The Green Paper and its subsequent Programme of Action have gone down in history, like the 1978 Warnock Report, as milestone publications and declarations of policy change. Like Warnock, the Green Paper both anticipated a change toward greater inclusion for *some*, while maintaining and endorsing continuing segregation for others.

36. IPPR: *Alternative White Paper*

It is not often that the link is made between the effects and the outcome of separate, segregated education and the probable poor employment prospects later on for the young people who attend such institutions, but a visionary document from the Institute of Public Policy Research (IPPR) made such a connection in 1993 in its *Alternative White Paper*. Its chapter on special educational needs makes important points both about employment issues and the problems of seeing children's difficulties in education as the result of some deficit. Exclusion, it makes clear, is no proper solution to the education system's difficulties with a proportion of the population it is supposed to serve.

> ❝ The history of special educational needs has been largely one of the exclusion of more and more children from mainstream education . . . the number of children excluded from ordinary education in a variety of ways, continues to rise. This is a serious social as well as educational issue because modern societies increasingly demand qualifications and credentials acquired via a 'normal' education. To be excluded from mainstream education is to be excluded from the prospects of employment and thus the mainstream of life.

The IPPR says employers seldom looked kindly on school leavers from special programmes. 'The majority of children who acquire any sort of a "special" label are usually destined for a special career.'

And in endorsing the conviction that all schools, colleges and educational agencies should be 'inclusive institutions' and not try to exclude minorities on grounds of disability, inability, difficult or different behaviour, the IPPR defends this principle 'on grounds of social and distributive justice'. It goes on:

> ❝ In any alternative consideration of special educational need, we need to bring together discussion of special educational needs, school failures, under or low achievers, disruptive and excluded pupils.
>
> We would also wish to make clearer that the majority of the children falling into the above categories experience problems whose genesis may lie more in poor school management and inflexible curriculum and inappropriate testing, poor teaching or poor teacher-pupil interaction than any deficit in the children themselves.
>
> Solutions to the problems must be found in school improvements, effective teaching and teacher support, rather than in more assessment, statementing or exclusion of children.
>
> Given the problems of definition and lack of clarity of the concept we should abandon the label of special educational need and envisage a broader concept which would embrace all children who find their encounters with the education system problematic.
>
> We wish all staff to be professionally developed to high levels to accept that *all kinds of children will enter their classes to be educated* and that the management will develop policies and allocate resources to help teachers.
>
> We thus wish to move beyond the arguments of integration versus segregation. In our view *all children* have a right to education in mainstream schools. We recognise, however, that a small number of those with severe disabilities who, with full parental consent, would need education

outside mainstream classes. But even these could be given a place on the books of a mainstream school, should it ever be possible to attend it.

We wish to end the legal coercion of parents whereby those who do not ultimately agree that their child will be placed in special provision can, under the 1981 (Education) Act, be fined or imprisoned. **99**

(IPPR 1993)

37. British Psychological Society: *Inclusive Education – Position Paper*

In 2002 the British Psychological Society (BPS) became a signatory to CSIE's *Inclusion Charter*. The BPS also produced a summarizing position paper describing its stance on inclusive education.

The paper is particularly interesting for two important reasons:

• it gives a full and helpful definition of what inclusive education is about;
• it offers a contrast between psychologists' views of their roles today and the views of their counterparts only twenty years ago, which are commented on elsewhere in this volume (for example, in Leyden's piece, 12).

66 Inclusive education – part of a changing society

The recent drive toward inclusive education is about more than 'special educational needs'. It reflects changes in the social and political climate wherein a new approach characterises thinking about difference.

In recent debate about inclusion, a premium is placed upon full participation by all and respect for the rights of others. Discussion about the benefits of an inclusive society assumes that a society which can nurture, develop and use the skills, talents and strengths of all its members will enlarge its collective resources and ultimately is likely to be more at ease with itself.

These changes in thinking are espoused in much recent discourse about education. Increasingly, this discourse emphasises learners' rights as well as their needs, and stresses the importance of an education free from discrimination and segregation.

Legislation

The new anti-discriminatory climate has provided the basis for much change in policy and statute, nationally and internationally. Inclusion has been enshrined as segregation and discrimination have been rejected and outlawed. Articulations of the new developments in ways of thinking, in policy and in law include:

- The UN *Convention on the Rights of the Child* (1989) which sets out children's rights in respect of freedom from discrimination and in respect of the representation of their wishes and views.
- The UNESCO Salamanca Statement (1994) which calls on all governments to give the highest priority to inclusive education.
- The Human Rights Act (1998) which contains an anti-discrimination article and brings the European Convention on Human Rights into UK legislation; British courts must now adhere to the convention.
- The SEN and Disability Act (2001).

What is inclusive education?

Inclusive education differs from previously held notions of 'integration' and 'mainstreaming', which tended to be concerned principally with 'special educational needs' and implied learners changing or becoming 'ready for' accommodation by the mainstream. By contrast, inclusion is about the child's right to participate and the school's duty to accept. It is about . . .

- rejecting segregation or exclusion of learners for whatever reason – ability, gender, language, care status, family income, disability, sexuality, colour, religion or ethnic origin;
- maximising the participation of all learners in the community schools of their choice;
- making learning more meaningful and relevant for all, particularly those learners most vulnerable to exclusionary pressures;
- rethinking and restructuring policies, curricula, cultures and practices in schools and learning environments so that diverse learning needs can be met, whatever the origin or nature of those needs.

Tensions and challenges

Whatever the arguments, it must be recognised that there are many tensions and challenges in moving toward a more inclusive education. Some of the tensions exist around issues of choice and diversity, and for whom; around what constitutes an inclusive learning environment, and whether this has to equate to schools as they are currently structured. Other challenges concern the competing demands of legislative frameworks such as the 1998 School Standards and Framework Act and the 2001 SEN and Disability Act. One of the most pressing issues is about the achievement and management of inclusion of young people who present the most challenging behaviour.

The contribution of applied psychology and psychologists

Not only educational psychologists, but all psychologists – occupational, health, developmental, counselling, clinical and academic – can help schools, colleges and other learning environments to become more inclusive.

- Educational psychologists have for many years laid stress on the environment and the systems within it as part of a move away from an individually orientated, deficit approach to failure. Continuing and developing this emphasis – designing effective learning environments for learners with diverse learning styles and needs – is consistent with the beliefs and precepts behind inclusive education.
- Psychologists will use their skills in applied psychology to help identify, assess and resolve issues of concern, drawing, as they do so, on the abilities and resources of their clients and others in a supportive community.
- Psychologists will use their expertise to engage in research into the development of new ways in which learning environments can become more inclusive.
- Psychologists have a key role to play in the process by which new technology can enhance the capacity of schools and other educational settings to meet the learning needs of all their members – including those learners most vulnerable to exclusion.
- Psychologists will demonstrate an acceptance of difference and diversity, in terms of abilities, values and aspirations held in a plural society.
- Psychologists will work in close collaboration with teachers, parents and others to help schools and other educational settings to develop as more inclusive educational environments.
- Psychologists will work closely with colleagues in all learning environments to foster in learners the attitudes and values expected of citizens of an inclusive society. **99**

(BPS 2002)

38. CSIE: *The Inclusion Charter*

The Inclusion Charter, written and launched by CSIE in 1989 was the first document in the UK to put inclusive education and the ending of segregation on a human rights platform. In so doing, CSIE had taken a lead from the UN Convention on the Rights of the Child (1989) and from new thinking and good practice in North America. Soon after the Charter was launched and signatures were being sought, other UK organizations and their publications began to refer to integration (and later, inclusion) as a human rights issue, but not before 1989.

Ten years later the list of signatories has grown to an impressive group of those wishing to support the long-term aims of the Charter to work towards the goal of ending all segregated education on the grounds of disability or learning difficulty.

The Charter's Six Points:

❝ 1. We fully support an end to all segregated education on the grounds of disability or learning difficulty, as a policy commitment and goal for this country.

2. We see the ending of segregation in education as a human rights issue which belongs within equal opportunities policies.

3. We believe that all students share equal value and status. We therefore believe that the exclusion of students from the mainstream because of disability or learning difficulty is a devaluation and is discriminating.

4. We envisage the gradual transfer of resources, expertise, staff and pupils from segregated special schools to an appropriately-supported, diverse and inclusive mainstream.

5. We believe that segregated education is a major cause of society's widespread prejudice against adults with disabilities or difficulties and that efforts to increase their participation in community life will be seriously jeopardised unless segregated education is reduced and ultimately ended. De-segregating special education is therefore a crucial first step in helping to change discriminatory attitudes, in creating greater understanding and in developing a fairer society.

6. For these reasons we call on Central and Local Governments to do all in their power to work as quickly as possible towards the goal of a de-segregated education system. ❞

It was originally entitled *The Integration Charter*, but with the change in thinking in the 1990s, 'integration' was replaced with 'inclusion' in 1996. The Charter has been sent out on five occasions over ten years to a wide list of potential signatories in an attempt to get key organizations and bodies in the field, along with LEAs to make a commitment to work towards ending segregation. Only a minority of requests have been met affirmatively.

Key mainstream bodies who have signed include Barnardos, The Children's Society, National Society for the Prevention of Cruelty to Children (NSPCC), MIND (National Association for Mental Health), the British Psychological Society and the Association of Educational Psychologists.

An interesting aspect of the Charter signatories list is those who have *not* signed over the years. The non-signers include the major organizations *for* disabled people, such as Royal National Institute for the Blind, Royal National Institute for the Deaf, National Deaf Children's Society, MENCAP (Royal Society for Mentally Handicapped Children and Adults), and the Spastics Society (now called Scope).

The Centre's regular requests for signatures have had the effect of forcing committees and executive councils in very many bodies to discuss the document and its aims; thus the subject of society working towards inclusion has been a topic for discussion and awareness-raising among hundreds of key organizations, all LEAs, MPs and peers and trades unions, even though signatures to the Charter might not be forthcoming.

By 2003, signatories included 57 organizations, five LEAs (Calderdale,

Carmarthenshire, Derbyshire, Leeds and Newham), four trade unions, 30 MPs, seven peers and the Green Party.

❝ *The Inclusion Charter – Explanatory Paper*
This CSIE explanatory paper on the six points in the Inclusion Charter, first written in 1989, was revised in 2002 to take account of latest developments and understandings of inclusion and segregation.

  1. We fully support an end to all segregated education on the grounds of disability or learning difficulty, as a policy commitment and goal for this country.

Segregation in education is exclusion from the mainstream in separate settings without a time limit or a plan for inclusion. It is also education under separate management from the mainstream.

This description applies to special schools and can also apply to special units in ordinary schools and to pupil referral units when they are run separately from the everyday life of schools, when the students are not members of the appropriate class for their age group and when there is no plan to include them.

Time spent out of the ordinary classroom for appropriate individual or group work on a part-time basis is not segregation. Neither is removal from the ordinary classroom for therapy or because of disruption, provided it is time-limited, for a specified purpose and based on a goal-oriented plan aimed at returning the student to his or her ordinary class. Settings are within the student's mainstream school if possible and certainly within the mainstream system. Any form of time-out from the ordinary classroom should not affect a student's right to full membership of the mainstream.

Parents and carers who have students in separate special schools because local policies make that the only option can still support a goal to end segregation. Working towards a de-segregated education system is working towards a better education for all students. The benefits of inclusion apply to all students, disabled and non-disabled alike.

  2. We see the ending of segregation in education as a human rights issue which belongs within equal opportunities policies.

The existence of special schools represents a serious violation of students' human rights, including – but not only – the right to properly supported, inclusive education in their local area.

Legal enforcement of segregation on the grounds of disability, learning difficulty or emotional need is against international human rights agreements including the UNESCO Salamanca Statement and Framework for Action (1994), the UN Standard Rules on the Equalisation of Opportunities for Persons with Disabilities (1993) and the UN Convention on the Rights of the Child (1989).

From a human rights perspective, which recognises the rights of all students to inclusive education, the existence of segregated special schools is a form of institutional discrimination. Students' rights to inclusive education are universal – they apply to all students, everywhere, including those whose parents would prefer them to go to separate, special schools.

Violating students' human rights means treating them in a way which does not recognise their equality and dignity; it undermines their humanity. A UN General Comment published in 2001 explained that discrimination, including on the basis of disability, 'offends the human dignity of the child and is capable of undermining or even destroying the capacity of the child to benefit from educational opportunities'.

Disabled adults, describing themselves as 'special school survivors' speak of similar negative feelings as a result of their segregated education.

> 3. We believe that all students share equal value and status. We therefore believe that the exclusion of students from the mainstream because of disability or learning difficulty is a devaluation and is discriminating.

Students with severe learning difficulties are of no less value than students who gain Oxbridge entry and their achievements are no less worthy of respect. To select a student out of the mainstream because of disability or learning difficulty is a devaluation of their worth as a person and discriminating on the basis of circumstances for which they are not responsible.

According to the social model of disability, barriers to learning and participation arise from the interactions between learners and the learning environment or from the nature of the setting itself. This contrasts with a medical model in which disabilities and difficulties are attributed to inherent 'deficits' in individuals to be identified and treated as 'abnormal' in segregated settings.

The Charter does not accept that segregating students with disabilities or difficulties in special schools can be classed as positive discrimination on the grounds that the separation is for their benefit.

There is no evidence that students who are selected for separate, special schooling are students who cannot benefit from mainstream education. Research shows that trends towards inclusion and segregation vary widely and are connected to local culture, policy and practice, not to 'deficits' in groups or individuals. Neither is there evidence that students do better in segregated special schools than in mainstream with support. Evidence continues to grow that students learn better and develop more social skills in mainstream schools.

The benefits of inclusion have been well demonstrated and inclusion is widely accepted by governments and local education providers in this country and overseas as the way forward.

The UK Government supports the 'strong educational as well as social and moral grounds' for students learning together in the mainstream and has declared inclusion as the 'keystone' of its education policy. The 2001 Statutory Guidance on Inclusive Schooling from the Department for Education and Skills gives a strong message to local education authorities (LEAs), schools and other bodies that the development of inclusion in schools is one of the Government's highest priorities.

Following its General Discussion on the rights of students with disabilities in October 1997, the Committee on the Rights of the Child, which monitors implementation of the UN Convention on children's rights, specifically stated that legislation which segregates disabled students in separate institutions 'for care, treatment, or education', is 'not compatible with the principles and provisions of the Convention'.

In July 1994, the Council for Disabled Children in the UK agreed a new policy statement on inclusion:

> The CDC believes that no child should be denied inclusion in mainstream provision. Mainstream provision should offer the full range of support and specialist services necessary to give all children their full entitlement to a broad and balanced education.

UNESCO's 1994 Salamanca Statement represents an agreement reached by representatives of 92 governments and 25 international organisations that inclusion should be the norm for the education of disabled students.

It argues that 'regular schools with this inclusive orientation are the most effective means of combating discriminatory attitudes, creating welcoming communities, building an inclusive society, and achieving education for all; moreover, they provide an effective education to the majority of students and improve the efficiency and ultimately the cost-effectiveness of the entire education system'.

The UN Standard Rules on the Equalisation of Opportunities for Persons with Disabilities (1993) calls on all countries to have a clearly stated policy on inclusive education that is understood at school and wider community levels; they should allow for a flexible curriculum as well as additions and adaptations and provide quality materials, on-going teacher-training and support teachers. Inclusive education and community-based programmes should be seen as complementary approaches to cost-effective education and training for disabled people. Communities should develop local resources to provide this education.

The Rules acknowledge that special education may be necessary in the short-term, but only in preparation for eventual mainstream inclusion of all students.

In May 1990, the Council of the European Communities and Education Ministers agreed:

> All education establishments should be in a position to respond to the needs of students with disabilities.

4. We envisage the gradual transfer of resources, expertise, staff and students from segregated schools to an appropriately supported and diverse mainstream.

Because of the paramount need to move appropriate support for students with disabilities or difficulties into the mainstream, the Charter envisages ending segregation by a transfer of resources from the segregated sector and the development of resources within the mainstream.

A 1999 study by the Organisation for Economic Co-operation and Development (OECD) found that it is no more expensive to provide a supported mainstream place for a student than to educate him or her in a special school. The study also concluded that it is far more expensive to operate a dual system of regular and special education than it is to run a properly resourced fully inclusive single system. These findings support similar findings by the UK Audit Commission seven years earlier.

In the Charter's vision of inclusion a restructured mainstream will change and adapt to accommodate diverse needs. A diverse mainstream would accept and cater for differences, not submerge, isolate or exclude them. The Charter does not intend that the autonomy and strength of culturally strong groups like the blind community and the deaf community would be weakened through assimilation. Nor does it want to isolate teachers who have relevant specific skills.

Total Communication would be used in the education of deaf students in ordinary schools and as many hearing adults and students as possible would be encouraged to have some facility with British Sign Language and finger spelling. The employment of adults with disabilities or difficulties as part of teaching and non-teaching staff teams would be another important development in preserving autonomy and giving students appropriate role models. All teachers and learning supporters with their individual skills and interests, including those with specific skills, would be equally valuable in a diverse mainstream.

5. We believe that segregated education is a major cause of society's widespread prejudice against disabled adults and those experiencing difficulties in learning and that efforts to increase their participation in community life will be seriously jeopardised unless segregated education is reduced and ultimately ended. De-segregating special education is therefore a crucial first step in helping to change discriminatory attitudes, in creating greater understanding and in developing a fairer society.

Continued segregation of disabled and non-disabled students can only help to foster stereotypes, while inclusion has the potential to get rid of stereotypes by enabling young people to learn about each other's common humanity as well as their uniqueness.

Fear of disability by non-disabled people has its roots, at least in part, in the denied relationships of earlier years. Segregation gives distorted messages about who is eligible to membership of the mainstream, and who is not. Status and self-esteem are undermined. Groups and individuals become categorised as 'other' and their segregation justified. Adults who have been educated within the special school system often identify early segregation as the key factor in creating conditions which lead to prejudice and barriers encountered in later life.

Unless education is de-segregated and efforts made to combat stereotyping and prejudice before it begins, it is unlikely that community care policies will be fully effective. Research suggests that the most effective way of combating stigma and stereotyping (the negative valuation of a whole person based on a single attribute) is through planned, personal interaction of those who have been 'labelled' and those who have not. UNESCO's Salamanca Statement recognises the role of inclusive schools in building an inclusive society. Discrimination in education leads to discrimination in society. As the 2002 UN Annual Report of the Special Rapporteur on the right to education explains:

> Discrimination breeds prejudice. Children learn through observation and imitation. They are likely to start perpetuating discriminatory practices much before they can understand the word 'discrimination' and to internalise underlying prejudices in the same way as they accept any other facet of the way of life in their family and community. Prejudice is sustained from one generation to another through social usage.

The same report points out that as education can be used as a means to both retain and eliminate inequality, international human rights law prioritises the elimination of inequality as a key purpose of education.

6. For these reasons we call on Central and Local Governments to do all in their power to work as quickly as possible towards the goal of a de-segregated education system.

Working towards the goal of a de-segregated education system means making a commitment to do everything possible to provide appropriate learning support for all students in ordinary schools and to resist segregation. It involves mainstream schools adapting and changing to accommodate diverse needs and receiving the financial and other resources they need to enable them to do this. It means making on-going efforts to overcome the problems and difficulties that will inevitably arise in the change process. Central Government, LEAs, and local schools all need to be involved.

Ending segregation and making inclusion for all students in their local schools a matter of routine entitlement guaranteed by law implies further legal reform of education and discrimination legislation to:

• remove LEA powers to run separate, special schools

- remove the remaining constraints on access to the mainstream
- make provision of necessary support for learning a legal entitlement for all students in local mainstream schools
- reduce reliance on current assessment and statementing procedures, which are based on an outdated view of disability as individual 'defect' and which hinder inclusion, as a main means of obtaining that support.

One of the main strengths of a human rights approach to education is the recognition that the rights of students to enjoy inclusive education are accompanied by the responsibilities of governments to provide it. In ratifying the Convention on the Rights of the Child in 1991, the UK Government accepted the obligations set out in the Convention and agreed to take responsibility for implementing its principles. Ending segregation in education is a responsibility yet to be fulfilled. **99**

(CSIE 2002)

39. Alison Wertheimer: *Inclusive Education: A Framework for Change*

In *Inclusive Education: A Framework for Change* (1997) Alison Wertheimer provides a succinct and hard-hitting commentary on the international movement toward inclusive schools that welcome all children, whatever their needs and abilities.

66 There is a growing consensus throughout the world that all children have the right to be educated together. In the last six years a number of major international statements have appeared, affirming the principle of inclusive education and the importance of 'working towards schools for all – institutions which include everybody, celebrate differences, support learning and respond to individual needs' (Salamanca Statement 1994).

The United Nations Convention on the Rights of the Child (1989), the UN Standard Rules on the Equalisation of Opportunities for Persons with Disabilities (1993) and UNESCO's Salamanca Statement and Framework for Action are all powerful tools in the struggle to abolish segregated education which denies children with disabilities the right to be part of mainstream schooling and reinforces society's prejudice and discrimination against them. These documents, which together make a strong case for inclusion, provide a unique opportunity to place inclusive education firmly on the agenda of national governments.

The rights enshrined in the UN Convention are applicable to all children without discrimination including the right to education on the basis of equal opportunity. This spirit of inclusion is further emphasised in the UN Standard Rule 6, requiring member states to provide education for people with disabilities in integrated settings. But it is the Salamanca document which provides the clearest and most unequivocal statement about inclusion with its guiding principle that ordinary schools should accommodate all children, regardless of their physical, intellectual, emotional, social, linguistic or other requirements. All educational policies, according to Salamanca's accompanying Framework for Action, should stipulate that disabled children attend their neighbourhood school.

The UK formally supports all these documents. The British government ratified the UN Convention on the rights of the Child in 1991 and the UK was one of the 92 countries that endorsed Salamanca in 1994. As a UN member state, the UK has also assumed responsibility for implementing the 1993 Standard Rules.

The weight accorded to international statements by individual countries varies widely and the UK's record has not been particularly positive. Nevertheless, Britain is a signatory to all these documents and we must use them in our 'domestic' struggle for inclusion. **99**

(Wertheimer 1997)

PART FOUR

Inclusion in action

40. Linda Shaw and Marsha Forest: Ontario: from integration to inclusion

Two education authorities in Ontario, Canada, led the world for a time with their approach to the inclusion of disabled children in the mainstream. This pioneering work in the Hamilton and Waterloo School Boards near Toronto began in the early 1980s.

A report written by Linda Shaw for CSIE in 1990 described the work and opened with the news that explained why thousands of people from all over the world had visited these school systems.

> 66 The Boards do not run any special schools and special classes in ordinary schools are virtually extinct. All children, including those with challenging needs, are welcomed and supported together. 99

In 1990, in the UK at least, educators were undergoing a change in thinking about 'integration' and beginning to understand – and practice – 'inclusion'. The CSIE report demonstrated this changeover period by itself quoting a variety of Canadian educators using the term 'inclusion' while then going on to report on progress with 'integration'.

Shaw wrote of the approach by Hamilton and Waterloo being known as 'full inclusion' or, as it is described in one of the Board's mottos, 'Each Belongs'.

> 66 Full inclusion challenges the traditional 'cascade' concept of special education and replaces it with the image of a diverse kaleidoscope. Instead of labelling children by their disability and placing them some-where along a continuum between integration and segregation, all children with their unique backgrounds, gifts and special needs, learn together in ordinary classrooms. This is integrated education.
>
> Marsha Forest, from the Centre for Integrated Education and Community in Toronto, Ontario, says that the most disturbing element of the 'cascade' model is the misunderstanding of integration.
>
> Integration is traditionally interpreted as an amount of time a child spends in a situation with children who do not have disabilities. In fact, says Dr. Forest, the deep meaning of integration is expressed by the terms 'inclusion', 'belonging', 'unity'. It is not a placement. It is a philosophy that says classrooms – and communities – are not complete unless all children with all needs and all gifts are welcome.
>
> The strong emphasis on integration as a moral and human rights issue is relevant in considering what visitors to schools in the Waterloo and Hamilton Board can reasonably expect to discover.
>
> They can see integration working in these two boards and learn about the wide range of support services readily available to help teachers and pupils in ordinary classrooms. They can see classroom structures and teaching practice which facilitate diverse ways of learning. They can talk to teachers who work in teams and share problems and achievements,

and to children who do the same. Commitment is regarded as vital, together with team work and problem solving, inspired and sustained by common values and known goals.

This experience of everyday life at schools in Waterloo and Hamilton is not offered as a definitive model for integration or proof that it will always be successful. On the contrary, visitors are warned that there is no perfect model, that there are risks, and that integration might fail. They are challenged to turn to their own resources and contributions rather than confine their search for knowledge to so-called experts.

(Shaw 1990)

An integration consultant visited one of the Canadian schools mentioned in the CSIE report to speak to students prior to the arrival of a disabled student into the school. The following conversation took place:

❝ Consultant: Hi, I've come to talk to you about May (the student) who will be coming to your class next week. You met her last week when she visited with her mother. For years May has gone to a segregated school or been in a self-contained life skills class. What does this mean?

Students: Places for retarded people. Schools for kids who are really bad. Like the one near my house where all the wheelchairs go.

Consultant: Well, May is coming here and I'll tell you a secret, everyone is scared. Her mother and father are scared, Mr Gorman (teacher) is scared, Mr Cullen (principal) is scared, I'm scared. Why do you think all of us are so scared?

Students: You think we'll be mean to her. You think we'll tease her. You think she'll be left out.

Consultant: There are some things we don't want you to do when she arrives. What do you think they are?

Students: Don't treat her like a baby. Don't pity her. Don't ignore her. Don't feel sorry for her.

Consultant: Why is May coming to this class? Why are we doing this?

Students: Why not? She's our age, she should be here. How would you feel if you were 12 and were never with kids your own age? It's dumb for her not to be here. She needs friends. She needs a boyfriend.

Consultant: What do you think we want you to do?

Students: Treat her like one of us. Make her feel welcome. Help her make friends. Help her with her work. Call her and invite her to our parties. ❞

The consultant then did an exercise with the students called Circle of Friends in which they all drew four concentric circles and in the inner circle were asked to name the people closest to them. Typically the students put their parents and their best friends because 'I love them and share my secrets. I can be myself. I trust them and go to them when I'm hurt.'

The students filled in circle two with people they really liked, but who were not close enough to go into the first one, such as teachers and other friends. In the third circle the students put clubs and groups such as Sunday school, the scouts and the street hockey group. The last circle was for people who they, or their parents paid to be in their lives, like the dentist and doctor. At the end the students completed a picture of the range of people in their lives from loved ones to professionals.

> 66 Consultant: Now I want you to think about another person's circle, a fantasy person named Sebastian aged 12. He put his Mom in circle one and the rest of his circles are empty apart from circle four which is filled with doctors, social workers, therapists etc. Think hard for a few minutes . . . how would you feel if your life looked like Sebastian's?
> Students: Lonely, depressed, unwanted, terrible, disgusted, like what's the use of living, like I'd want to commit suicide, like dying, awful, crazy, hurt, nobody cares, angry, furious, mad.
> Consultant: How do you think you'd act?
> Students: I'd act like a vegetable. I'd hide and keep my head down all day. I'd hit people. I'd cry all day. I'd hate everyone. I'd kill myself. I'd want to kill others. I'd steal and curse and spit and fight.
> Consultant: Remember we were talking about May who will be in your class soon? Well, right now her life looks a bit like Sebastian's imaginary circle. So why did I do this?
> Students: To help us understand about all the new kids who are coming into our classes – about how they must feel.
> Consultant: I'd like a group of you to act as a welcome committee and another group to act as a telephone crew . . . a phone caller for each day of the week.
> Students: Wow, yeah . . . what a neat idea!
> Consultant: Friends don't develop overnight. This is just the start. Not all of you will be May's friends, but all of you can be friendly. My dream is that May will have at least six friends who will do things with her in school and after school and on weekends. Who wants to help? 99
>
> (Forest 1988)

41. Mark Vaughan and Ann Shearer: *Mainstreaming in Massachusetts*

In *Mainstreaming in Massachusetts* (1985) Vaughan and Shearer found the English situation comparing badly with the US with regard to rights to integration and to mainstreaming. The US Public Law 94–142 (see 28 of this volume) had given a stimulus to mainstream education. From its enactment in 1978 all handicapped children aged 3–21 years had to be educated in the 'least restrictive environment'. This meant that a child had to be educated 'to the maximum extent appropriate with non-handicapped children. It must include non-academic and extra curricular activities. The placement must be as close to the child's home as possible.'

Eight years before implementation of England's 1981 Act in 1983, US legislation guaranteed school students and their parents a host of rights surrounding assessment and placement in the mainstream. For example, each child assessed as in need of help had to have an individualized education plan (IEP) giving a profile of his or her needs, together with specific ways in which goals and objectives would be reached over a one year period. The IEP was only finalized after a meeting which had to include parents, and child where appropriate, and the plan was not valid without the parent's consent. The IEP had to be written within 30 days of it being decided that the child needed special education, and a review of the plan had to take place at least once a year. Parents had the right to have their child tested in non-discriminatory test materials, and parents had the right to see and obtain copies of all records and reports and to have confidentiality maintained. Parents had to be informed of all meetings early enough to ensure their opportunity to attend; they had the right of appeal if any rights were denied or if they disagreed with the school or the LEA.

Parents could request that an appeal be heard in public and they had to have copies of all relevant documents five days before the hearing; they also had the right to present evidence and to confront, cross-examine and compel witnesses to attend. Where parents withheld or revoked their consent, the child was still guaranteed all normal education services and where parents disagreed with an assessment of their child, they had the right to a further independent assessment at public expense.

In Massachusetts, the State brought in Chapter 766 a year earlier in 1974 and this went further than the Federal Law by abolishing all categories of handicap such as mentally retarded or speech impaired, which were listed in the Federal Law; in their place Massachusetts brought in a system that described children according to the degree of time they spent *out* of the mainstream classroom (known as program prototypes). Chapter 766 also ruled that assessments could only go ahead with parents' written permission; parents had the right to participate in all meetings where the IEP was being developed; they could be accompanied or represented at these meetings by someone of their choice; and a student aged 18 or older could act on his or her behalf.

In addition, Chapter 766 brought in a remarkable list of rights for *students* (aged 14 and older). They included:

- The right to have a pre-assessment meeting.
- The right to be present at a team meeting (a group brought together to design a child's IEP) and to help write their own IEP (under 14 they need the permission of the team's chairperson).
- The right to have language used at the team meetings which is the same as that used at home.
- The right to bring two people of their parents' choice to the meeting.
- The right to have the assessment completed within 30 school days.
- The right to see all records that the school has on file.
- The right to a copy of the IEP on request.
- The right to stay in their present programme during the assessment process (unless parents or the education officer felt otherwise).

- The right to progress reports every six months, on request (sent to parents).
- The right to an annual review of their IEP, their needs, and the appropriateness of their programme.
- The right to have records protected and kept confidential. (The only people allowed to see their records without their special permission were the school officials, teachers who work with them and certain State education people.)

For students between the ages 18 to 22, all the above rights applied, plus the following:

- The right to refer himself or herself for an assessment.
- The right to refuse an assessment.
- The right to deny parents access to records and other information.
- All parents' rights under Chapter 766 become the student's rights upon reaching the age of 18.

It is worth noting that part of the background to this early assertion in the US that all children had fundamental rights was the landmark court decision in the case brought by the Pennsylvania Association for Retarded Children against the Commonwealth of Pennsylvania in 1971, which found that the State, having undertaken to provide all its children with a free public education, could not deny access to that education to any mentally retarded child. Interestingly this court decision was made at about the time the English 1970 Education Act came into force, bringing the last small group of disabled children out of the care of English health authorities and guaranteeing them a right to a full education.

Another aspect of Chapter 766 in Massachusetts that contrasted starkly with the contemporary practice in the UK was the time limits placed on various authorities and education officials to complete different parts of the process. The importance of these time-lines was that parents, students and their advocates knew and understood the framework within which everyone was operating. For example, under Chapter 766, the assessment of the child must, by law, be completed within 30 school working days following the parents' written consent to go ahead. As has been well documented elsewhere, the total absence of any time limits placed on English education officers to complete different parts of the assessment and placement procedures when the 1981 Education Act came into operation in this country, led to widespread abuse of the process and extremely long delays. The depressing part about this was that members of the Warnock Committee on special education (see also 29) had visited Massachusetts and knew the full detail of the US Federal and State laws, including the detail of the rights given to parents and students and the duty covering time limits. They chose, however, not to prioritize this knowledge when it came to recommending change for England, Scotland and Wales. Similarly, the government's drafters of the new British law were aware of the Federal and Massachusetts legislation but produced, instead, a much weaker and inadequate version in the 1981 Education Act.

42. Richard Rieser and Micheline Mason: *Disability Equality in the Classroom*

In the UK there was one document more than any other that put equality and segregation in special education on the national agenda in 1990. It permanently changed the national debate in education surrounding attitudes towards special education generally and disabled people more specifically. That book is *Disability Equality in the Classroom: A Human Rights Issue* by Richard Rieser and Micheline Mason. It is constructed around the politics of disability, good practice and practical tasks that can be carried out in classrooms by teachers and others. It contains many powerful stories by disabled people, which demonstrate the validity and appropriateness of inclusion.

Rieser and Mason write from their experiences as disabled people, as well as Rieser being a teacher and Mason the parent of a disabled child. In the extract from their introduction below they acknowledge the support and backing they received from the ultimately disbanded Inner London Education Authority (ILEA), the original publishers of this book, and they make a call for awareness of the lives, needs and aspirations of disabled children and adults to become a much higher priority in ordinary schools than they had been in the past. Much has been achieved in this field since the book's launch more than a decade ago, but as the authors remind us, there is still a long way to go.

❝ Disability is the neglected dimension of equal opportunities. This pack has been written by disabled people for teachers in both mainstream and special schools and nurseries. It aims to open up areas for reflection, discussion and action for both staff and pupils, which will lead to greater understanding of the issues facing disabled people and to changed attitudes and practice.

The discrimination and prejudice directed at people with disabilities in our society has not been challenged in schools generally. In ILEA's equal opportunities policy it receives recognition in the Authority's equal employment policy, but has not been challenged in the school curriculum in the same way as sexism and racism. This major oversight is in urgent need of rectification, particularly in the 'mainstream' or ordinary curriculum.

Discriminatory attitudes and prejudices must be tackled by all teachers in the curriculum content, teaching methods and materials that they use in removing barriers to disabled people's full participation in mainstream schools both physical and educational.

Why was disability left out of the race, class, gender formulation of disadvantage adopted by ILEA in 1981? Was it because negative attitudes to, and fears of, people with disabilities are so deeply rooted in our society that most people are not even aware they hold such views? Was it because regardless of class background, race or gender we all can, at any time, become disabled physically or mentally?

So the 'non-disabled' majority classify people with disabilities in such a way as to distance themselves from disabled people. This is extremely damaging; not only to people with disabilities, but more fundamentally, it is damaging to the essential humanity of the whole of society.

As long as stereotyping and prejudice exist towards people with disabilities, scapegoating and violence towards people with disabilities is never far away, whether it be individual, institutional or in society as a whole . . .

Our approach is based on the assumption that children are not born with prejudices against disabled people, but acquire them from adults, the media, and the general way society is organised. When children become adults they reinforce and legitimise the misinformation and fear in the form of policies and practices over which they have varying amounts of control depending on how much power and influence they have. Able-bodied people always have more power than us with respect to our particular impairment.

As with racism, sexism, heterosexism and class bias we believe that the education system has to make positive attempts to reach the truth when attempting to inform people about history, politics, and life experiences of the different groups within our society. The best way to approach the truth is to enable each group to express and represent themselves, including disabled people. We also believe that each group has a right not only to be consulted, but for their opinions to be legitimized in action and policy which will give equality of opportunity to all.

Disabled people believe that our problems as adults will continue to be exacerbated by the able-bodied community, unless the education system accepts its responsibility towards us. We believe it to be our right to be part of the best, most flexible mainstream education system possible in order to prepare us for a useful active adult life within the mainstream. We also believe it is a right for all non-disabled children to grow up informed, unafraid and close to disabled children, teachers, parents, grandparents and to be able to maintain those relationships without enforced segregation at any point. We therefore hope that teachers, parents, governors and all those concerned will join with us to campaign for the resources to be made available without delay. 99

(Rieser and Mason 1992)

43. Mark Vaughan: Kirsty Arrondelle – early integration

In the UK in the early 1980s it was a pioneering school or LEA that agreed to integrate a child with severe learning difficulties in a mainstream class. The general practice was automatically to direct all such children to segregated special schools with little or no discussion on the possibilities of educating them in ordinary schools. Most children with Down Syndrome were placed in segregated special schools.

Over the years the Centre for Studies on Inclusive Education (CSIE) acted as advocates for a number of families with children or young people with Down Syndrome in their bid to try to secure ordinary school placements. Elizabeth and David Arrondelle and their daughter Kirsty were the first of these; a number of CSIE publications testify to the ongoing story of the Arrondelles' battle with LEAs and professionals to keep Kirsty in the mainstream. In 1983 the Centre published a brief account of some of the parents' feelings about school for Kirsty (who was then six), about the pressures they faced from authorities to send her to special school and their continuing anxiety about whether or not their daughter would be admitted to local, ordinary education, like the education of their neighbours' non-disabled children.

Kirsty's story was one of the earlier reported stories in the UK but it was a repeated scenario in very many families up and down the country; there are families today who will identify with the experiences the Arrondelles had two decades ago, in spite of progress and improvements in inclusive education. The following extract is a poignant account of a family continually being, as they described it, 'on tenterhooks'. It begins with a comment from the parents.

    ❝ There isn't a week that goes by without Kirsty being invited to a party in the neighbourhood. She went to the local integrated pre-school play-group at the age of three – we looked at several in the area and the closest turned out to be the one we liked the best – and it has been this normal contact with other children and their families, whether in their homes, or here in ours, which has made us feel so sure that pressing for integrated schooling was the right thing to do. **❞**

The report continues:

    ❝ Kirsty's parents feared there would have been a great upheaval out of the community if they had responded to pressure from the local authority, and the special school in particular, that segregated schooling was the proper kind for their child and not normal schooling somewhere in the neighbourhood. It was not an easy decision to take as Kirsty approached the age of five: she had earlier attended this ESN(S) school once a week for physiotherapy to help get her walking. These . . . sessions stopped at about two when she began walking. Nevertheless, following this first contact with the special school, which is three and a half miles away, it was always inferred that Kirsty would go there for both her nursery education and then her full-time schooling from the age of five.

    Her parents felt otherwise. 'The weekly sessions to help get her walking were wonderful, but we saw that the other children were very protected in the special school – it's just the way things are. We're not critical of the school, or that kind of school: the staff are extremely dedicated, there's no doubting that. What we *are* critical of is the concept of withdrawing a particular child from its natural environment, its local community, and educating it in a place where children with a variety of handicapping conditions are brought together in a concentration.'

Having the support of the peripatetic home-teacher (home tutor) while trying to secure a place in a local ordinary school where Kirsty's friends from the playgroup naturally progressed on to, was obviously of great help to the parents. But they said that even with this support they felt very much on their own in their pursuit of an integrated setting for Kirsty's schooling; the pressure for Kirsty to take the traditional (special) educational route was 'enormous' and rested on the fact that no alternative was ever offered. 'From the word go, all the different people involved in caring for her let us know that they expected an ESN(S) education for Kirsty and nothing more.'

It was an uphill struggle for the parents who soon came to realise they were going against the majority of attitudes and opinions held by individuals as well as those in authority, the most devastating of which was shown early on by a senior hospital doctor soon after Kirsty was born, when the parents were told 'Don't expect her to live very long: don't look too far into the future as far as your life with Kirsty is concerned.' The local education authority (LEA) also certainly expected her parents to follow the traditional route for children categorised as ESN(S) . . .

From the moment she was born Kirsty's parents, who had had no previous experience of disability at all, exposed her to a lot of stimulation, particularly in the first six months and they now feel they have seen clear benefits at various stages of her life. She is a great mimic, according to her parents, and this has been put to good effect both in playing and learning at home, in the playgroup and in teaching social and behavioural skills in the infants' school where she has been for a year and two terms (April 1983).

Her progress in the playgroup, where she mixed easily with all the other children and often helped the smaller ones with various tasks, allowed her to benefit considerably from a normal environment. At that time Kirsty was the only handicapped child in the playgroup but they were fully supportive of the parents' wishes for an ordinary education. Thinking back to the pressure they faced to place her in the ESN(S) school, the parents commented: 'Without any malice to the children there, to their parents or to the staff, we could so easily see Kirsty regressing, or staying still in that kind of environment. Putting her in the special school's nursery unit at three years of age definitely wasn't the right thing to do for her at that moment. The playgroup was not a particularly unusual playgroup – which was fine – but it did prove to us what we had felt for a long time, that Kirsty could mix, take part and benefit from remaining in the "normal" community.'

A major factor in this example of integrated education is the clear support for integration shown by the headmistress of the [local] infants school: without it, Kirsty's parents said they would have probably given in to those pressures. For her part, the headmistress said that from the moment she was first approached by the parents and met Kirsty, she was convinced by their arguments as well as their enthusiasm, and she agreed to take Kirsty on a term-to-term basis. 'We have had tremendous support from the parents and we could not have come this far without it: with considerable enthusiasm they have always been involved with the school, they have talked with the staff and carried on with Kirsty's education at home in conjunction with her teacher.'

It was agreed that a case conference at the end of each term would decide whether or not it was working. The ESN(S) school was aware of the arrangements and ready and willing to take Kirsty at a moment's notice if the scheme 'failed': everyone involved knew this as they embarked on the scheme.

The parents said they felt they could not ask for anything more in terms of rights or a guaranteed future for Kirsty and they described this arrangement for them as being 'on tenterhooks' at times: 'It does highlight the difference in parental rights and security of a school place which parents of ordinary children enjoy compared to that enjoyed by us.'

The headmistress felt that bringing Kirsty into her school was a challenge to everyone concerned: 'If we are not educating Kirsty, then we are failing. There is always a place in the special school, so it is up to us to prove it works here.'

Kirsty's parents have observed her in the ordinary infants school and commented: 'She isn't protected from the outside world in that school, and that is just what we wanted. The greater the chance she has in taking part in so-called "normal" society when she grows up, the better. Yes, we have made a direct connection between this ultimate goal of trying to achieve some kind of normality for her when she leaves school, and our seeking an integrated educational setting. We think ordinary schooling makes that goal much more likely than a special school does. She isn't molly-coddled at this school; she has become much more self-reliant; she has to speed up – literally. Downs children tend to be slower and appear to be lazy, but she has adapted and she can keep up with a lot of things in the classroom and elsewhere in the school.

'We are delighted with her progress, which is greater than we had dared hope for, particularly with her reading ability which has also impressed the speech therapist'. The infants school has given her greater independence as well as self-reliance, and this comes out after school and at weekends: for example the regular Saturday morning visit to the adventure playground will see Kirsty moving from one activity to another under her own steam; when she comes home from school she will happily sit down and decide to read to her parents from her *Kathy and Mark* reader for 20 minutes to a half-an-hour before going upstairs to play on her own in her bedroom for a further half an hour to an hour. The headmistress said that the strongest benefit to Kirsty in the first year had been a social one. She had not learned 'academic' skills as fast as other children of her own age, but she had gained more by being in the ordinary school, than if she had been in the special school. She added: 'The plus side has been for people already in the school as much as for Kirsty: if it is going to make the ordinary children realise that there are others with greater special needs than themselves, then that alone makes it all worthwhile.

'I feel that for far too long some children have been kept away from the "ordinary" environment. In Kirsty's case, I will still have doubts until she has learned more concentration and until her spoken language improves. The elder middle infants fussed her when she first came and she lapped it up: even though she could do things herself she let her peers do things for her, and it was something we had to look out for and stop, because it was obviously holding her back.'

Everyone felt the first term was a great success. Kirsty had learned from the other children who played and chatted to her as much as she did to them, and as they did to each other; she was included in the class group for *all* activities, in spite of the stumbling block of being behind in language development compared with the others. She was also included in all the joint school activities involving other classes.

Those taking part in the first case conference were the headmistress, the class teacher, the support teacher, the home tutor, the area speech therapist, the educational psychologist, and, when this group had finished the bulk of their discussions, Kirsty's parents were brought in. They felt the decision had been made before they went in to the meeting, but of course they were extremely pleased that it went in their favour: Kirsty was to stay another term, by a unanimous decision.

The school staff, as well as Kirsty's parents, noticed that other children *made* her say things properly, rather than letting her get away with less than clear words and actions: in her parents' words – 'Some of the best teachers Kirsty could ever have are other children in the ordinary school.' The end of the first term also proved that one anxiety of the head and the parents was quite unfounded – that of complaints from parents of other children in the school: nor have there been complaints or any opposition since then.

The second term – the spring term – was not as good: the headmistress said progress had not been as marked as before, and said she was worried about Kirsty staying in the same class, mainly because the older children wanted to do too much for her and not get on with their own work, or they vied with each other for her attention. It was clear to see how the other children were benefiting and learning after two term's schooling. The other professionals involved in the second case conference were in agreement with the head and it was decided to put Kirsty in the new reception class for the summer term, rather than stay with the group she had come to know and work with.

Kirsty's parents felt they had to go along with the decision, and although they felt that this change might be construed as 'failure', they agreed with the head's advice and the decision of the case conference.

It worked. Kirsty's behaviour according to her parents changed significantly: suddenly she was older than the others, and it was the same as when she was in the playgroup – the new reception class of children were six months younger, and she found she could teach them things in the class and around the school, because she had experienced school for eight months more than them. This third term, the summer of 1982, was crucial so far as Kirsty's continued integrated education was concerned – it was the end of the first year and the parents approached the case conference in June with a considerable degree of anxiety.

Things had gone well in the term and included a new dimension of Kirsty joining a small group of six Asian children who were getting half-an-hour's tuition a day on their own from a teacher of English as a second language: in addition Kirsty's mother started taking her to the local welfare clinic for half-an-hour's speech therapy each week, something suggested by the second case conference . . . The term ended with the case conference deciding that Kirsty should continue in September, a decision possibly influenced more than anything else by the head's sincere belief that the school was doing the right thing for Kirsty, that it could cope with her special needs and that it wanted to educate Kirsty, rather than simply 'contain' her.

By the new year (January 1983), Kirsty's fifth term in school and at the age of six and a half, her achievements included knowing all her colours and most of her numbers; writing her name with a little help; reading five word sentences from her *Kathy and Mark* reader with ease; a marked improvement in language development; a real understanding of what the teacher was saying; an ability to get herself around the whole of the school competently; a healthy appetite without any problems at school dinner time, and, according to a teacher at the ESN(S) school, much more self-sufficiency than children of a similar age and handicap at the special school. Her ability to concentrate on her own work was improving slowly, and it was decided that this and her language development, which clearly marked her out from the rest of the class, were the areas where most effort was going to be put in future. On a comparative basis with the rest of the children, Kirsty's parents were told she was 'not bottom of the class in everything': there were one or two others, who at that point in time, had greater problems in some areas.

The head stressed that while her commitment to integration had increased markedly since the scheme had been in operation, she felt she would not let the theory dominate the practice. If she and the staff felt they could not cope or adapt to meet Kirsty's needs, she would recommend that the scheme be ended. At the same time, she agreed that Kirsty's presence in the school implied a lot more than Kirsty simply fitting in with existing structures and curriculum goals. All the staff and some parents of other children had gone through various educational processes and changes in attitude as well as a readjustment of expectations, as a result of Kirsty being in the school; the headmistress added 'While the future might not be certain, nobody – from the director of education downwards – had said we are doing the completely wrong thing. Nothing has happened so far to make me think it has been anything but good.'

In her first four terms Kirsty had three different teachers which might have had a slightly unsettling effect, although she has always adapted quickly, once familiar with the teacher. In an effort to understand the problems involved, the head, and all the teachers who had Kirsty, went over to the special school 'to see what a child like Kirsty would be doing in that setting, to see if she was actually missing out on anything, and to see how we could improve the provision we were already making'. Kirsty's arrival at the infants school also lead to some in-service training on special needs for the head and two staff.

In looking to the future the head and other staff are firm about needing extra support, if only part-time, although no formal application had yet gone into the LEA: so far, the class teacher was able to cope with the needs of all the children in the class, but everyone agreed that some degree of regular withdrawal for special tuition would be necessary in the near future; some has already taken place with the headmistress teaching Kirsty on her own.

The ESN(S) school was recently asked if it felt that Kirsty was losing out by not being there: the firm reply to the parents was 'No'. It was true that the pupil-teacher ratios were much better in the special school, but the interaction in the infants school, as well as the chance to find greater independence in a wider variety of activities, far outweighed the advantages of being in the special school. Other skills such as training and domestic skills could be caught up with in later life.

Kirsty's parents added: 'We're still in the dark about the future, about where Kirsty should go. We have approached one local junior school, but like Kirsty's present school, they too would be breaking new ground, and the head there is not 100 percent certain that he would take her. He said: "The door is open – there's no objection so long as we can cope with Kirsty's needs". We feel that raises a lot of questions not only about Kirsty's education, but also about the attitude of ordinary schools, so we have to keep a number of options open; one possibility is Kirsty staying on an extra year at the infants school.

'Any parent in the same position as us is going to experience doubts as well as certainties: we both feel very strongly that we're doing the right thing for Kirsty at the moment. You see, we want to give her the greatest possible chance of looking after herself, of living an independent life when we're not around, and to us, the best starting point for that is integrated schooling. After the success of the playgroup and now the local infants school, our hopes and aspirations have grown and changed as we have seen Kirsty thrive and develop from being in those environments.'

(Vaughan 1983)

44. Kenn Jupp: *Everyone Belongs*

There appeared in the mid-1980s in the UK a small group of pioneering special school head teachers who were committed to emptying their schools and transferring the students across to the mainstream with support. Kenn Jupp at Overdale School in Stockport, Cheshire was one of these and in the following extract from his book, *Everyone Belongs* (1992), he outlines the philosophical underpinning behind the radical moves he undertook with the support of students, parents, governors and the LEA. It was a philosophy that set out to challenge the fabric and very existence of special schools, as well as challenging a culture of enforced separate living that segregated schools imposed on children and their families.

While the following excerpt concentrates on the reasons that caused Jupp and his colleagues to make changes to inclusion, the book itself proceeds to outline in detail how the changes were made.

66   The immorality of a segregated system

The mark of a civilised society is that it supports its weakest member, rather than following its strongest. If we subscribe to the belief that people who have learning difficulties should take their place in the community and are entitled to the same choices, opportunities and status that the rest of us enjoy, then it seems to make very little sense for us to create abnormal experiences and environments during their childhood and school years by segregating them from other children. A deaf child, after all, will be living in a hearing world and a physically disabled child in a mobile one.

In our bid to protect children who have special needs, by sheltering them within special establishments, we inevitably, even if unwittingly, discriminate against them. In recent years Local Educational Authorities have started to become more aware of multiracial and multicultural issues within schools, along with issues of gender. When I was at school, most establishments catered either for girls or boys, but not for both. Where co-education existed, boys and girls were made to use different playgrounds. Not so long ago in the United States, the same sort of segregation took place on the basis of skin colour. In the United Kingdom now, there would undoubtedly be an outcry if blacks were made to attend different schools from whites, or if they were compelled to eat at special tables or were kept in a special class or unit away from other children in the school. The choice of local school that is given to most parents is not afforded to parents of children who have severe learning difficulties. These children, we say, must be segregated into special schools 'for their own good'.

Our society uses numerous euphemisms to make the unpalatable sound more acceptable, 'Asylums for the insane' became 'psychiatric hospitals', 'wards in sub-normality hospitals' became 'villas', and now we have 'special schools'. This conveys to people the idea that the school is in some way specially beneficial and advantageous quite different from all other run-of-the-mill schools. It creates the notion that the building itself is special and utterly unlike all other school buildings, so that it can accommodate special children in particular. And what is inside these special schools? Why, special teachers, of course, who have special teaching methods and special educational equipment which somehow prepares special pupils, at school leaving age, to be launched into the real world outside where they can live more meaningfully and independently than they otherwise would. Strange that we have to take them from the real world outside to do this. I suppose it is easy to think of children who have special needs in terms of protection, but it is important that we examine closely our true motives. Segregation, after all, is a two-way process. Adolf Hitler segregated the Jews, those who had a disability and homosexuals from other Germans, in order to protect the master race from 'impurities'. South Africa segregated its blacks in order to protect its whites. When it comes to segregating those who have special needs, we should not flinch from asking ourselves who it is that we are attempting to protect.

Once a child has been identified as having severe learning difficulties, we can be fairly confident about the route which that child will be destined to take throughout the system of future provision that will be made available to him. Having attended a special school all through his childhood, he will most likely attend an adult training centre. Often, however, a place is unavailable, in which case he or she will stay at home all day, looked after by parents. Those who take up a place in the adult training centre . . . will be destined to spend the rest of their lives in this establishment. The word 'training' in adult training centre is often confusing, since it is unclear what people are being trained for. It is surely not for a job, since very few 'trainees' actually leave the centre to go into open employment. Not all youngsters go into adult training centres directly from special school of course. Some attend a college of further education for two years; then they go into an adult training centre, or remain at home. Sooner or later, due to the death or total fatigue of those who care for them, most people who have severe learning difficulties will end up living in a place provided by the District Health Authority or Social Services Department. This will take the form of a hospital, a twenty-four bedded unit or, for those most fortunate, a group home, which will be either supported or unsupported.

With the exception perhaps of group homes, the majority of residential provision will mean that people who have learning difficulties will be cared for by medical and paramedical staff or social workers, or both. They are likely to have little choice about what they wear, what they eat, where they go on holiday, who they live with, what furniture and decor they are surrounded by. They will have little privacy, few hobbies, even fewer real friends and will be accountable for almost everything they do. Whilst most Health Authorities and Social Services Departments are these days aware of these laws in the provision they make available, they have as yet only been able to develop more ideal support for a minority.

As things stand, equal opportunity is not something that people who have a severe learning difficulty can realistically expect, either during their school years or in adulthood. After leaving their special school, we can with some degree of reliability predict the way in which their lives will continue to be severely limited in opportunity, status and just about everything else. They are destined to be restricted in the same way as someone serving a prison sentence, although they have committed no crime and will not qualify for remission. The field of special education seems full of nice people doing terrible things quite unintentionally. They build sparkling new special schools which will only serve further to incarcerate, no matter how well resourced they may be. Raising funds to provide any special equipment or facility, when it can perfectly well be provided in the ordinary way, will only serve to exclude people and deny them the opportunities and experiences that the rest of us seem able to take for granted. Anything which highlights the differences between us will only take away from the overwhelming sameness that we share with one another.

Why not integrate and bring normality into what are said to be the best years of people's lives?   99

Jupp uses his experience as a teacher and later headteacher to construct a powerful case for fundamental change in the whole approach to special education. He concludes:

66   Whatever normality is, it is rarely to be found in special places. Those of us who are engaged in the planning and provision of human services must come to understand that, whilst some of the needs of some people may be regarded as special, the people themselves are not special at all. So often in our bid to enrich people's lives, we can and do, unwittingly, restrict severely the experience and opportunity of whole populations, who simply become the prisoners of our provision and the victims of our charity. Once they have been established, our conditioned attitudes can be passed down from parent to child and to their children's children, in family after family. Our stilted perceptions of those who are elderly, mentally ill, disabled or have a learning difficulty have now become so entrenched that any bid to alert us to our own shortcomings towards them, in our role as parents, relatives, professionals or neighbours, seems always to be viewed with suspicion and disdain. No matter how compassionate we may think we are, smug complacency can make us blind to the restraints, condescension and injustice that we inflict upon other people. Whether we are parents, relatives or professionals, it is useful for us to address the part we play in the lives of those near to us, who have special needs, and to ask ourselves, what is it precisely that we are contributing to, and is it what we would want for ourselves?

The education of young children is meant to equip them to live together in their adult lives, in a way that will build a peaceful, caring and prosperous future for each new generation that is to come. If we really believe in the pursuit of equal opportunity in our schools and in our society, if there is to be commitment to the underlying merits of a comprehensive education system, then everyone should belong. **99**

(Jupp 1992)

45. Bishopswood School: Good practice transferred

The staff at Bishopswood Special School in Oxfordshire wrote in 1992 that they believed the UN Declaration of the Rights of Disabled People (1975) applied to their school and that children and young people with 'severe learning problems' had the right to receive their education alongside children in mainstream schools. This was a special school for pupils with complex and severe disabilities and learning difficulties. It was a new school and purpose-built with all the latest facilities. The staff wrote a report; below is an extract:

66   Special schools and segregated units were created to house a population of children whose disability it was felt prevented them from receiving an education in ordinary schools. Those special schools, generally speaking, have provided a useful and very good education.

However, because of the existence of segregated provision, some schools, instead of looking at their curricula and ways of reorganising to enable them to provide for special needs pupils, have taken the easy alternative and moved their more disabled children to separate provision.

Special schools have, quite rightly, been allowed to operate a system of positive discrimination in terms of staff to pupil ratio and capitation allowance. In some cases they have been centres of expertise.

This element of positive discrimination and the pool of expertise is essential if special needs are to be met. What we hope we are doing at Bishopswood is proving that it is possible to transfer an example of good practice to ordinary schools and by doing so provide an even better education for our pupils.

. . . At Bishopswood we certainly do not want to protect our children from society by hiding them away. On the contrary, we want the children to be accepted as valued and important members of society, and this will not come about by their segregation. *We do not need to protect anyone from our children* [emphasis added]. **99**

(Bishopswood Staff 1992)

This special school was unusual at the time in that it gradually transferred all of its pupils, staff, equipment, expertise and other resources to mainstream settings at a nursery, primary, secondary and further education level. It was an important example of integration and inclusion in the 80s and 90s because the original special school was purpose built with a lot of capital as well as emotional investment to get it established as a highly segregated school for students of all ages with severe and complex disabilities and learning difficulties.

The story of how Bishopswood School transferred itself completely and successfully to the mainstream began with the head teacher and staff investigating the fundamental principles underpinning the school's existence. With a new philosophical goal in place the school first set about moving all the younger pupils to mainstream nursery and primary school locations and offering expertise and support to their mainstream colleagues. The success of these placements led later on to the transfer of secondary age pupils and ultimately those of college level.

At the time Bishopswood insisted on maintaining the name and funding arrangements for the special school even though all of the pupils had transferred to mainstream placements and the Bishopswood staff were on the campuses of ordinary schools. The arguments in favour of this strategy, according to the head and staff, included securing and maintaining adequate financial resources; the school was concerned that if the formal and legal entity of 'Bishopswood School' was dismantled then it would lose control of the necessary finances being used to fund inclusive placements of its pupils.

The financial and administrative model adopted by Bishopswood was not one used widely across other LEAs in the UK.

46. Rick Rogers: *Developing an Inclusive Policy for Your School*

This report by Rogers (1996, updated 1999) highlights the discriminatory message given to children and young people and their families when they experience 'integration' rather than 'inclusion'. A key item on the agenda, says the report, is one of 'eligibility'. The guide opens with this call to ordinary schools:

> ❝ Inclusion in education is an approach by your school that says all pupils in the catchment area who have a disability, or who experience difficulties in learning, should enjoy the same rights of membership of the mainstream as all other pupils. They should be fully part of your school community and receive an education and social life according to their age, needs, aptitude and ability.
>
> Many ordinary schools 'integrate' disabled children by bringing them into their premises – on a full or part-time basis – but on the ordinary school's terms. The pupils can stay if they can benefit from what is already

on offer; schools do not expect to change to accommodate and support diverse needs. Other children experience a warmer welcome and their place is more secure. Why do schools do this? Whatever the answer, it is a discriminatory message being given to disabled pupils, their peers, their parents and others about entitlement to education at a local primary or comprehensive school.

Inclusive education, by comparison, demands that a mainstream school considers all pupils in its area as fully belonging to the school and all of its varied activities. Each child has the same rights of access – each belongs and each is entitled to appropriate support to meet individual needs. The issue here is one of eligibility. And the question to ask your school is: 'Who do we say is eligible for full membership and who is not – and why?'

Inclusive education also demands that ordinary schools change their systems and structures for educating and socialising children and young people. Adaptations to the school curriculum, the buildings, the language, images and role models in the ordinary school are some of the changes required to make inclusion work. Restructuring is at the core of these changes.

This guide from CSIE aims to help your school on this challenging journey, the principle message of which is that disabled children and non-disabled children being educated together and developing relationships through shared educational and social experiences, is fundamentally worthwhile. 99

(Rogers 1999)

47. Linda Jordan and Chris Goodey: *Human Rights and School Change: The Newham Story*

Between 1984 and 1996 the London Borough of Newham undertook a series of pioneering radical reforms of its education service that resulted in it becoming – at that time – the leading education authority in the UK to have travelled down the inclusion road. In a study published in 1996 (updated 2002), the account is told of this authority's unique response to reducing segregated special education provision and developing inclusion at the end of the 20th century. It reveals well thought-through policies and actions to establish new principles, to move resources and expertise from a separate, special sector to the mainstream and to close the vast majority of its special schools between 1984–96.

Jordan and Goodey were among the leading local figures in the transition from exclusion to inclusion. The 2002 edition begins:

66   The London Borough of Newham has taken the first important step along the road towards inclusive education. Ending the segregation

of disabled people is a change requiring fundamental shifts in the way that people think and what they believe in. However, change is possible and segregation can be stopped. Where the change has been made it can clearly be seen to improve the health of schools and colleges and to make for better experiences for everybody. We hope that by telling some of what has happened in Newham during the past 18 years it can be shown that ending segregation requires one very important ingredient – the commitment to do it. Once a community decides to end segregation, the rest is much easier. Examining how schools are run and looking at how they can be changed for the better is challenging but it is also invigorating.

During the 18 years 1984 to 2002 the number of children attending segregated schools has declined dramatically in Newham. In 1984 there were 711 pupils attending eight special schools and three separate classes, and 202 attending out borough special schools. Today there are 56 pupils at one special school in the borough and a similar number placed outside, including children in residential placements who are a joint responsibility with social services.

Newham Council's aim can be summed up by the following 1995 mission statement: 'The ultimate goal of Newham's Inclusive Education policy is to make it possible for every child, whatever special educational needs they may have, to attend their neighbourhood school, and to have full access to the curriculum and to be able to participate in every aspect of mainstream life and achieve their full potential.'

This mission statement may sound unexceptional. But for tens of thousands of children and adults with disabilities in many other education authorities it is the assertion of a civil right which for them still requires a major struggle to achieve. The important first step that Newham has taken is that desegregation has been firmly stated as council policy and is well under way. The job now in hand is to make all schools genuinely inclusive, in line with the mission statement.

Jordan and Goodey put the task facing Newham into perspective:

❝ It has to be explained that if you have a vision the important thing is to try to achieve it rather than fail to do things along the route which do not immediately look like the ultimate goal. To get over 100,000 people (children, families and workers in the borough's education system) sharing a vision of inclusion, sharing an understanding of the vision and then all willing to work hard to achieve it is not an easy task. Even if the whole process were to begin again, it is not easy to see how things could have been done differently. Working with an imperfect system with over a 100 years of history and traditions is not like starting from scratch. You have to work with what you have got.

And there certainly have been constraints, as always happens when you are actually doing something rather than talking about it. In the early 1980s there were very few people advocating an end to all segregated education – at least in the public arena. The 1981 Education Act had built in conditions in its integration section, which could be used to resist integration by anyone who was even slightly concerned about what was happening in Newham. Legislation makes closing a special school quite difficult. The council had to confront a predictable series of situations: petitions to the then Department for Education and Science, meetings with ministers, judicial reviews in the High Court, threats of physical violence against members, and visibly disabled children being pushed to the front of the public gallery at education committee meetings to try and sway public opinion against desegregation.

The increasing autonomy of schools and the opportunity for grant maintained status brought in by subsequent education legislation acted against creativity and progress. In this context it was absolutely essential to be clear about what the aim was and why it was being done. It meant being opportunistic and seizing any chance to take inclusion forward. To get from A to B in this case had to be a process, even though many people would have liked to move faster. To end segregated education overnight would have required different legislation and probably a different social context. **99**

The authors report 'one of the really important milestones' as being when the authority's inclusion policy was acknowledged as positive because Newham headed two national league tables:

66   One was for having the lowest percentage of children in special schools in England, the other was the Department for Education and Employment's (DfEE) table of local authority areas with the most improved GCSE results over a four-year period. There was a lot of media publicity which focused on how including all children has a positive effect on improving education for everybody. These improvements have continued. When the inclusion policy began, in 1986, the LEA average for GCSE A*–C passes was 8 percent, in 2002 it was 42 percent, and in no year since league tables were introduced, have the results decreased. Perhaps even more importantly, A-G passes have risen to among the highest in the country.

In 1999 the Ofsted inspection of Newham LEA was a significant success, inasmuch as it remarked about achievement that Newham 'serves the country well, in demonstrating . . . that it is possible to successfully challenge the assumption that poverty and ethnic diversity must necessarily lead to failure.' In respect of inclusion, it said 'Much of what the LEA does is well done and in some respects a model for others to follow . . . It has successfully implemented a policy of inclusion of pupils with special educational needs,' acknowledging that Newham has the lowest percentage of children in special schools of any authority in the country, and that the policy is not particularly expensive 'because its additional expenditure on mainstream support is more than offset by much lower expenditure on special school places.' **99**

Today, say the authors, people from Newham are asked to speak around the country on the lessons learned from changes in the borough over the past two decades:

> 66   There are young adults emerging from this system who have had full social lives, have participated in further and higher education and have begun living independently, who would not have done so if they had spent their school years in a segregated setting. For those coming after, inclusion has been the norm. This has meant that younger families have not had to fight for their children to be included. Any child born or arriving in Newham has for a number of years been directed by the LEA to a mainstream school.
>
> What has been learned from this experience? Change occurs when people with a vision have an opportunity to use their power positively and to recognise where power lies. Change also occurs when they are prepared to take chances and to be opportunistic. We have learned that people respond to strong leadership; most people are nervous about change and being seen to go against the grain, but if there is strong leadership, people respond positively. The majority of people respect the setting out of a strong, radical vision, enabling other people to take leadership roles at different levels and in different settings. Many people felt enabled to articulate views that they previously felt might be thought lunatic or wacky; the policy gave people permission to be at the cutting edge. We have learned that schools that include all children from the community are better schools all round: they focus much more on children as fully individual humans and cope with issues of bullying, friendship and mutual caring, as well as being able to raise academic standards, often more quickly than other schools.   99

(Jordan and Goodey 2002)

Langdon school

Langdon Comprehensive School in Newham has become a prominent example of how an inclusive school can operate very effectively and in a 1999 report, students from Langdon spoke eloquently about the importance of inclusion to them. The Langdon students made the following presentation at a CSIE national conference on disaffection and inclusion in London, March 1999:

> 66   Our school is well known as an inclusive school. Our school reflects our community. We have male and female students from all cultures, races and religions with all abilities and disabilities. There are many languages spoken in our school. There are students who are good at academic subjects and go on to university, students who are good at being guides

around the school, students who volunteer to take part in extra activities, even those who take part in big conferences. There are also students who take part in sports. There are students who have special needs – some with difficulties in learning, some with behaviour problems, some with problems with communication and some with physical problems. However, we don't actually think that often about being an inclusive school because the school population with all the differences is what we are used to. 〞

(CSIE 1999)

48. Dorothy Lipsky: Inclusion across America

In 1995, a national study of inclusive education across America was published by the National Center on Educational Restructuring and Inclusion (NCERI), City University of New York. The survey revealed remarkable degrees of inclusion in mainstream settings and gave details of successful curricular and administrative restructuring in many schools across the United States. Interestingly it pointed to the ways in which inclusion had enabled thought to take place about improved experiences for all children. As one teacher from Texas put it: 'Emphasis has been shifting from a focus on content toward a focus on learning strategies.'

The following points were among the key findings of the NCERI report:

*   The number of school districts reporting inclusive educational programmes has increased significantly since 1994.
*   Outcomes for students in inclusive educational programmes, both general and special education, are positive.
*   Teachers participating in inclusive education programmes report positive professional outcomes for themselves.
*   Students with a wider range of disabilities are in inclusive education programmes.
*   School restructuring efforts are having an impact on inclusive education programmes and vice versa.

NCERI conducted the study to identify the key factors of inclusive education practices as identified by the school districts implementing inclusive education programmes. The areas studied include:

*   the initiation and planning process;
*   the role of inclusive education in school and district restructuring;
*   the extent of inclusive education;
*   staff attitudes;
*   instructional strategies and classroom supports;
*   parental response; and
*   fiscal issues.

The following extracts give a flavour of the study.

❝   For many school districts, the development of inclusive education programs has been integral with broader educational restructuring. In others, it has been a consequence of such restructuring, and in a few districts, the development of inclusive education programs has led to broader restructuring.

The initiation and process
The data indicate that there is no single or even general pattern of initiation of inclusive education programs in local school districts. Rather, programs have been initiated based on the interests of individuals or groups. Among these are the following: parents; teachers, both general and special education; administrators, both school principals and district superintendents; clinicians and related services providers; state or district reform initiatives; federally funded systems change projects; and court decisions.

The initiation of inclusive education programs does not begin at any single point of entry. Programs are initiated at all grade levels: pre-school and kindergarten, in the elementary grades, at middle schools, and in high schools. In most school districts, however, programs are started at the elementary level. When success is established or students transitioned, inclusive education programs are initiated at the next grade level(s). In a few instances, school districts initiate the changes at all levels at the same time as part of a larger restructuring effort and a new district philosophy.

As states and school districts engage in broad educational restructuring, inclusion programs are implicated. Often, inclusion is a component of a state's restructuring efforts. This is true in Connecticut, Delaware, Florida, Hawaii, Illinois, Indiana, Michigan, Minnesota, Ohio and Texas. In Kentucky, a state committed to broad educational restructuring, inclusion is an integral component.   ❞

The NCERI study quoted a number of reports from local school districts:

❝   *Springfield Public Schools, Massachusetts.* We have experienced several unexpected outcomes from our restructuring efforts. Teachers who would never have had the opportunity to work together have for the first time crossed educational lines. Bilingual teachers teach with general education teachers. Special education teachers teach with bilingual and regular education teachers. Inclusion has caused educators to cross cultural, educational, and philosophical boundaries. It has produced a model for ongoing professional development. Educators team teaching are learning new techniques from one another on the job. Experimentation is at an all time high. The need to retool is apparent, and there is a thirst for knowledge not seen in some time. Teachers are reading professional magazines and forming study groups in an effort to better understand the diverse needs of students before them. The inclusion of a multicultural curriculum is another critical aspect of successful inclusive practices.

Alvarado Independent School District, Texas. Inclusion has had a tremendous impact on curriculum restructuring and instruction for all our diverse learners. Structural arrangements provided through co-operative learning models have been advocated to facilitate academic and social learning. Problem solving has been increasingly stressed to assist students. Teachers are encouraged to assist students in learning how to learn through approaches such as the 'Strategies Intervention Model'. Emphasis has been shifting from a focus on content toward a focus on learning strategies, such as teaching skills, processes, and practices that allow learners of all ages to sustain and update their acquisition and application of specific knowledge. More emphasis is being placed on teaching the child and not just the text.

Burbank Unified School District, California. Deaf children are included in an inclusive model, with classes taught by a general education teacher and a deaf education teacher, both of whom sign; teachers who sign are given a 'bilingual education' bonus. There is no isolation of the deaf students, in the classroom or playground. Hearing students sign. Indeed, at the eighth grade graduation ceremony, three hearing students who were chosen as speakers (the fourth was deaf) each signed their speech.   **99**

The following is the remarkable response by the Ontario School District, Oregon in the survey:

66   The only criteria for a student to attend any of our six elementary schools, our middle school or our high school is that they must be breathing. Our school district does not view inclusion as a program. It is part of our total belief and practice. It goes part and parcel with the idea that our responsibility is to all children. If inclusion is only used as a way to deal with special education students, it will never accomplish anything.

Our school has adopted the site-based management philosophy, where the building principal has total control of all of the money, power and responsibility. Students are assigned to the neighborhood school they would have gone to if they were not disabled.

The Director of Special Education's role changed from being in charge and control of the program to a quality control officer and technical assistance person. Special educational personnel evolved into support specialists for the regular education teachers. We added personnel at the high school level who find jobs for students with disabilities and job coaches who support them in regular job placement within the community.

Parents who feel they are in an elite class have had a harder time accepting students with disabilities, or students with brown skin, or students who come from low income families.

Before inclusion we were bussing students all over our county in order for them to receive services at different sites. When we allowed all students to attend their neighborhood school, the money no longer was needed in transportation and was moved to support services in the regular classroom. Because of this transfer of money the increase for supporting students with disabilities in the regular classroom was almost nothing.   **99**

(Lipsky 1995)

49. Gary Thomas *et al.*: *The Making of the Inclusive School*

In the early 1990s Barnardo's, a national UK charity working with children, started a major discussion within the organization around its educational activities. That discussion was to lead to substantial change and a move to embrace inclusion in its educational activities.

This root change in the organization led to a number of initiatives, including the gradual closure of a 'successful' and financially secure Barnardos special school in Taunton, Somerset, the Princess Margaret School (PMS).

This account is from the headteacher of that school, who, with colleagues and parents, managed to convert the special school into an *inclusion service*. The school at the centre of the narrative was a school for physically disabled children, but the experiences gained from its closure and the setting up of the inclusion service are relevant for all schools.

It was a major event at a local level sending shock waves through the education service and many battles had to be fought and won before the changes were implemented. The school's transition was monitored by a team of writers who retold the story in their book *The Making of the Inclusive School* (Thomas *et al.* 1998).

Part of the story related in the book includes an extensive interview with the headteacher of the school, Dave Walker, about the sequence of events that led to the transfer of pupils to the mainstream, the closure of the school and its conversion to an 'inclusion service'. The following are some edited extracts from the interview conducted by one of the book's authors, Julie Webb.

66 *Could you tell me about how the inclusion initiative came about originally?*

. . . there's two things that happened. If you like, there's the outer events and for me personally there were some inner things that were going on as well. In 1991, I'd been head teacher at the school three years, and in that time we increased the occupancy, we built the school up from a position where it had been in some difficulties, and it was doing well. So we agreed that at that point we would just look around and see what was on the horizon in special educational needs. And we looked at a lot of things, not just at inclusion . . . things like conductive education, special therapies, all sorts of stuff. One of the things that I and Steve Connor [assistant divisional director for Barnardo's responsible for the whole school] went to, was the first Inclusion Conference, which was held in Cardiff . . . they invited the Canadians over, George Flynn, Marsha Forest, John O'Brien and Judith Snow. And Barnardo's committed resources to staff going, so there were quite a lot of Barnardo's staff there . . . something like ten Barnardo's staff. Some of the things that George Flynn was saying about the outcomes for people who'd been in special education: joblessness, alcoholism, potential for crime, vulnerability . . . all those things hit me very powerfully at a time when I was personally feeling quite vulnerable . . . There was an alternative to the special school . . . it affected me a lot.

The other important element was that Steve Connor had gone as well. So I wasn't going to something and then coming away on my own – I actually had somebody I could talk things through with. Steve and I did talk it through, an awful lot . . . Between us . . . we . . . formed a very good alliance . . . It was shortly after that that Vivian Upton was appointed as deputy and we had a clear ally in Vivian . . . Peggy [the administrator] . . . was also an ally. So as the senior management team we were quite strong.

So would you say that those issues, of outcomes for segregated schooling, were something that you hadn't really devoted much time to before? . . .

My own background before being at PMS was children who have emotional and behavioural difficulties. And I suppose at some level I'd always been concerned with those children that there was very little follow-up after school as to what happened to them. I think . . . I was busy doing the job, and, in a way, not knowing about what happens afterwards is kind of – useful. You don't have to think about it. And once it had been articulated for me by George Flynn, I think there were two things: one was, it felt right when he said . . . 'These are the outcomes.' I thought, yes, at some level I knew this, and . . . the second thing was, once you know something, once *I* know something I can't ignore it, can't leave it alone.

So . . . at that point it was clear for me . . . I was being faced with two choices: one was to leave and go and do something else somewhere else, or two was to take this school through the process . . . notions about including children and so on were talked about at that point about five years down the line . . . we were quite clear . . . it would take about five years to do this. And we held to that in fact. But by doing that we gave ourselves time . . . to say, '. . . are there some small things that we can do now?' . . . That was actually . . . quite important.

So you're saying you held to that view, that it would take about five years but it's taken a lot less than that hasn't it?

No, [it was] 1991 when the idea first came up – and 1996 [for the closure of PMS]. If you look at what's happened in that time there have been a number of steps . . . The first . . . was that we fairly quickly got into the partnership with Somerset [Education Authority], around Val Lane – the joint appointment of an advisory teacher.

So that was a direct result of your going to . . . [the Cardiff] conference and seeing the need for links with the mainstream?

We'd talked about it before but it certainly gave added impetus, and it clarified for me a route for the children back into mainstream.

So that was seen as . . . [Val Lane's] main role?

Yes, that's right . . . before, the discussion had been about her acting as a support to the teachers here rather than being a route out.
    . . . The other thing was we took on the first consultant that we had – Angie Ash . . . [She] did . . . some important stuff around . . . helping us as a management team to get our heads clear as to where we needed to be concentrating our efforts . . . [including] a basic round-up of research. So the value for us as managers was that that round-up of research almost became . . . a mantra: inclusion would work if it was resourced properly, if there was commitment, and if it was planned properly. And having a simple message about the research becomes very valuable because if you're talking to sceptical parents or whatever, getting into the 'perhapses' and 'maybes' is not going to help you.

They need a clear message to take away and talk about?

That's right. So having it presented in that way . . . was actually really useful . . . There [were] a number of things that happened as a result of Val Lane's appointment. There were voices within the school who were sceptical about the possibility of any child being able to manage in mainstream – that kind of ethos: 'They're here therefore they must need to be here and they could never possibly manage outside.' The first child . . . went into mainstream and that voice changed [to] 'Well, maybe *some* . . .' And . . . the next thing that happened was we had a whole-school training day, which gave people, the whole staff, a chance to talk about what they thought was best for the children and what their hopes and fears were . . . What . . . was powerful . . . was that I did have some com- plaints from some members of staff afterwards that they had felt afraid of putting forward a view that said that segregation was best. [That was] . . . the power of the message . . . we've got enough people here saying inclusion's best [and] that the people who are promoting segregation are on the defensive. That's not what I'd expected at all. It was quite the opposite.

I suppose you have to allow for one being seen as politically correct?

Of course. That's right. But it did say to me that those people who'd promoted segregation are actually on the defensive. And that told me we could be bolder. So the next thing . . . that happened was . . . as a management team . . . we knew we had to make a big step forward . . . Looking back it's quite obvious that what we had to do was set a date for closing the school . . . We did everything but that – we just avoided that, for all sorts of purely internal reasons . . . And in a way . . . we were rescued a bit . . . by two things. One was we had projected that the numbers at FE [Further Education] were going to go right down . . . so suddenly we had a window of opportunity to actually close the FE painlessly. And the second was that Carol Bannister [a class teacher] came to us and said, 'I want to take the class to West Hill' [the first primary school to become involved in the project]. [This] enabled us to . . . avoid the big decision . . . 'When does this close!' . . . Carol's initiative [at] West Hill . . . [developed] a bridgehead . . . we'll have some children there, we're going to have some staff working there: that's a very powerful message . . . I was very clear in my own mind that . . . if that required five teachers and twenty-seven assistants I didn't care what it cost – at that point. It was vital that we got in – it was going to succeed.

The implication of that is that once those kids are out there's nobody coming into the PMS secondary department?

That's right.

At no point was Barnardo's providing the impetus for any of that?

No – and it is unusual for Barnardo's but I think it's fair to say that we were pushing Barnardo's. There was a process with Barnardo's where we were writing papers, in effect saying 'This is what we're doing.' And gaining permission.

So Barnardo's wasn't involved at all at that level. And equally, really and truly, neither were the LEA. You know, we just did it and then involved them afterwards. And I'm actually really pleased now that that's how we did it because I think if we'd once got ourselves tangled up with the bureaucracy we'd still be faffing about.

So . . . then . . . we had to do two things . . . One was to develop a proposal for . . . the 16+ project . . . The second was . . . the decision about how . . . to close the rest of the school . . . It was clear to us that . . . it couldn't be achieved in one year. And so two was where we got to . . . As the impact of that hit me I really began to feel very vulnerable . . . I was actually in tears at that point 'I don't know if I'm the person who can actually do this.' But . . . that was also the point at which we realised, as a group, that we could do it, so long as we stuck together and supported one another which we've done.

There was still no partnership with the [Somerset] LEA at this stage?

There were talks with the LEA but they were fairly aimless. They weren't going anywhere. I think from the LEA's point of view we were not a high priority, that they were having all sorts of problems with EBD [emotional and behavioural difficulties], and . . . something . . . might happen three, four, five years down the line.

So we got agreement that we would involve the stakeholders . . . and two things followed from that: one, we had to tell the staff; two, we had to tell the parents.

. . . At that stage did you envisage all the children going into mainstream?

Yes. That's what we were saying, that we would close the school and we would work to make it possible for all the children to be in mainstream. I think we did realise that there would be some parents [who] would take their children away. Of course we got into all sorts of time-wasting, stupid, games trying to second-guess what parents would do. A few we even got right!

So the parents [who] . . . wanted to keep their children in special education – that didn't necessarily relate to the severity of the children's disabilities?

Oh absolutely not, no. It was purely their parental wishes. Kids' needs didn't come into it.
   . . . We were asking parents, I think, to take a great leap of faith, and clearly some parents felt able to do that and others didn't. I think in addition to that the Dorset . . . LEA was giving . . . [parents] very clear messages . . . [that] 'Integration in our schools is not actually an option for disabled children – Victoria School will be the alternative.' So they clearly were not giving a supportive message. Certainly in the early days the Somerset LEA *were*.

. . . Are you saying that Dorset wouldn't have provided funding for them to attend mainstream education here?

We . . . put a proposal to Dorset [which] . . . would actually have cost them less: there would have been more Barnardo's money for the children, and they still said 'No'.
   . . . We then set up the parents' consultative group, to represent all the views of the parents. They certainly represented *some* views very well but not all of them! They didn't represent those parents who were

in favour of what we were doing . . . because the group . . . in the main was composed of parents who were opposed to what we were going to do.

But why didn't the others join and put their point of view forward?

Because . . . if they tried to put a positive stamp, they just got drowned by the anxieties and worries of those people who were nominally in charge of the parents' representative group.

. . . [The] group clearly formed itself into a 'We are going to fight the closure' group. That was their point of view. I think they also had an agenda of . . . perhaps I'm being unfair, but there was a sense of 'If we can't stop the school closing we'll do everything we can to oppose any alternative.'

But we . . . also had set up another group that would meet with every parent to run through what they wanted for their child . . . a massive undertaking, really, meeting with sixty parents . . . The workload was just phenomenal. And trying to hold on to all the things that parents were saying and wanting. But we did actually achieve that. And we were able, at the end of the consultation period, to say quite clearly . . . everybody's had a chance to put their view . . . to Barnardo's and to the LEA, and it was agreed and ratified by both organisations that we would go ahead: it would close in 1995/96.

. . . The LEA were now much more heavily involved . . . The parents did set off one hare which we had to follow, which was an idea for a unit attached to a school, primary to start with. And again, looking back, it's interesting how far we were prepared to run with that without actually doing any checking ourselves. Because when we actually did check, the school that they'd spoken to had had a completely different notion of what was being talked about from what the parents had. And had no intention of wanting a unit at all. We were so embroiled in the process we allowed that notion for quite a while before we really dealt with it. And the LEA got themselves wound up about that as well. The . . . thing that struck me, looking back, is actually the disparity of power between the professionals and the parents was very disempowering.

. . . We went through this consultation process – we did try to listen to what parents had to say, and we did modify aspects of what we were proposing – but the bottom line was that it was a consultation exercise and at the end of that . . .

. . . the school would close anyway?

That's right. So on the really principled issue, on the substantive issue we weren't going to change.

Were you prepared to give them help with finding alternatives if they did go for special education . . .?

Yes. That was the intention behind the individual meetings . . . We could have been more hard-nosed in terms of, 'Well, we will support those parents who want inclusion but not other parents: they'll have to go and make their own arrangements.' We didn't do that but there was quite a lot of support for it. But the other element I was thinking about . . . we'd taken on Sue Rickell as [a] consultant, and I think Sue had a number of important roles, really. One was, in the meetings with parents I think she was a very powerful influence: some things became not sayable because Sue was there – about disabled people. And two, she was able to challenge some of the assumptions parents had about children not being able to cope in mainstream school. And Sue's own experience had been that she had transferred to a mainstream school in her last year at school and it had been the most important year of her life. So that was a very powerful message.

. . . The LEA now began to work rather harder than they had done. We'd clearly moved up their priorities list. Barnardo's began to pull in people like Personnel and Training and so forth, in a way that they hadn't done before. And of course we were now talking to *actual* schools, about *actual* children. So I think achieving our own clarity was perhaps the single biggest step forward that we took. Whether people were for us or against us, they actually knew where we were. Now those people who were against us, I think, the parents who were upset with what we were doing and so on, we were able to say to them at least: we can be fair about what we're not going to do. There are some uncertainties about the future . . . and in a way, it's hard, it's like a bereavement or a separation or something like that: suddenly the partner is very clear that they're going to be somewhere else but at least it is clear. And I think that was quite powerful. And of course some of the parents took their kids off and went.

Did you have any sort of official agreement with the LEA by then?

Well, we had the agreement, yes, because . . . it had gone through committee in the June, and [the] Barnardo's council at the same time, and both parties had agreed that over the next two years they would work in partnership to get an agreement and to work that up into a contract.

So the financial aspect hadn't been decided at that point?

Hadn't been decided, but . . . we talked in terms of the same sum of money being available as had always been, historically, so between £550,000 and £600,000 . . . that was the kind of sum that we had in our minds . . . In effect what we were trying to do was run two services with no additional increase in staffing, and some people would be facing redundancy at the end of that first year: all of that stuff had to be dealt with. It was a complicated process, really. And inevitably a bit messy, I think . . . The other thing that . . . happened . . . was . . . Barnardo's dropped a bombshell on us. We thought we had an absolute agreement about the money that would be available to make the change happen and suddenly found that that had been pulled back. And in itself I think that that was fair enough – the organisation found it was harder up than it thought it was.

[Does Barnardo's] have other special schools for physically disabled children?

No. We were the last. But EBD [emotional and behavioural disorders] schools, and others: my perception is that those schools are increasingly on the defensive. They'll have to address the issues sooner or later. Barnardo's has signed up to CSIE's Inclusion Charter, so that's a step – it is beginning to move. It hasn't developed its own policy and statement about inclusion yet but it has had its conference. But there are steps, you know, so I feel pleased really that we've had a part to play in that. We've moved the organisation rather than the other way round . . . We have had a part in the wider debate. Our staff have had an impact in the schools that we're working with, and that won't go away. We haven't achieved all that we wanted to, but then maybe you never do. I think the biggest disappointment was that we have not been able to impact significantly on Somerset's special needs policy.

I suppose there's always the wish that we could have done more, [but] I wouldn't have missed any of this. Sue Rickell said: 'You are moving from being an oppressor to an ally, and that is always a painful process.'

A bit of an extreme way of putting it, isn't it? You wouldn't have seen yourself as an oppressor?

No, but I . . . do think that the more I've been with disabled people – articulate, thoughtful, disabled people – the more I've had to recognise that the whole segregation process is a form of oppression. It is what able-bodied people do to disabled people. And they do it with the absolute best of intentions – but that doesn't make it right.

But are you implying that they shouldn't have the choice? In which case you're still oppressing them?

But they don't have a choice: that's the issue.

But you're removing a choice by closing the school?

But it's not a real choice. If the power imbalance is such that for disabled people there isn't a real choice between mainstream and segregated, and actually they don't want that choice, increasingly: a lot of the parents are saying, 'I don't want that choice. All I want is the same choice as any other parent.' So actually, if you shut all the special schools you, on one level maybe, are reducing choices but on another, you'd actually be funding to provide the resources to make it possible for the parent of a disabled child to have the same choices as any others do – and actually that is the *key* choice: you know, the choice to go to one of the three primary schools in the area.

Rather than the only one that's accessible . . .?

Yes, that is the real choice. But we're a long way from that . . . And the present system, it seems to me, is incredibly wasteful. You have two systems, both of which have to be managed, both of which have to be resourced. It just doesn't make economic sense, and increasingly it doesn't make educational sense. And some kind of mechanism . . . will need to be created . . . to make it possible for special schools to be absorbed into mainstream.

(Thomas *et al.* 1998)

50. Sam Harris: *A seven year sentence*

In 1992, teenager Sam Harris from Harrow wrote about his educational experiences revealing insulting and stereotypical attitudes towards disabled children and young people by non-disabled adults. Happily, his experiences in an inclusive comprehensive school toward the end of his school career were more positive, and he concludes this excerpt with these words: 'Here they treat me just like all the other pupils, but also provide the backup that I need to "level the playing field".'

❝ *We couldn't possibly cope with him here – he should be at the special school.*

These words, from the head of the local infants school, sentenced me to seven years at the local education authority's physical handicap day school. It was six miles from where I live and operated in a time warp all of its own. People arrived late and went home early. Lessons in English and maths only – took second place to physiotherapy, riding and swimming. There was to be no pressure and so there were no apparent goals.

He has cerebral palsy so he'll have spatial problems. He won't be able to do maths.

Staff at the special school were always stereotyping the pupils. They saw the problem first and not the child. If I didn't understand a concept – such as fractions – after one explanation, they gave up. In fact, everyone in my family has trouble with maths, but they never thought about that. It took me four attempts to get a grade C at GCSE, but I did it in the end. They did try to get us to mix with the able-bodied pupils at the junior school on site, but it didn't work because it was an artificial arrangement.

If he's going to mainstream school, he'll have to control that dribbling.

Well, they might just as well have asked an amputee to grow a new leg before he was entitled to an education. I can control the dribbling, if I concentrate on that alone, but not if I'm concentrating hard on something else. I know it's unpleasant, but having an unattractive feature shouldn't preclude me from the human race.

What a clever boy, doing GCSEs.

If my friend from the special school hadn't been present when her mother said this, I'd have exploded! Everyone in the country does GCSEs. It's normal and should be expected. So I passed eight GCSEs. What's the big deal?

We aim to help every pupil develop to his or her full potential, regardless of race, gender or any disability that her or she might have.

My last quote comes from the brochure of the comprehensive school where I took my GCSEs and am doing my A levels this summer. Here they treat me just like all the other pupils, but also provide the backup that I need to 'level the playing field'. Everyone should have this opportunity . . .   99

(Harris 1992)

51. Tony Booth and Mel Ainscow: *Index for Inclusion*

The practice of inclusive education in schools across the UK and in a growing number of overseas countries was given a significant boost from 2000 onwards with the launching of CSIE's *Index for Inclusion*.

This document is a unique set of materials, written by Tony Booth and Mel Ainscow, which support ordinary schools in a process of inclusive school development and is a process of investigation the schools undertake in order to improve school attainments for all students through inclusive practices.

It involves ordinary local primary and secondary schools in a process of self-review looking at all aspects of school life through the three key dimensions of

.s, policies and practices. This is how the Index sets out the dimensions
. the diagram below.

❝❞   Inclusion and exclusion are explored along three interconnected
dimensions of school improvement . . .

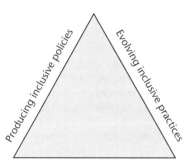

Creating inclusive cultures

These dimensions have been chosen to direct thinking about school
change. Experience with the *Index* indicates that they are seen, very
widely, as important ways to structure school development.

The three dimensions are all necessary to the development of inclusion
within a school. Any plan for school change must pay attention to all of
them. However, the dimension, 'creating inclusive cultures' is placed,
deliberately, along the base of the triangle. At times, too little attention
has been given to the potential for school cultures to support or under-
mine developments in teaching and learning. Yet they are at the heart of
school improvement. The development of shared inclusive values and
collaborative relationships may lead to changes in the other dimensions.
It is through inclusive school cultures, that changes in policies and
practices can be sustained by new staff and students.   ❞❞

At the time of its launch in March 2000, the UK government placed a copy
of the Index in every school and local education authority in England (27,000
copies). Later the National Assembly in Wales placed a copy in all schools and
LEAs in that country. By 2003, CSIE had sold a further 10,000 copies in the UK
and overseas where it has been translated and adapted for use in 21 other
countries.

The Index challenges any school to move forward, regardless of how
inclusive that school believes itself already to be.

A key aspect of the Index process, which many users say has positively transformed schools' approaches to education, is that it works with 100 per-cent of
students – not only the often-referred to '2 per-cent' of disabled students, nor
the '20 per-cent' said to have 'special educational needs'.

The Index came about after three years of government-sponsored trials that
were co-ordinated by CSIE and involved a team of 11 people drawing on input
from heads, teachers, academics, disabled adults, parents, governors and CSIE

staff. Two earlier versions of the Index were tested by a total of 22 schools across the country. In such a wide-ranging project the Index team and the authors were duty bound to come up with definitions of 'inclusion' and the updated (2002) edition of the Index introduces its definitions of inclusion in this way:

> ❝ The key concepts of the *Index* are 'inclusion', 'barriers to learning and participation', 'resources to support learning and participation', and 'support for diversity'. These provide a language for discussing inclusive educational development.
>
> Everyone has his or her own view of a complex idea like inclusion . . . Many people find that the notion of inclusion becomes clearer as they engage with the [Index] materials.
>
> Some of the ideas which make up the view of inclusion within the *Index* are summarised [below]. Inclusion involves change. It is an unending process of increasing learning and participation for all students. It is an ideal to which schools can aspire but which is never fully reached. But inclusion happens as soon as the process of increasing participation is started. An inclusive school is one that is on the move.
>
> Inclusion in education involves:
>
> • Valuing all students and staff equally.
> • Increasing the participation of students in, and reducing their exclusion from, the cultures, curricula and communities of local schools.
> • Restructuring the cultures, policies and practices in schools so that they respond to the diversity of students in the locality.
> • Reducing barriers to learning and participation for all students, not only those with impairments or those who are categorised as 'having special educational needs'.
> • Learning from attempts to overcome barriers to the access and participation of particular students to make changes for the benefit of students more widely.
> • Viewing the difference between students as resources to support learning, rather than problems to be overcome.
> • Acknowledging the right of students to an education in their locality.
> • Improving schools for staff as well as for students.
> • Emphasising the role of schools in building community and developing values, as well as in increasing achievement.
> • Fostering mutually sustaining relationships between schools and communities.
> • Recognising that inclusion in education is one aspect of inclusion in society.
>
> Participation means learning alongside others and collaborating with them in shared learning experiences. It requires active engagement

with learning and having a say in how education is experienced. More deeply, it is about being recognised, accepted and valued for oneself.

Developing inclusion involves reducing exclusionary pressures. 'Disciplinary exclusion' is the temporary or permanent removal of a student from school for breaches of school rules. It is the result of one set of exclusionary pressures. Like inclusion, exclusion is thought of in a broad way. It refers to all those temporary or longer lasting pressures which get in the way of full participation. These might result from difficulties in relationships or with what is taught, as well as from feelings of not being valued. Inclusion is about minimising all barriers in education for all students.

Inclusion starts from a recognition of the differences between students. **99**

The materials in the Index include questionnaires aimed at teachers, students, parents, governors and others; there are a dozen different activities for all members of the school community to undertake and five specific phases or cycles of work, all of which are designed, over time, to build on the wealth of knowledge and experience that people in mainstream schools already have.

Below each of the three dimensions – cultures, policies and practices – are a series of indicators (44 in total) and below each indicator is an associated set of questions (over 500) for schools to ask themselves (see example of indicator A.2.5 on page 185). The Index carefully and logically guides users through this process and the work creates a lot of new and useful information for a school.

From the beginning, the language by the authors in the Index is deeply inclusionary, replacing the phrase 'special educational needs' with the new term, 'barriers to learning and participation', a phrase now widely adopted and promoted by the UK government, LEAs, schools, academics and educational organizations. The Index process invites a school to reduce those barriers, by undertaking a deep scrutiny of everything that makes up the life of a school and setting new priorities for development. The schools themselves design these priorities and locate them formally in the school development plan.

But the Index does not offer pre-designed improvements and changes; rather it facilitates investigation using the three dimensions, the indicators and questions. The Index – and the process – is also expected to be adapted by individual schools as they progress and own the process themselves. It is a flexible, not prescriptive, approach to school development, which encourages restructuring of ordinary schools.

Experience has shown that whatever comes up in a particular school turns out to be the right thing for action and change in *that* school. All members of a school – teachers, heads, students, support staff, parents and governors – contribute to this process. The Index cycle (see figure below) is designed to last about one year, though only a limited amount of the full Index process can be achieved in that time and the document strongly recommends a commitment to using it in an on-going manner – perhaps over a five-year period.

One large, urban education authority in England, Sheffield, has declared it wants 100 per-cent of its schools to be using the Index process within five

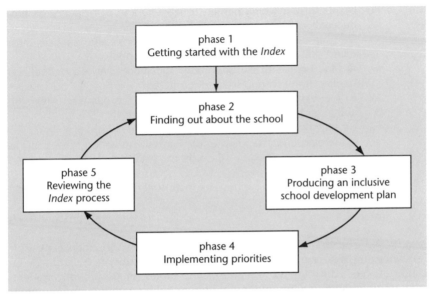

years, while in other areas it is clear that only a minority of schools have started using it. Another large, rural authority in England, East Sussex, has adapted the Index for use in pre-school and childcare settings. This work led to CSIE launching in 2004 an Index for Early Years and Childcare, also written by Booth and Ainscow. Importantly, the Index takes the social model of disability as a starting point.

The gathering of students' views of how a school performs is also a strong characteristic of the Index in action. It may seem glaringly obvious that the consumers of the education service should be asked what they think of the product they are getting, but in the UK and elsewhere, teachers and other professionals have always been most reluctant to do this. After all, the children might just tell them the truth.

Below is a sample indicator from the Index (Indicator A.2.5) with its associated questions. This indicator is within the first dimension, 'Creating inclusive cultures' and in the second part of this dimension where the focus is on 'Establishing inclusive values'.

> 66 INDICATOR A.2.5 Staff seek to remove barriers to learning and participation in all aspects of the school
>
> i) Do staff understand that they can make a difference to the barriers to learning and participation experienced by students?
> ii) Are barriers to learning and participation seen to arise in a relationship between students and their teaching and learning environment?
> iii) Is the teaching and learning environment understood to include student and staff relationships, buildings, cultures, policies, curricula and teaching approaches?

iv) Do staff avoid seeing barriers to learning and participation as produced by deficiencies or impairments in students?

v) Do staff and students understand that policies and practices must
reflect the diversity of students within the school?

vi) Are the barriers that arise through differences between school and
home cultures recognised and countered?

vii) Is it understood that anyone can experience barriers to learning
and participation?

viii) Do staff avoid labelling children according to notions of ability?

ix) Is there an understanding of the way categorisation of students as
'having special educational needs' can lead to their devaluation and
separation?

x) Do staff avoid contrasting mainstream and 'special needs'
students?

(Booth and Ainscow 2002)

In its short history (2000–04) there is clear evidence of the Index's positive
influence on UK government ministers and their departments, local chief education officers, education administrators and professionals, schools, academics, parents and others. The government has recently promoted it in its official
literature to schools and education authorities.

Schools have reported that it can be an extremely powerful process of
investigation and development, sometimes too powerful, and sometimes
revealing more issues for action than they are able to deal with at that time.
Some schools have experienced difficulties in implementing the Index
process alongside other pressures facing them, but many have successfully
incorporated it into their normal school development process and annually
revised school development plans.

It is helpful at this stage to mention a few priorities for change created by
ordinary schools in the UK after a short time of using the Index process.

Index-inspired priorities for school change

- introducing rituals for welcoming new students and staff and marking
  their departure;
- establishing staff development activities to make lessons more responsive
  to diversity;
- introducing clear management and career structures for teaching
  assistants;
- improving all aspects of access in the school for disabled students and
  adults;
- promoting positive views of ethnic diversity in teaching and displays;
- integrating all forms of support within the school;
- arranging joint training for teaching assistants and teachers;
- developing collaborative learning amongst students;
- revising anti-bullying policies;

- improving the induction process for new students;
- increasing the involvement of students in decision-making about school policies;
- improving communication between the school and parents/carers;
- improving the reputation of the school amongst local communities.

Very many schools using the Index have said the process has worked well and that it has been a genuine empowering process. Feedback from schools and LEAs given to CSIE over the Index's first three years includes:

- The Index is versatile and can be used flexibly.
- It brings together different groups in the school community.
- It is a rich source of ideas, particularly the indicators and questions.
- It gives structure to speaking about the massive issues of inclusion.
- It is good for awareness raising and bringing equal opportunity initiatives together.
- The questionnaires provide excellent focus for information gathering.
- It underpins the whole school development process.
- It creates discussion of difficulties which would not otherwise have happened.

Away from the UK, versions of the Index have been prepared or are being prepared in: Arabic, Basque, Bulgarian, Chinese (for use in Hong Kong), Danish, Finnish, French (for use in Quebec), German, Hindi, Hungarian, Japanese, Maltese, Norwegian, Portuguese, Romanian, Spanish (for use in South America and another version for use in Spain), Swedish, Urdu, Vietnamese and Welsh. English versions are being used in: Australia (in Melbourne, Perth, Queensland and Tasmania) and in South Africa. UNESCO has funded work to look at ways of developing an Index for countries in the South.

Conclusion

In this book we have tried to give an idea of the streams of thought that have led education in an inclusive direction – that have provided shape to contemporary thinking about inclusion rather than segregation. We have done this by giving extracts from articles, papers, books, legislation and reports that we feel exemplify in some way those streams of thought.

Those documents stretch back over quite a period – in the case of Thomas Paine's, more than two hundred years. Early treatises such as his contributed to discourses that led eventually to a more progressive political agenda, with gradual improvements in people's living conditions eventually following, in terms of political life, equity and social justice.

Those foundational changes were vital, but the real acceleration in the move to inclusion has been in the last third of the twentieth century, where there has been focused attention on not just the injustices generated by a segregated education system, but also on the system's efficacy. Does it, in other words, effectively do the job it sets out to do?

We have tried, in the documents, extracts and accompanying commentaries that comprise this volume, to show that both on principled and practical grounds there is no justification for a segregated system. The last 40 years have produced a hefty portfolio of evidence and argument against the system as well as more than enough practical examples of effective inclusive education, and some of that argument and evidence is marshalled here.

In the 1960s came the first questions about the system as discriminatory in a society that claimed to be eliminating discrimination. The 1970s brought research that destabilized earlier assumptions about the efficacy of the special education system and its particular pedagogies. Late in that decade and in the 1980s, against the grain of an increasingly competitive social climate, came many innovations and experiments that aimed at equity and that showed inclusion not only to be possible but successful. The dominant political discourse of the time, at least in the UK and the US, was of the justice of meritocracy and the power of competition in achieving supposedly improved social arrangements. That discourse provided justification for continuing segregative forms of provisic whether in special schools or in selective mainstream sch at least in part the lack of movement to inclusion, despit(progressive legislation of the 1981 Education Act in the UK.

Much changed in the political climate of the 1990s. 1 oriented ethic of the 1980s was largely displaced – although i ... uic fondness of governments for performativity, selection and competition among schools. In the new ethic that took shape around the mid-1990s, talk of an 'inclusive society' and a 'stakeholder society' came to replace the earlier ethic of competition and winner-takes-all.

Changes have been possible in thinking about inclusion in education not only because of the broader change in social climate, but also (and perhaps more significantly), because of changes in the way that 'difficulty' is conceptualized; there seems far less willingness now to locate the difficulties that children may experience at school unproblematically *in* the children themselves – whether the 'in-ness' is about children's learning or behaviour, or about their social background, family income, gender or race.

In the next few years there is likely to be an extension of the changes that took place at the end of the twentieth century, with an increasing recognition of the interconnectedness of the issues that surround inclusion.

Education should be moving in a more inclusive direction. But is it really? Where in fact are we now? In the UK government's discussion paper on the future of special provision (DfEE 1997, see 35) a number of suggestions were made for promoting inclusion. It was suggested, amongst other things, that:

- special schools should have targets for numbers of children whom they successfully reintegrate;
- mainstream schools that reach high standards in improving their provision for a wide range of special needs should be awarded a 'kite mark';
- special schools should become more like services, providing resources and expertise to local mainstream schools; – *Akin with Removing Barried Doc*
- all children should be registered on the roll of a mainstream school. This, if the money for the child also went to the mainstream school, would encourage creative thinking about inclusive solutions.

At the time that we are compiling this book, six years after that discussion paper, few of these suggestions have been realized. In fact, only the third in the list could be said to be happening, though even here the position is very patchy. It is interesting to ponder on the lack of movement. Three years after the Green Paper (35) a short letter appeared in *The Times Educational Supplement*, under the banner, False Sympathy for Inclusion. From a group of teachers, it said:

> 66 As learning support staff in a multi-racial school we support the principles of inclusion and of raising academic standards.
>
> We feel strongly that unrealistic target-setting, an over-prescriptive curriculum and league tables are not sympathetic to the principle of

inclusion. They negatively affect the status of children with special educational needs or those for whom English is an additional language.

We have seen such children become 'unwanted' because they affect the league tables in a negative direction and we have evidence of schools refusing to take such children before national tests.

(Chambers *et al*, 2000: 23)

Continuing pressure to be at the same time competitive *and* inclusive, these thirteen teachers were saying, looks remarkably like tokenism. Pressures of all kinds – to be successful in examinations, to meet targets – lead schools to reject rather than accept children who are likely to drive down results.

The sentiment expressed by Maggie Chambers and her colleagues is often heard in schools, and it recalls the findings of Croll and Moses (2000) that appeared to indicate a willingness amongst teachers to support inclusion in the right circumstances, but which indicated also that those same teachers thought that the circumstances were not currently right. The concern has to be that 'inclusion' is merely a headline for governments, a slogan contradicted by other policy and unscaffolded by structural, financial and legislative supports.

Change, of course, in a matter as major as the move to inclusion is inevitably slow. However, there are signs – that we have tried to show in this book – that the journey is progressing: that there is a historical pulse behind inclusive education and that it is gaining in strength.

References

In this section, the first reference under each numbered heading refers to the main source from which the piece has been taken. Where there are embedded references from within the extract, these have been added, indented after the main reference.

PART ONE THE CONTEXT – RIGHTS, PARTICIPATION, SOCIAL JUSTICE

1. Thomas Paine
Paine, T. (1999) *The Rights of Man*. Dover: Dover Publications.

2. R.H. Tawney
Tawney, R.H. ([1931] 1964) *Equality*. London: George Allen & Unwin.

3. John Rawls
The first, explanatory, piece is from:

Nussbaum, M. (2001) The enduring significance of John Rawls: the Chronicle review, *Chronicle of Higher Education*, 20 July at: http//chronicle.com/free/v47/i45/45b00701.htm

The second piece is from Rawls himself:

Rawls, J. (1972) *A Theory of Justice*. Oxford: Oxford University Press.

4. Martin Luther King
King Jr, M.L. (1963) 'I have a dream', in J.M. Washington (ed.) *Writings and Speeches that Changed the World*. San Francisco: Harper.

5. Caroline Roaf and Hazel Bines
Roaf, C. and Bines, H. (1989) Needs, rights and opportunities in special education, in C. Roaf and H. Bines (eds) *Needs, Rights and Opportunities: Developing Approaches to Special Education*. London: Falmer.

References in this piece:
Adams, C. (1988) Gender, race and class: essential issues for comprehensive education, in C. Chitty (ed.) *Redefining the Comprehensive Experience*, Bedford Way Papers 32. London: University Institute of Education.

Bandman, B. (1973) Do children have any natural rights? *Proceedings of the 29th Annual General Meeting of the Philosophy of Education Society*, (2): 34–42.

Booth, T. (1983) Integrating special education, in T. Booth and P. Potts (eds) *Integrating Special Education*. Oxford: Blackwell.

Brennan, W.K. (1981) *Changing Special Education*. Milton Keynes: Open University Press.

Byrne, E.M. (1985) Equality or equity? A European overview, in M. Arnot (ed.) *Race and Gender Equal Opportunities Policies in Education*. Oxford: Pergamon.

Department of Education and Science (1978) *Special Educational Needs Report of the Committee of Enquiry into the Education of Handicapped Children and Young People* (Warnock Report). London: HMSO.

Dessent, T. (1987) *Making the Ordinary School Special*. Lewes: Falmer Press.

Evetts, J. (1973) *The Sociology of Educational Ideas*. London: Methuen.

Freeman, M. (1987) Taking children's rights seriously, *Children and Society*, 1(4): 229–319.

Hargreaves, D. (1983) *The Challenge for the Comprehensive School*. London: Routledge and Kegan Paul.

Hegarty, S. (1987) *Meeting Special Needs in Ordinary Schools*. London: Cassell.

ILEA (Inner London Education Authority) (1985) *Educational Opportunities for All?* (Fish Report). London: ILEA.

Kirp, D. (1983) Professionalization as policy choice: British special education in comparative perspective, in R.G. Chambers and W.T. Hartman (eds) *Special Education Policies*. Philadelphia: Temple University Press.

Lynch, M. (1986) *Multicultural Education: Principles and Practice*. London: Routledge and Kegan Paul.

Straker-Welds, M. (ed.) (1984) *Education for a Multicultural Society*. London: Bell and Hyman.

Tomlinson, S. (1982) *The Sociology of Special Education*. London: Routledge and Kegan Paul.

6. Sharon Rustemier

Rustemier, S. (2002) *Social and Educational Justice: The Human Rights Framework for Inclusion*. Bristol: Centre for Studies on Inclusive Education.

7. David Hevey

Hevey, D. (1992) *The Creatures Time Forgot: Photography and Disability Imagery*, 1–2. London: Routledge.

PART TWO ARGUMENTS AND EVIDENCE AGAINST SEGREGATION – 1960s TO TODAY

8. Erving Goffman

Goffman, E. ([1961] 1968) *Asylums: Essays on the Social Situation of Mental Patients and Other Inmates*. London: Pelican.

9. L.M. Dunn

Dunn, L.M. (1968) Special education for the mildly retarded – is much of it justifiable? *Exceptional Children*, September 35: 5–24.

References in this piece:

Bereiter, C. and Engelmann, S. (1966) *Teaching Disadvantaged Children in the Pre-school*. Englewood Cliffs, NJ: Prentice-Hall.

Coleman, J.S. *et al.* (1966) *Equality of Educational Opportunity.* Washington, DC: USGPO.

Goffman, E. *Asylums:* (1961) *Essays on the Social Situation of Mental Patients and Other Inmates.* Garden City, NY: Anchor.

Guilford, J.P. (1967) *The Nature of Human Intelligence.* New York: McGraw-Hill.

Hoelke, G.M. (1966) *Effectiveness of Special Class Placement for Educable Mentally Retarded Children.* Lincoln, Neb: University of Nebraska.

Hollingworth, L.S. (1923) *The Psychology of Subnormal Children.* New York: Macmillan.

Johnson, G.O. (1962) Special education for mentally handicapped – a paradox, *Exceptional Children,* 19: 62–9.

Kirk, S.A. (1964) Research in education, in H.A. Steven and R. Heber (eds) *Mental Retardation.* Chicago, ILL: University of Chicago Press.

Mackie, R.P. (1967) *Functional Handicaps Among School Children Due to Cultural or Economic Deprivation.* Paper presented at the First Congress of the International Association for the Scientific Study of Mental Deficiency, Montpellier, France, September.

Meyerowitz, J.H. (1965) Family background of educable mentally retarded children, in H. Goldstein, J.W. Moss and L.J. Jordan (eds) *The Efficacy of Special Education Training on the Development of Mentally Retarded Children.* Urbana, ILL: University of Illinois Institute for Research on Exceptional Children.

Meyerowitz, J.H. (1967) Peer groups and special classes, *Mental Retardation,* 5: 23–6.

Passow, A.H. (1967) *A Summary of Findings and Recommendations of a Study of the Washington, D.C. Schools.* New York: Teachers College, Columbia University.

Rosenthal, R. and Jacobson, L. (1966) Teachers' expectancies: determinants of pupils IQ gains, *Psychological Reports,* 19: 115–18.

Rubin, E.Z., Senison, C.B. and Retwee, M.C. (1966) *Emotionally Handicapped Children in the Elementary School.* Detroit: Wayne State University Press.

Smith, H.W. and Kennedy, W.A. (1967) Effects of three educational programs on mentally retarded children, *Perceptual and Motor Skills,* 24: 174.

Thurstone, T.G. (1948) *Learning to Think Series.* Chicago, ILL: Science Research Associates.

Wright, Judge J.S. (1967) *Hobson vs Hansen: U.S. Court of Appeals Decision on the District of Columbia's Track System.* Civil Action No. 82–66. Washington, DC: US Court of Appeals.

10. F. Christoplos and P. Renz

Christoplos, F. and Renz, P. (1969) A critical examination of special education programs, *Journal of Special Education,* 3(4): 371–9.

References in this piece:

Atkinson, J.W. and O'Connor, P. (1963) *Effects of Ability Grouping in Schools Related to Individual Differences in Achievement Related Motivation,* Cooperative Research Project 1283. Washington, DC: Dept. HEW, Office Education.

Bacher, J.H. (1965) The effect of special class placement on the self-concept, social adjustment and reading growth of slow learners, *Diss. Abstr.,* 25: 70–1.

Baker, H.J. (1959) *Introduction to Exceptional Children.* New York: Macmillan.

Baldwin, W. (1958) The social position of the educable mentally retarded child in the regular grade in the public school, *Except. Child.,* 25: 106–8, 112.

Balow, B. and Curtin, J. (1965) Ability grouping of bright pupils, *Elem. Sch. J.,* 321–6.

Barker, R.G. (1948) The social psychology of physical disability, *J. Soc. Issues,* 4: 28–38.

Bateman, B. (1962) Sighted children's perception of blind children's abilities, *Except. Child,* 29: 42–6.

Billings, Helen K. (1963) An exploratory study of the attitudes of non-crippled children toward crippled children in three selected elementary schools, *J. Exp. Educ.*, 31: 381–7.

Blackman, L.S. (1967) The dimensions of a science of special education, *Ment. Retard.*, 5(4): 7–11.

Blatt, B. (1958) The physical, personality, and academic status of children who are mentally retarded attending special classes as compared with children who are mentally retarded attending regular classes, *Amer. J. Ment. Defic.*

Carlson, R.O. (1964) Environmental constraints and organizational consequences: the public school and its clients, in D.E. Griffiths (ed.) *Behavioral Science and Educational Administration*, 63rd Yearbook of the NSSE. Chicago: Chicago University Press.

Carroll, A.W. (1967) The effects of segregated and partially integrated school programs on self-concept and academic achievement of educable mentally retarded, *Except. Child.*, 34: 93–6.

Cassidy, V.M. and Stanton, J.E. (1959) *An Investigation of Factors Involved in the Educational Placement of Mentally Retarded Children: A Study of Differences Between Children in Special and Regular Classes in Ohio*, Cooperative Research Project 043. Washington, DC: Dept. HEW, Office Education.

Cruickshank, W. and Johnson, G.O. (1958) *Education of Exceptional Children and Youth*. Englewood Cliffs, NJ: Prentice-Hall.

Cutsforth, T.D. (1962) Personality and social adjustment among the blind, in P.A. Zahl (ed.) *Blindness*. New York: Hafner.

Diggs, E.A. (1964) A study of change in the social status of rejected mentally retarded children in regular classrooms, *Diss. Abstr.*, 25: 220–1.

Doll, E.A. (1966) Retrospect and prospect, *Educ. Train. Ment. Retard.*, 1: 3–7.

Dunn, L.M. (1963) *Exceptional Children in the Schools*. New York: Holt, Rinehart & Winston.

Dunn, L.M. (1967) Education of the handicapped, *Amer. Educ.*, July–August, 3: 30–1.

Dunn, L.M. (1968) Special education for the mildly retarded – is much of it justifiable? *Except. Child*, 35: 5–24.

Empey, La M.T. (1967) *Alternatives to Incarceration*. Washington, DC: Dept. HEW, Office Juvenile Delinquency and Youth Development.

Flanders, N.A. (1964) Teacher and classroom influences on individual learning, in A.H. Passow (ed.) *Nurturing Individual Potential*. Washington, DC: Assoc. Super. Curr. Dev.

Franseth, J. and Koury, R. (1966) *Survey of Research on Grouping as Related to Pupil Learning*. Washington, DC: US Printing Office, Dept. HEW, Office Educ., CE 20089.

Goldstein, H., Moss, J.W. and Jordan, L.J. (1965) *The Efficacy of Special Class Training on the Development of Mentally Retarded Children*, Cooperative Research Project 619. Washington, DC: Dept. HEW, Office Education.

Ingram, T.T.S. (1965) Education – for what purpose? in J. Loring (ed.) *Teaching the Cerebral Palsied Child*. Lavenham, Suffolk, England: Lavenham Press, Ltd.

Jordan, S. (1963) The disadvantaged group: a concept applicable to the handicapped, *J. Psychol.*, 55: 313–22.

Jordan, T.E. (1962) *The Exceptional Child*. Columbus, OH: Charles E. Merrill.

Keppel, F. (1966) *The Necessary Revolution in American Education*. New York: Harper & Row.

Kern, W.H. and Pfaeffle, H. (1962) A comparison of social adjustment of mentally retarded children in various educational settings, *Amer. J. ment. Defic.*, 67: 407–13.

Kirk, S.A. (1962) *Educating exceptional children*. Boston: Houghton-Mifflin.

Mackie, R.P. (1965) Spotlighting advances in special education, *Exceptional Children,* 32: 77–81.

Mayer, L. (1966) The relationship of early special class placement and the self-concepts of mentally handicapped children. *Except. Child,* 33: 77–80.

Meyerowitz, J.H. (1962) Self-derogations in young retardates and special class placement, *Child. Dev.,* 33: 443–51.

Meyerowitz, J.H. (1967a) Parental awareness of retardation, *Amer. J. Ment. Defic.,* 71: 637–43.

Meyerowitz, J.H. (1967b) Peer groups and special classes, *Ment. Retard.,* 5(5): 23–6.

Meyerson, L.A. (1963) Psychology of impaired hearing, in W.M. Cruickshank (ed.) *Psychology of Exceptional Children and Youth.* Englewood Cliffs, NJ: Prentice-Hall.

NEA (1967) *Programs for Handicapped Children.* Washington, DC: NEA Research Div.

Pintner, R. (1942) Intelligence testing of partially sighted children, *J. Educ. Psychol.,* 33: 265–72.

Porter, R.B. and Milazzo, T.C. (1958) A comparison of mentally retarded adults who attended a special class with those who attended regular school classes, *Except. Child.,* 24: 410–2, 420.

Pressey, S.L. (1963) *Acceleration and the Gifted.* Columbus, OH: Ohio State Dept. Educ.

Reynolds, M.C. (ed.) (1967a) *Early School Admission for Mentally Advanced Children.* Washington, DC: NEA.

Reynolds, M.C. (1967b) The surge in special education, *Net. Educ. Assn. J.,* 56(8).

Robinson, H.B. and Robinson, N.M. (1965) *The Mentally Retarded Child.* New York: McGraw-Hill.

Sears, P.S. (1963) *The Effects of Classroom Conditions on the Strength of Achievement Motive and Work Output of Elementary School Children,* Cooperative Research Project 873. Washington, DC: Dept. HEW, Office Education.

Stanton, J.E. and Cassidy, V.M. (1964) Effectiveness of special classes for educable mentally retarded, *Ment. Retard,* 2: 8–13.

Tenny, J.W. (1953) The minority status of the handicapped, *Except. Child,* 18: 260–4.

Thelan, H.A. (1967) *Classroom Grouping for Teachability.* New York: John Wiley.

Thurstone, T.G. (1959) *An Evaluation of Educating Mentally Handicapped Children in Special Classes and in Regular Classes,* Cooperative Research Project OE-SAE 6452. Washington, DC: Dept. HEW, Office Education.

Trippe, M.J. (1959) The social psychology of exceptional children: Part 11, *Except. Child,* 26: 171–5, 188.

Warren, E. (1954) *Brown vs. Board of Education.* Washington, DC: US Supreme Court.

Wright, B.A. (1960) *Physical Disability: A Psychological Approach.* New York: Harper & Row.

11. R.A. Weatherley and M. Lipsky

Weatherley, R.A. and Lipsky, M. (1977) Street-level bureaucrats and institutional innovation: implementing special education reform, *Harvard Educational Review,* 47(2): 171–97. Quoted text is from the Introduction and Conclusion.

Reference in this piece:
Audit Commission/HMI (1992) *Getting in on the Act: Provision for Pupils with Special Educational Needs.* London: HMSO.

12. Gerv Leyden

Leyden, G. (1978) The process of reconstruction: an overview, in B. Gillham *Reconstructing Educational Psychology.* London: Croom Helm.

References in this piece:

Bruner, J. (1966) *Towards a Theory of Instruction*. New York: Norton.

Burden (1973) If we throw tests out of the window what is there left to do? *Journal of the A.E.P.*, 3(5): 6–9.

Ghodsian, M. and Calnan, M. (1977) A comparative longitudinal analysis of special education groups, *British Journal of Educational Psychology*, 47(2): 162–74.

Miller, P. (1973) All children are special, *Journal of the Association of Educational Psychologists*, 3(3): 40–6.

Morgan, G. (1977) Integration versus segregation in Ontario, *Special Education*, 4(1): 18–21.

Moseley, D. (1975) *Special Provision for Reading: When Will They Ever Learn?* Windsor: NFER-Nelson.

Presland, J. (1970) Who should go to ESN schools? *Special Education*, 59(1): 11–16.

Tizard, J. (1966) Schooling for the handicapped, *Special Education*, 55: 2, 4–7.

Williams, P. and Gruber, E. (1967) *Response to Special Schooling*. London: Longman.

13. Will Swann

Swann, W. (1982) *Psychology and Special Education*, Unit E241. Milton Keynes: The Open University.

14. Tony Booth

Booth, T. (1983) Integration and participation in comprehensive schools, *Forum*, spring, 25(2): 40–1.

Reference in this piece:

Booth, T. (1981) Demystifying integration, in W. Swann (ed.) *The Practice of Special Education*. Oxford: Blackwell.

15. Sally Tomlinson

Tomlinson, S. (1982) *A Sociology of Special Education*. London: Routledge & Kegan Paul.

References in this piece:

Archer, M.S. (1979) *The Social Origins of Education Systems*. London: Sage.

Barton, R. (1973) The institutionalised mind and the subnormal mind, in H. Gunzberg (ed.) *Advances in the Care of the Mentally Handicapped*. London: Bailiere-Trindall.

Becker, H.S. (1963) *Outsiders*. New York: Free Press.

Berger, P. and Luckman, T. (1971) *The Social Construction of Reality*. Harmondsworth: Penguin.

Bourdieu, P. and Passeron, J.C. (1977) *Reproduction in Education, Society and Culture*. London: Sage.

Bowles, S. and Gintis, H. (1977), I.Q. in the US Class Structure, in J. Karabel and A.H. Halsey (eds) *Power and Ideology in Education*. Oxford: Oxford University Press.

Dexter, L.A. (1958) A social theory of mental deficiency, *American Journal of Mental Deficiency*, 63.

Downes, D. (1966) *The Delinquent Solution*. London: Routledge & Kegan Paul.

Eggleston, J. (1979) Introduction to P. Broadfoot, *Assessment, Schools and Society*. London: Methuen.

Gulliford, R. (1971) *Special Educational Needs*. London: Routledge & Kegan Paul.

Karabel, J. and Halsey, A.H. (eds) (1977) *Power and Ideology in Education*. Oxford: Oxford University Press.

Mowat, C. (1961) *The Charity Organisation Society*. London: Methuen.

Scott, R. (1970) The social construction of the conception of stigma by professional experts, in J. Douglas (ed.) *Deviance and Respectability*. New York: Basic Books.

Spectre, M. and Kitsuse, T. (1977) *Constructing Social Problems*. California: Cummings.

Stein, Z. and Susser, M. (1960) Families of dull children, Pt. II. Identifying family types and subcultures, *Journal of Mental Science*, 106(445).

Weber, M. (1972) Selections on education and politics, in B. Cosin (ed.) *Education Structure and Society*. Harmondsworth: Penguin.

Williams, P. and Gruber, E. (1967) *Response to Special Schooling*. Longman: London.

Woods, P. (1979) *The Divided School*. London: Routledge & Kegan Paul.

Woods, P. (ed.) (1980a) *Pupil Strategies*. London: Croom Helm.

Woods, P. (ed.) (1980b) *Teacher Strategies*. London: Croom Helm.

16. Seamus Hegarty *et al.*

Hegarty, S., Pocklington, K. and Lucas, D. (1981) *Educating Pupils with Special Needs in the Ordinary School*. Windsor: NFER-Nelson.

Reference in this piece:
Hegarty, S. and Pocklington, K. (1982) *Integration in Action*. Windsor: NFER-Nelson.

17. ILEA

ILEA (Inner London Education Authority) (1985) *Educational Opportunities for All?* (Fish Report). London: ILEA.

18. Doug Biklen

Biklen, D. (1985) *Achieving the Complete School: Strategies for Effective Mainstreaming*. New York: Teachers College Press.

References in this piece:
Blatt, B. ([1969] 1974) *Exodus from Pandemonium*. Boston: Allyn & Bacon.

Brightman, A. and Sullivan, M. (1980) *The Impact of Public Law 94–142 on Parents of Disabled Children: A Report of Findings*. Cambridge, MA: The Cambridge Workshop, Inc., 37 Goden St., Belmont, MA 02146, October 15.

Children's Defense Fund (1974) *Children Out of School in America*. Washington, DC: Children's Defense Fund.

Dunn, L.M. (1968) Special education for the mildly retarded – is much of it justifiable? *Exceptional Children*, 35: 5–22.

Dybwad, G. (1980) Avoiding misconceptions of mainstreaming, the least restrictive environment, and normalization, *Exceptional Children*, 47: 85–8.

Kugel, R.B. and Wolfensberger, W. (1969) *Changing Patterns in Residential Services for the Mentally Retarded*. Washington, DC: Presidents Committee on Mental Retardation.

Lippman, L. and Goldberg (1973) *1. Right to education*. New York: Teachers College Press.

PARC v. Penn (Pennsylvania Association for Retarded Children v. the Commonwealth of Pennsylvania) 334 F. Supp. 1257 (E.D. Pa. 1971).

Public Law 94–142 (1975) Right to Education for All Handicapped Children Act 20 U.S.C. §1412.

Reynolds, M.D. (1962) A framework for considering some issues in special education, *Exceptional Children*, 28: 367–70.

Task Force on Children out of School (1969) *The Way We go to School*. Boston: Beacon Press.

Wolfensberger, W. (1983) Social role valorization: a proposed new term for the principle of normalization, *Mental Retardation*, 21: 234–9.

19. Tony Dessent

Dessent, T. (1987–88) Making the Ordinary School Special, *Children and Society*, 4: 279–87.

References in this piece:

Department of Education and Science (1978) *Special Educational Needs* (Warnock Report). London: HMSO.

Department of Education and Science (1981) *Education Act 1981.* London: HMSO.

Gipps, C. and Goldstein, H. (1984) Remedial service to special needs support team: is it more than a change in name? *Occasional Paper No. 4. Screening and Special Educational Provision in Schools Project.* London: University of London, Institute of Education.

House of Commons (1987) Third Report from the Education, Science and Arts Committee, *Special Educational Needs: Implementation of The Education Act 1981.* London: HMSO.

20. L. Anderson and L. Pellicer

Anderson, L.W. and Pellicer, L.O. (1990) Synthesis of research on compensatory and remedial education, *Educational Leadership*, 48(1): 10–16.

References in this piece:

Anderson, L.W. and Reynolds, E. (1990) The Training, Qualifications, Duties and Responsibilities of Teacher Aides in Compensatory and Remedial Programs in South Carolina. Unpublished manuscript, University of South Carolina.

Anderson, L.W., Cook, N.R., Pellicer, L.O. and Spradling, R.L. (1989) A *Study of EL4-Funded Remedial and Compensatory Programs in South Carolina.* Columbia, SC: South Carolina Educational Policy Center.

Anderson, L.W., Pellicer, L.O., Spradling, R.L., Cook, N.R. and Sears, J.T. (1990) *No Way Out: Some Reasons for the Stability of Student Membership in State Compensatory and Remedial Programs.* Paper presented at the Annual Meeting of the American Educational Research Association, Boston.

Carter, L.F. (1984) The Sustaining Effects Study of Compensatory and Elementary Education, *Educational Researcher*, 13(7): 4–13.

Davidoff, S.H., Fishman, R.J. and Pierson, E.M. (1989) *Indicator Based Evaluation for Chapter 1.* Paper presented at the Annual Meeting of the American Educational Research Association, San Francisco.

Johnston, P., Allington, R. and Affierbach, P. (1985) The congruence of classroom and remedial instruction, *Elementary School Journal*, 85(4): 465–77.

Lee, G.V., Rowan, B., Allington, P. *et al.* (1986) *The Management Delivery of Instructional Services to Chapter 1 Students. Case Studies of 12 Schools.* San Francisco: Far West Laboratory Educational Research and Development.

OERI (Office of Educational Research and Improvement) (1987) *The Current Operation of the Chapter 1 Program.* Washington, DC: OERI.

Peterson, J.M. (1989) Remediation is no remedy, *Educational Leadership*, 46(6): 24–5.

Pogrow, S. (1990) Challenging at-risk students: findings from the HOTS program, *Phi Delta Kappan*, 71: 389–97.

Potter, D. and Wall, M. (1990) *An Analysis of Five Years of State Remedial/Compensatory Program Evaluation Data.* Paper presented at the Annual Meeting of the South Carolina Educators for the Practical Use of Research, Columbia, SC.

Rowan, B., Guthrie, L.F., Lee, G.V. and Guthrie, G.P. (1986) *The Design and Implementation of Chapter 1 Instruction Services. A Study of 24 Schools.* San Francisco, CA: Far West Laboratory Educational Research and Development

21. John O'Brien and Marsha Forest

O'Brien, J. and Forest, M. (1989) *Action for Inclusion: How to Improve Schools by Welcoming Children with Special Needs into Regular Classrooms.* Toronto: Inclusion Press.

22. Sam Carson

Carson, S. (1992) Normalisation, needs and schools, *Education Psychology in Practice*, 7(4): 218–22.

References in this piece:

Bennett, N. and Cass, A. (1989) The effects of group composition on group interactive processes and pupil understanding, *British Educational Research Journal*, 15: 19–32.

Bluhm, H.P. (1977) The right to work: employers, employability and retardation, in C.T. Drew, M.L. Hardman, H.P. Bluhm and B. Blott (eds) *Mental Retardation Social and Educational Pespectives*. St. Louis: The C.V. Mosby Co.

Brinker, R. and Thorpe, M. (1983) *Evaluation of Integration of Severely Handicapped Students in Regular Classrooms and Community Settings*. Princeton, NJ: Educational Testing Service.

Chapman, J.W. (1988) Learning disabled children's self concepts, *Review of Educational Research*, 57(3): 347–71.

Ferguson, R. and Asch, A. (1989) Lessons from life: personal and parental perspectives on school, childhood and disability, in D. Biklen, A. Ford and D. Ferguson (eds) *Disability and Society*. Chicago: NSSE.

Forest, M. and Pearpoint, J. (1990) Supports for addressing severe maladaptive behaviours, in W. Stainback and S. Stainback (eds) *Support Networks for Inclusive Schooling*. Baltimore: Paul H. Brooks Publishing Company.

Galloway, D. and Goodwin, C. (1987) *The Education of Disturbing Children: Pupils with Learning and Adjustment Difficulties*. New York: Longman Inc.

Illyes, S. and Erdosi, S. (1981) The special school and the social integration of the educable mentally young adults, *Studia Psychologica*, 23: 245–53.

O'Brien, J. and Lyle, C. (1985) *What We Want from Residential Programs*. Washington, DC: People First.

O'Brien, J. and Tyne, A. (1981) *The Principle of Normalisation*. London: VIA Publications.

Oliver, M. (1989) Disability and dependency: a creation of industrial societies, in L. Barton (ed.) *Disability and Dependency*. London: Falmer Press.

Redding, S.F. (1979) Life adjustment patterns of retarded and non-retarded low functioning students, *Exceptional Children*, 45: 5.

Reiter, S. and Levi, A.M. (1980) Factors affecting social integration of non-institutionalised mentally retarded adults, *American Journal of Mental Deficiency*, 85: 25–30.

Slavin, R.E. and Madden, W.A. (1986) The integration of students with mild academic handicaps in regular classrooms, *Prospects*, 16(4): 443–81.

Vanier, J. (1971) *Eruption to Hope*. Toronto: Griffin House.

Wang, M. and Birch, J. (1984) Effective special education in regular classes, *Exceptional Children*, 50: 391–9.

Wolfensberger, W. (1972) *The Principle of Normalisation in Human Services*. NIMR Publications.

23. Seamus Hegarty

Hegarty, S. (1993) Reviewing the literature on integration, *European Journal of Special Needs Education*, 8(3): 194–200.

24. Tom Hehir

Audit Commission/HMI (1992) *Getting in on the Act: Provision for Pupils with Special Educational Needs, The National Picture*. London: HMSO.

Dessent, T. (1987–80) Making the Ordinary School Special. London: Falmar.

Miller, E. (1996) Changing the way we think about kids with disabilities: a conversation with Tom Hehir, in E. Miller and R. Tovey (eds) *Inclusion and Special Education, Harvard Education Letter* (HEL) Focus Series No. 1. Cambridge, MA: Harvard Educational Publishing.

25. Gary Thomas and Andrew Loxley
Thomas, G. and Loxley, A. (2001) *Deconstructing Special Education and Constructing Inclusion.* Buckingham: Open University Press.

References in this piece:
Clark, C., Dyson, A. and Millward, A. (1998) Theorising special education: time to move on? in C. Clark, A. Dyson and A. Millward (eds) *Theorising Special Education.* London: Routledge.
Laing, R.D. (1965) *The Divided Self.* London: Penguin.
Ryle, G. (1990) *The Concept of Mind.* London: Penguin.
Smail, D. (1993) *The Origins of Unhappiness.* London: Harper Collins.
Szasz, T.S. (1972) *The Myth of Mental Illness.* London: Paladin.
Thomas, G. (1992) Ecological interventions, in S. Wolfendale *et al.* (eds) *The Profession and Practice of Educational Psychology.* London: Cassell.

26. CSIE
Centre for Studies on Inclusive Education (2003) *Reasons Against Segregated Schooling.* Bristol: Centre for Studies on Inclusive Education.

References in this piece:
Abbott, D., Morris, J. and Ward, L. (2001) *The Best Place To Be? Policy, Practice and the Experiences of Residential School Placements for Disabled Children.* York: Joseph Rowntree Foundation.
Alliance for Inclusive Education (2003) Report of the Working Group on the Future Role of Special Schools. Consultation meeting held between disabled special school survivors and representatives of the DfES, 5 July 2003. London: Alliance for Inclusive Education.
Allport, G.W. (1954) *The Nature of Prejudice.* Reading, MA: Addison-Wesley.
Armstrong, B., Johnson, D.W. and Balow, B. (1981) Effects of Cooperative vs. Individualistic Learning Experiences on Interpersonal Attraction Between Learning-disabled and Normal-progress Elementary School Students, *Contemporary Educational Psychology*, 6: 102–9.
Audit Commission (1998) *Getting in on the Act: A Review of Progress on Special Educational Needs.* London: Audit Commission.
Audit Commission (2002) *Statutory Assessment and Statements of SEN: In Need of Review?* London: Audit Commission.
Audit Commission/HMI (1992) *Getting in on the Act: Provision for Pupils with Special Educational Needs – The National Picture.* London: HMSO.
Baker, E.T., Wang, M.C. and Walberg, H.J. (1995) The effects of inclusion on learning, *Educational Leadership*, 52: 33–5.
Ballard, K. and McDonald, T. (1999) Disability, inclusion and exclusion: some insider accounts and interpretations, in K. Ballard (ed.) *Inclusive Education: International Voices on Disability and Justice.* London: Falmer Press.
Barton, L. and Armstrong, F. (2001) Cross-cultural issues and dilemmas, in C.L. Albrecht, K.D. Steelman and M. Bury (eds) *Handbook of Disability Studies,* London: Sage Publications.
British Council of Organisations of Disabled People (1998) *Response to the Green Paper: Excellence for all Children.* Derby: BCODP.

Brown, R. (1995) *Prejudice: Its Social Psychology.* Oxford: Blackwell Publishing.

Carson, S. (1992) Normalisation, needs and schools, *Educational Psychology in Practice,* 7(4): 216–22.

Centre for Studies on Inclusive Education (2002) *The Inclusion Charter and Explanatory Paper.* Bristol: CSIE.

Cook, T., Swain, J. and French, S. (2001) Voices from segregated schooling: towards an inclusive education system, *Disability and Society,* 16(2): 293–310.

Corbett, J. (1996) *Bad-Mouthing.* London: Falmer Press.

Crandell, C.S. (2000) Ideology and lay theories of stigma: the justification of stigmatization, in T.F. Heatherton, R.E. Kleck, M.R. Hebl and J.G. Hull (eds) *The Social Psychology of Stigma.* London: The Guilford Press.

Crocker, J. and Quinn, D.M. (2000) Social stigma and the self: meanings, situations, and self-esteem, in T.F. Heatherton, R.E. Kleck, M.R. Hebl and J.G. Hull (eds) *The Social Psychology of Stigma.* London: The Guilford Press.

Crowther, D. *et al.* (1998) Costs and outcomes for pupils with moderate learning difficulties (MLD), Special and Mainstream Schools, *DfEE Research Brief* No.89. London: DfEE.

Dockrell, J., Peacey, N. and Lunt, I. (2002) *Literature Review: Meeting the Needs of Children with Special Educational Needs.* London: Institute of Education.

Dolan, C. (1997) My journey, *Bolton Data for Inclusion,* No.16. Bolton: Bolton Institute.

Dovidio, J.F., Major, B. and Crocker, J. (2000) Stigma: introduction and overview, in T.F. Heatherton, R.E. Kleck, M.R. Hebl and J.G. Hull (eds) *The Social Psychology of Stigma.* London: The Guilford Press.

EPPI-Centre (2002) *A Systematic Review of the Effectiveness of School-level Actions for Promoting Participation by all Students.* London: Institute of Education, Social Science Research Unit.

Falk, G. (2001) *Stigma: How We Treat Outsiders.* New York: Prometheus Books.

Farrell, P. (2000) The impact of research on developments in inclusive education, *International Journal of Inclusive Education,* 4(2): 153–62.

Farrell, P. and Tsakalidou, K. (1998) Recent trends in the re-integration of pupils with emotional and behavioural difficulties in the United Kingdom, *School Psychology International,* 20(4): 323–37.

Fisher, D., Roach, V. and Frey, N. (2002) Examining the general programmatic benefits of inclusive schools, *International Journal of Inclusive Education,* 6(1): 63–78.

Fisher, M. and Meyer, L.H. (2000) *A Comparison of Developmental and Social Competence Outcomes after Two Years of Inclusive vs. Segregated Special Education,* submitted for publication.

Foucault, M. (1977) *Discipline and Punish: The Birth of the Prison.* London: Penguin.

Fryxell, D. and Kennedy, C. (1995) Placement along the continuum of services and its impact on students' social relationships, *Journal of the Association for Persons with Severe Handicaps,* 20: 259–69.

Goffman, E. (1963) *Stigma: Notes on the Management of Spoiled Identity.* Englewood Cliffs, NJ: Prentice-Hall.

Gordon, B.O. and Rosenblum, K.E. (2001) Bringing disability into the sociological frame: a comparison of disability with race, sex and sexual orientation statuses, *Disability and Society,* 16(1): 5–19.

Green, H. ([2001] 2002) Special schools lacking in music provision, University of London Institute of Education press release cited in J. Dockrell, N. Peacey and I. Lunt *Literature Review: Meeting the Needs of Children with Special Educational Needs.* London: Institute of Education.

Guralmick, M.J., Connor, R.T. and Hammond, N. (1995) Parent perspectives of peer relationships and friendships in integrated and specialised programs, *American Journal on Mental Retardation*, 99(5): 457–76.

Harrower, J.K. and Dunlap, G. (2001) Including children with autism in general education classrooms: a review of effective strategies, *Behavior Modification*, 25(5): 762–84.

Hegarty, S. (1993) Reviewing the literature on integration, *European Journal of Special Needs Education*, 8: 194–200.

Hunt, P., Farron-Davis, F., Beckstead, S., Curtis, D. and Goetz, L. (1999) Evaluating the effects of placement on students with severe disabilities in general education versus special classes, in G. Bunch and A. Valeo (eds) *Inclusion: Recent Research*. Toronto: Inclusion Press.

Jahnukainen, M. (2001) Experiencing special education: former students of classes for the emotionally and behaviourally disturbed talk about their schooling, *Emotional and Behavioural Difficulties*, 6(3): 150–66.

Johnson, D.W., Johnson, R.T. and Maruyama, G. (1984) Goal independence and interpersonal attraction in heterogeneous classrooms: a meta-analysis, in N. Miller and M.B. Brewer (eds) *Groups in Contact: The Psychology of Desegregation*. Orlando, FL: Academic Press.

Jordan, L. and Goodey, C. (2002) *Human Rights and School Change: The Newham Story*. Bristol: Centre for Studies on Inclusive Education.

Jussim, L., Palumbo, P., Chatman, C., Madon, S. and Smith, A. (2000) Stigma and self-fulfilling prophecies, in T.F. Heatherton, R.E. Kleck, M.R. Hebl and J.G. Hull (eds) *The Social Psychology of Stigma*. London: The Guilford Press.

Karagiannis, A., Stainback, W. and Stainback, S. (1997) Rationale for inclusive schooling, in W. Stainback and S. Stainback (eds) *Inclusion: A Guide for Educators*. Baltimore: Paul H. Brookes Publishing.

Kenworthy, J. and Whittaker, J. (2000) Anything to declare? The struggle for inclusive education and children's rights, *Disability and Society*, 15(2): 219–23.

Kulik, C. and Kulik, J. (1982) Effects of ability groupings on secondary school students: a meta-analysis of evaluation findings, *American Educational Research Journal*, 19: 415–28.

Kulik, J. and Kulik, C. (1992) Meta-analytic findings on grouping programs, *Gifted Children*, 36: 73–7.

Lipsky, D. and Gartner, A. (1996) Inclusion, school restructuring and the remaking of American society, *Harvard Educational Review*, 66(4): 762–96.

Lipsky, D. and Gartner, A. (1997) *Inclusion and School Reform: Transforming America's Classrooms*. Baltimore: Paul H. Brookes Publishing.

Loevy, R.D. (ed.) (1997) *The Civil Rights Act of 1964: The Passage of the Law that Ended Racial Segregation*. New York: State University of New York Press.

Logan, K.R. *et al.* (1998) The impact of typical peers on the perceived happiness of students with profound multiple disabilities, *Journal of the Association for Persons with Severe Handicaps*, 23: 309–18.

Maras, P.F. (1993) *The Integration of Children with Disabilities into the Mainstream*. PhD Thesis, University of Kent.

Maras, P. and Brown, R. (1995) Effects of contact on children's attitudes toward disability: a longitudinal study, cited in R. Brown *Prejudice: Its Social Psychology*. Oxford: Blackwell Publishing.

Meadows, N.B., Neel, R.S., Scott, C.M. and Parker, G. ([1994] 1999) Academic performance, social competence and mainstream accommodations: a look at mainstreamed and non-mainstreamed students with serious behavioural disorders,

Behavioral Disorders, 3(19): 170–80, reviewed in Bunch, G. and Valeo, A. (eds) *Inclusion: Recent Research*. Toronto: Inclusion Press.

Meyer, L.H. (2001) The impact of inclusion on children's lives: multiple outcomes, and friendship in particular, *International Journal of Disability, Development and Education*, 48(1): 9–31.

Miller, N. and Davidson-Podgorny, F. (1987) Theoretical models of intergroup relations and the use of cooperative teams as an intervention for desegregated settings, in C. Hendrick (ed.) *Group Processes and Intergroup Relations: Review of Personality and Social Psychology*. Beverly Hills, CA: Sage.

Morris, J. (1995) *Gone Missing? A Research and Policy Review of Disabled Children Living Away from their Families*. London: Who Cares? Trust.

Morris, J. (1998a) *Still Missing? Vol 1: The Experience of Disabled Children and Young People Living Away from their Families*. London: Who Cares? Trust.

Morris, J. (1998b) *Still Missing? Vol 2: Disabled Children and the Children Act*. London: Who Cares? Trust.

Muscroft, S. (ed.) (1999) *Children's Rights: Reality or Rhetoric?* London: International Save the Children Alliance.

Nakken, H. and Pijl, S.J. (2002) Getting along with classmates in regular schools: a review of the effects of integration on the development of social relationships, *International Journal of Inclusive Education*, 6(1): 47–61.

Norwich, B. (2002) *LEA Inclusion Trends in England 1997–2001: Statistics on Special School Placements and Pupils with Statements in Special Schools*. Bristol: Centre for Studies on Inclusive Education.

Oliver, M. (1994) Does special education have a role to play in the twenty-first century? in *REACH Journal of Special Educational Needs in Ireland*, 8(2): 67–76.

Polat, F. and Farrell, P. (2002) What was it like for you? Former pupils' reflections on their placement at a residential school for pupils with emotional and behavioural difficulties, *Emotional and Behavioural Difficulties*, 7(2): 97–108.

Polat, F., Kalambouka, A., Boyle, W.F. and Nelson, N. (2001) Post-16 Transition for Pupils with Special Educational Needs, *DfES Research Brief No.315*. London: DfES.

Rieser, R. and Mason, M. (1992) *Disability Equality in the Classroom: A Human Rights Issue*. London: Disability Equality in Education.

Robinson, L. (n.d.) From segregation to integration, *Bolton Data for Inclusion No.18*. Bolton: Bolton Institute.

Rosenthal, R. and Jacobson, L. (1968) *Pygmalion in the Classroom: Teacher Expectations and Student Intellectual Development*. New York: Holt, Rinehart & Winston.

Rosenthal, R. and Rubin, D.B. (1978) Interpersonal expectancy effects: the first 345 studies, *Behavioral and Brain Sciences*, 3: 377–86.

Rustemier, S. (2002) *Social and Educational Justice: The Human Rights Framework for Inclusion*. Bristol: Centre for Studies on Inclusive Education.

Rustemier, S. (2003a) The case against segregation in special schools: a look at the research evidence, *Occasional Paper No.1*. Bristol: Centre for Studies on Inclusive Education.

Rustemier, S. (2003b) *Inclusion in Further Education: The Experiences of Young People Designated 'Students with Learning Difficulties and/or Disabilities', 1997–2000*, PhD Thesis, University of Kent.

Rustemier, S. with Edwards, G. (2003) Selection by attainment in Birmingham, in P. Potts (ed.) *Inclusion in the City: Selection, Schooling and Community*. London: RoutledgeFalmer.

Salters, J., Neil, P. and Wright, M. (1998) Modern languages and special educational needs: a review of research, *Educational Research*, 40(3): 364–74.

Sebba, J. with Sachdev, D. (1997) *What Works in Inclusive Education?* Ilford: Barnardo's.

Shaw, L. (1997) CSIE talk given at the Alliance for Inclusive Education Conference, London, December.

Shaw, L. (1998) Children's experiences of school, in C. Robinson and K. Stalker (eds) *Growing Up With Disability.* London: Jessica Kingsley Publishers.

Schelling, G. (1996) Key concerns of people who have received special education: implications for inclusion, in G. Thomas, D. Walker and J. Webb (1998) *The Making of the Inclusive School.* London: Routledge.

Slavin, R.E. (1983) *Co-operative Learning.* New York: Longman.

Smith, A., Jussim, L., Eccles, J. *et al.* (1998) Self-fulfilling prophecies, perceptual biases, and accuracy at the individual and group level, *Journal of Experimental Psychology,* 34: 530–61.

Thomas, G. and Loxley, A. (2001) *Deconstructing Special Education and Constructing Inclusion.* Buckingham: Open University Press.

Thomas, G. (1996) *Exam Performance in Special Schools.* Bristol: CSIE.

Thomas, G. (1998) The myth of rational research, *British Educational Research Journal,* 24(2): 141–61.

Thomas, G., Walker, D. and Webb, J. (1998) *The Making of the Inclusive School.* London: Routledge.

Thomson, G.O.B., Ward, K.M. and Wishart, J.G. (1995) The transition to adulthood for children with Down's syndrome, *Disability and Society,* 10(3): 325–40.

Tomlinson, S. (1982) *A Sociology of Special Education.* London: Routledge & Kegan Paul.

United Nations Committee on the Rights of the Child (1997) *Children with Disabilities,* CRC/C/66/Annex V, 16th Session, 6 October.

Wade, B. and Moore, M. (1993) *Experiencing Special Education: What Young People with Special Educational Needs Can Tell Us.* Milton Keynes: Open University Press.

27. Mike Oliver

Oliver, M. (1995) Does special education have a role to play in the 21st century? *REACH, Journal of Special Needs Education in Ireland,* 8(2): 67–76.

References in this piece:

DES (Department of Education and Science) (1978) *Special Educational Needs,* Report of the Committee of Enquiry into the Education of Handicapped Children and Young People, Cmnd 7212. London: HMSO.

ILEA (Inner London Education Authority) (1985) Educational Opportunities for All? (Fish Report). London: ILEA.

Oliver, M. (1988) The political context of educational decision-making: the case of special needs, in L. Barton (ed.) *The Politics of Special Needs.* London: Falmer Press.

Rieser, R. and Mason, M. (1990) *Disability Equality in the Classroom: A Human Rights Issue.* London: ILEA.

Special Education Review Committee (1993) *Report of the Special Education Review Committee.* Dublin: HMSO.

PART THREE   LEGISLATION, REPORTS, STATEMENTS

28. Public Law 94–142

Public Law 94–142 (1975) *Federal Education of All Handicapped Children Act.* Washington, DC: United States Department of Education.

29. Warnock Report

Department of Education and Science (1978) *Special Educational Needs,* Report of the Committee of Enquiry into the Education of Handicapped Children and Young People, Cmnd 7212. London: HMSO.

30. Education Acts 1944–2001
These are Education Acts in 1944, 1970, 1976, 1981, 1993 and 1996. Also included are the Disability Discrimination Act 1995 and the Special Educational Needs and Disability Act (SENDA) 2001. London: HMSO.
CSIE (1986) Caught in the Act. Bristol: Centre for Studies on Inclusive Education.

31. European Convention on Human Rights
Application by four families supported by the Centre for Studies on Inclusive Education (1987) to the European Commission. For European Convention on Human Rights see http://conventions.coe.int/

32. UNESCO
UNESCO (1994) *The Salamanca Statement and Framework for Action on Special Needs Education.* Paris: UNESCO.
Wertheimer, A. (1997) *Inclusive Education: A Framework for Change. National and International Perspectives.* Bristol: Centre for Studies on Inclusive Education.

33. UN
United Nations (1989) *The UN Convention on the Rights of the Child.* London: UNICEF. See also http://www.unhchr.ch/html/menu3/b/k2crc.htm

34. UNESCO
UNESCO (1998) *Inclusive Education on the Agenda.* A paper for the World Bank http://www.eenet.org.uk/bibliog/unespubs.shtml

35. DfEE
DfEE (1997) *Excellence for All Children: Meeting Special Educational Needs.* London: Department for Education and Employment.

36. IPPR
IPPR (Institute for Public Policy Research) (1993) *Education: A Different Vision: An Alternative White Paper.* London: IPPR.

37. British Psychological Society
BPS (2002) *Inclusive Education – A Position Paper.* Leicester: BPS.

38. CSIE
CSIE (2002) *The Inclusion Charter.* Bristol: Centre for Studies on Inclusive Education.

39. Alison Wertheimer
Wertheimer, A. (1997) *Inclusive Education: A Framework for Change. National and International Perspectives.* Bristol: Centre for Studies on Inclusive Education.

PART FOUR   INCLUSION IN ACTION

40. Linda Shaw and Marsha Forest
Forest, M. (1988) *Circles for May: An Occasional Paper.* Toronto: Centre for Integrated Education and Community, Inclusion Press.
Shaw, L. (1990) *Each Belongs. Integrated Education in Canada.* Bristol: Centre for Studies on Inclusive Education.

41. Mark Vaughan and Ann Shearer
Vaughan, M. and Shearer, A. (1985) *Mainstreaming in Massachusetts.* Bristol: Centre for Studies on Inclusive Education.

42. Richard Rieser and Micheline Mason
Rieser, R. and Mason, M. (1992) *Disabililty Equality in the Classroom: A Human Rights Issue.* London: Disability Equality in Education.

43. Mark Vaughan
Vaughan, M. (1983) *Kirsty: The Struggle for a Place in an Ordinary School.* Bristol: Centre for Studies on Inclusive Education.

44. Kenn Jupp
Jupp, K. (1992) *Everyone Belongs: Mainstream Education for Children with Severe Learning Difficulties*, Human Horizon Series. London: Souvenir Press.

45. Bishopswood School
Bishopswood Staff (1992) *Bishopswood: Good Practice Transferred.* Bristol: Centre for Studies on Inclusive Education.

46. Rick Rogers
Rogers, R. (1999) *Developing an Inclusive Policy for Your School: A CSIE Guide.* Bristol: Centre for Studies on Inclusive Education.

47. Linda Jordan and Chris Goodey
Jordan, L. and Goodey, C. (2002) *Human Rights and School Change: The Newham Story.* Bristol: Centre for Studies on Inclusive Education.

References in this piece:
Forest, M. and Lusthouse, E. (1989) *Maps and Circles.* Toronto: Centre for Integrated Education in the Community, Inclusion Press.
Goodey, C. (ed.) (1991) *Living in the Real World: Families Speak About Down's Syndrome.* London: Newham Parents' Centre.
Hegarty, S. (1983–2004) *Boosting Educational Achievement, Report of the Independent Enquiry into Educational Achievement in Newham.* Slough: NFER.
Newham agreement with teacher unions (1990).
Newham inclusive education audit (1998).
Newham inclusive education charter (1997).
Newham inclusive education strategy (2001–04).
Newham integration development plan (1989).
Newham integration policy statement (1986).
Newham review of inclusive education strategy. Consultation document (1995).
Newham strategy for inclusive education (1996–2001).
Reports on the 1981 Education Act to Newham Education Committee and reports from the Integration Working Party (1983–85).
All available from Newham Education Department.
Shaw, L. (1999) *Follow-up Papers, An inclusive approach to difficult behaviour.* Bristol: Centre for Studies on Inclusive Education.

48. Dorothy Lipsky
Lipsky, D.K. (1995) *National Study on Inclusion in America: Overview and Summary Report.* New York: National Center on Educational Restructuring and Inclusion, Graduate School and University, City University of New York, 2(2). (Reprinted and published in the UK 1997 by CSIE, Bristol.)

49. Gary Thomas *et al.*
Thomas, G., Walker D. and Webb, J. (1998) *The Making of the Inclusive School.* London: Routledge.

50. Sam Harris

Harris, S. (1992) A seven year sentence, *National Integration Week Magazine*. Bristol: Centre for Studies on Inclusive Education.

51. Tony Booth and Mel Ainscow

Booth, T. and Ainscow, M. (2002) *Index for Inclusion: Developing Learning and Participation in Schools*. Bristol: Centre for Studies on Inclusive Education.

Conclusion

Chambers, M. (2000) False sympathy for inclusion, *Times Educational Supplement* (letters), March 17, p 23.

Croll, P. and Moses, D. (2000) *Special Needs in the Primary School*, London: Cassell.

Index

Page numbers in **bold** indicate main discussion.

Related books from Open University Press
Purchase from www.openup.co.uk or order through your local bookseller

ICT AND SPECIAL EDUCATIONAL NEEDS
A TOOL FOR INCLUSION

Lani Florian and John Hegarty (eds)

Information and Communications Technology (ICT) is indispensable to those who teach learners with special educational needs. This book gives the broader context for the use of ICT in special and inclusive settings. It gives a wide range of examples of ICT in use and considers the role of technology in overcoming barriers of access to the curriculum; includes in-depth examinations of the uses of ICT as a teaching tool to promote inclusion and raise standards for all; and features contributions from researchers and practitioners who explore the development of ICT, recent innovations, assessment, and specialist knowledge. This book will be invaluable to teachers on professional development courses and those preparing to teach learners with special educational needs, as well as experienced professionals seeking to update their knowledge and gain new inspiration in this rapidly developing area.

Contents
Introduction – ICT and SEN: issues and debates – ICT, SEN and schools: a historical perspective of government initiatives – From integration to inclusion: using ICT to support learners special educational needs in the ordinary classroom – Using computer-based assessment to identify learning problems – Integrated learning systems, literacy and self-esteem – ICT and SEN: a whole school approach – Innovations in ICT – Using virtual environments – Managing SEN provision with ICT – Service development and staff training – References – Index.

160pp   0 335 21195 X (Paperback)   0 335 21196 8 (Hardback)

SPECIAL EDUCATIONAL NEEDS, INCLUSION AND DIVERSITY
A TEXTBOOK

Norah Frederickson and Tony Cline

This book has the potential to become *the* textbook on special educational needs. Written specifically with the requirements of student teachers, trainee educational psychologists, SENCOs and SEN Specialist Teachers in mind, it provides a comprehensive and detailed discussion of the major issues in special education. Whilst recognising the complex and difficult nature of many special educational needs, the authors place a firm emphasis on inclusion and suggest practical strategies enabling professionals to maximise inclusion at the same time as recognising and supporting diversity.

Key features include:

- Takes full account of linguistic, cultural and ethnic diversity unlike many other texts in the field
- Addresses the new SEN Code of Practice and is completely up to date
- Recognises current concerns over literacy and numeracy and devotes two chapters to these areas of need
- Offers comprehensive and detailed coverage of major issues in special educational needs in one volume
- Accessibly written with the needs of the student and practitioner in mind

Contents

Introduction – Part one: Principles and concepts – Children, families, schools and the wider community: an integrated approach – Concepts of special educational needs – Inclusion – Special educational needs: pathways of development – Part two: Assessment in context – Identification and assessment – Reducing bias in assessment – Curriculum based assessment – Learning environments – Part three: Areas of need – Learning difficulties – Language – Literacy – Mathematics – Hearing impairment – Emotional and behaviour difficulties – Social skills – References – Index.

528pp   0 335 20402 3 (Paperback)   0 335 20973 4 (Hardback)

STRUGGLES FOR INCLUSIVE EDUCATION
AN ETHNOGRAPHIC STUDY
Anastasia D. Vlachou

This is a lucid, authoritative and original study of teachers' views and attitudes towards the integration into mainstream schooling of a particular group of children defined as having special educational needs. It offers one of the clearest and most comprehensive analyses of the socio-political mechanisms by which the 'special' are socially constructed and excluded from the normal education system that has so far been produced.

Sally Tomlinson, Professor of Educational Policy at Goldsmiths College,
University of London

In its detailed analysis of primary school teachers' and pupils' attitudes towards integration, this book locates the question of inclusive education within the wider educational context. The wealth of original interview material sheds new light on the reality of everyday life in an educational setting, and shows us the nature and intensity of the struggles experienced by both teachers and pupils in their efforts to promote more inclusive school practices. The author's sensitive investigation of the relationship between teachers' contradictory views of the 'special' and their integration, and the wider social structures in which teachers work, adds to our understanding of the inevitable difficulties in promoting inclusive educational practices within a system which functions via exclusive mechanisms.

The book will be of interest to students of education, sociology and disability as well as teachers and policy-makers involved in inclusive education. The original methodologies adopted when working with the children will also appeal to students of attitudinal, disability and educational research.

Contents
Introduction – Part 1: Setting the theoretical scene – Disability, normality and special needs: political concepts and controversies – Towards a better understanding of attitudes – Part 2: Teachers' perspectives – Teachers and the changing culture of teaching – Teachers' attitudes towards integration (with reference to pupils with Down's syndrome) – Part 3: Children's perspectives – Integration: the children's point of view – Disabled children and children's culture – Conclusion – Appendices – References – Index.

208pp   0 335 19763 9 (Paperback)   0 335 19764 7 (Hardback)

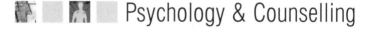